THE LORD OF GLORY

The Lord of Glory

A STUDY OF

THE DESIGNATIONS OF OUR LORD IN THE NEW TESTAMENT WITH ESPECIAL REFERENCE TO HIS DEITY

BENJAMIN B. WARFIELD

BAKER BOOK HOUSE
Grand Rapids, Michigan

Paperback edition
Reprinted 1974 by
Baker Book House

from the 1907 edition
by American Tract Society

ISBN: 0-8010-9548-4

Printed in the United States of America

Notable Books on Theology

Why theology? After the ebb and flow of theological study and discussion for the last fifty years, we are witnessing a renaissance of interest and inquiry. The denigration of preaching, the decline in moral standards, the demand that personal experience become the authority in religious values, and the dismissal of dogmatic theology as irrelevant for life — these have caught up with a new generation suspicious of dogma yet wistful for faith and certitude. This gives reply to the question, Why theology, for basic to all questions of life and destiny is theology.

The Biblical revelation has been made in life and recorded in the Scriptures, so that the teacher-preacher becomes an interpreter. Behind the formulation of truth and in the teaching-preaching function is theological conviction. Theology is spelled out in this way in Jonathan Edwards and in Karl Barth. Theology implies proclamation. Here we need the spirit of openness of mind and breadth of understanding to read widely and know the various theological insights in the depth of our reflection and study.

In 1967 the series *Notable Books on Preaching* began the reprint of a selection of books which were not easily found, but which were once more regarded as relevant. A similar aim is proposed in this series, *Notable Books on Theology*. The books chosen for reprint will set forth points of view on crucial doctrines, interpretations sometimes overlooked. They will recall contributions still enriching for our age. All volumes selected for this series will be broadly evangelical, and in the mainstream of historic Protestantism. They will present not only the scholarly and technical writer, but also the pastor working out his thought in more practical ways to meet life situations in the ministry. It is hoped that the discovery of emphases overlooked and insights of other minds will stimulate thought and reflection on themes which require restudy in our space age.

The first four books to be reprinted in this series are representative of titles to follow. They are: *The Atonement* by Archibald A. Hodge; *The Lord of Glory* by Benjamin B. Warfield; *A Help to the Study of The Holy Spirit* by William E. Biederwolf; *The Supernaturalness of Christ* by Wilbur M. Smith.

Theology is too often thought of as technical, scientific, and with special language not easy to understand. This series will demonstrate that this need not be the case. Many of the theologians of the past had as their aim the goal so well expressed by John Wesley: "I desire plain truth for plain people.... I labour to avoid all words which are not easy to be understood, all which are not used in common life...."

Notable Books on Theology can feed the mind, fortify the faith, and freshen the work and worship of many who need and desire theological instruction and illumination in our age.

RALPH G. TURNBULL

Introduction

Benjamin Breckinridge Warfield (1851-1921)

Like his predecessor at Princeton, A. A. Hodge, Warfield also served at Western Seminary, Allegheny (1878-1887), before his period as Professor of Systematic Theology (1887-1921). He was fortunate to have taught New Testament Language and Literature at Western, for the grammarian has the advantage in looking at the Scriptures before systematizing their revealed doctrines.

Warfield continued the Hodge tradition; his output of articles, reviews, and books indicate his influence as a teacher. Reprints of many of Warfield's works are still available through The Presbyterian and Reformed Publishing Company or Baker Book House. Among these are *The Inspiration and Authority of the Bible, The Person and Work of Christ, Biblical and Theological Studies, Calvin and Augustine, Perfectionism, The Warfield Collection* (five volumes), *Selected Shorter Writings of Benjamin B. Warfield—I,* and *Selected Shorter Writings of Benjamin B. Warfield—II.*

Much of Warfield's writing was the result of a forceful polemic in controversial battle. The areas of chief concern were Biblical criticism and authority. Warfield, like the younger Hodge, stood for the "Princeton doctrine of inspiration," which became a major defense of Biblical inerrancy. The struggle between theological conservatism and liberalism was acute then and is not overlooked in each succeeding generation.

Out of that period came *The Lord of Glory* (1907), which has as a subtitle, "A Study of the Designations of Our Lord in the New Testament with Especial Reference to His Deity." In the dust of controversy, Warfield has been forgotten as the exegete and expositor. In this volume he examines the intellectual and emotional statements of eye-witnesses, recorded in the text of the New Testament. Detailed references and words in context are studied minutely. Other authors, critical and believing, are weighed with care. Appraisal is made by the scholar and theologian who, like Thomas, confesses, "My Lord and my God!"

A careful examination of this book will stimulate the student and Bible reader to do his own "homework" with care in collating the facts before expressing a conviction.

RALPH G. TURNBULL

To

WILLIAM PARK ARMSTRONG, JR.

CASPAR WISTAR HODGE, JR.

ΜΑΘΗΤΑΙΝ · ΣΥΝΕΡΓΟΙΝ · ΔΙΔΑΣΚΑΔΟΙΝ

ΣΥΝΔΟΥΔΟΙΝ ΟΜΟΨΥΧΟΙΝ

ΧΑΡΙΝ ΕΧΩΝ.

Plurima quæsivi, per singula quæque cucurri,
Sed nihil inveni melius quam credere Christo.
                              —PAULINUS OF NOLA.

CONTENTS

Contents

Contents

Contents

This man so cured regards the curer, then,
As—God forgive me!—who but God Himself,
Creator and sustainer of the world,
That came and dwelt on it awhile! . . . .
And must have so avouched himself in fact, . .
The very God! think Ahib; dost thou think?
—ROBERT BROWNING.

THE DESIGNATIONS OF OUR LORD
IN THE NEW TESTAMENT

They . . . crucified the Lord of Glory.
—I CORINTHIANS ii. 8.

Who is this King of Glory?
The LORD of hosts,
He is the King of Glory.
—PSALM xxiv. 10.

THE DESIGNATIONS OF OUR LORD

The proper subject of the New Testament is Christ. Every page of it, or perhaps we might better say **Pervasive Witness of N. T. to Christ** every line of it, has its place in the portrait which is drawn of Him by the whole. In forming an estimate of the conception of His person entertained by its writers, and by those represented by them, we cannot neglect any part of its contents. We can scarcely avoid distinguishing in it, to be sure, between what we may call the primary and the subsidiary evidence it bears to the nature of His personality, or at least the more direct and the more incidental evidence. It may very well be, however, that what we call the subsidiary or incidental evidence may be quite as convincing, if not quite as important, as the primary and direct evidence. The late Dr. R. W. Dale found the most impressive proofs that the Apostles themselves and the primitive Churches believed that Jesus was one with God, rather in the way this seems everywhere taken for granted, than in the texts in which it is definitely asserted. " Such texts," he remarks, " are but like the sparkling crystals which appear on the sand after the tide has retreated; these are not the strongest—though they may be the most apparent—proofs that the sea is salt: the salt is present in solution in every bucket of sea-water. And so," he applies his parable, " the truth of our Lord's divinity is present in solution in whole pages of the Epistles, from which not a single text could be quoted that explicitly declares it."[1]

We need offer no apology, therefore, for inviting somewhat extended attention to one of the subsidiary **Scope** lines of evidence of the estimate put **of this** upon our Lord's person by the writers **Discussion** of the New Testament and by our Lord as reported by them. We certainly shall not, by so doing, obtain anything like a complete view of the New Testament's evidence for the dignity of His person. But it may very well be that we shall obtain a convincing body of evidence for it. What we purpose to do is to attend with some closeness to the designations which the New Testament writers apply to our Lord as they currently speak of Him. These designations will be passed rapidly under our eye with a twofold end in view. On the one hand we shall hope, generally, to acquire a vivid sense of the attitude, intellectual and emotional, sustained by the several writers of the New Testament, and by the New Testament as a whole, to our Lord's person. On the other, we shall hope, particularly, to reach a clearer notion of the loftiness of the estimate placed upon His person by these writers, and by those whom they represent. We are entering, then, in part upon an exposition, in part upon an argument. We wish to learn, so far as the designations applied to our Lord in the New Testament are fitted to reveal that to us, how the writers of the New Testament were accustomed to think of Jesus; we wish to show that they thought of Him above everything else as a Divine Person. For the former purpose we desire to pass in review the whole body of designations employed in the New Tes-

[1] *Christian Doctrine,* 1895, p. 87.

tament of our Lord; for the latter purpose, in passing this material in review, we desire to order it in
such a manner as to bring into clear relief its testimony
to the profound conviction cherished by our Lord's
first followers that He was of divine origin and nature. In prosecuting our exposition we shall seek to
run cursorily through the entire New Testament; in
framing our argument we shall lay primary stress on
the Gospels, or rather on the Synoptic Gospels, and
adduce the remaining books chiefly as corroborative
and elucidative testimony to what we shall find in
the evangelical narratives. Thus we hope to take at
once a wide or even a complete view of the whole field,
and to throw into prominence the unitary presupposition by the entire New Testament of the deity of our
Lord.

We turn, then, first to the Gospels, and in the first
instance to the Synoptic Gospels. We observe at once

**Designations
of Our Lord
in the
Synoptic Gospels**
that, on a *prima facie* view, the designations they apply to our Lord fall into
three general classes. They seem to be
either purely designatory, generally honorific, or specifically Messianic. Of all purely designatory designations, the personal name is the most natural
and direct. We can feel no surprise, therefore, to learn
that our Lord is spoken of in the Gospels most commonly by the simple name of ' Jesus.' Nor shall we
feel surprise to learn that the simplest honorific titles
are represented as those most frequently employed in
addressing Him,—' Rabbi,' with its Greek renderings,
' Teacher ' and ' Master,' and its Greek representative,
' Lord.' No Messianic title again is more often met
with in the narrative of the Gospels than the simple

'Christ,' although on our Lord's lips 'the Son of Man' is constant. The general effect of the narrative on the reader, who passes rapidly through it, noting particularly the designations employed of our Lord, is a strong impression that He is thought of by the writers, and is represented by them as thought of by His contemporary followers and by Himself, as a person of high dignity and unquestionable authority; and that this dignity and authority were rooted, both in their and in His estimation, in His Messianic character.   If we are to take the designations employed in the Gospel narratives as our guide, therefore, we should say that the fundamental general fact which they suggest is that Jesus was esteemed by His first followers as the promised Messiah, and was looked upon with reverence and accorded supreme authority as such. Whether this impression is fully justified by the evidence when it is narrowly scrutinized; and if so what the complete significance of the fact so established is; and whether more than appears upon the surface of it is really contained in the fact—these are matters which must be left to a closer examination of the details to determine.

In undertaking such a closer examination of the details, it will conduce not only to clearness of treat-
Starting ment, but also to surety of result, to
Point of the take up the several Gospels separately.
Survey And perhaps it may be as well to begin with the Gospel of Mark. It is the briefest and in some respects the simplest and most direct narrative we have of the career of our Lord. It may be supposed, therefore, to present to us the elements of our problem in their least complicated shape.

THE DESIGNATIONS OF OUR LORD IN MARK

In Mark what we may call the narrative designation of our Lord is uniformly the simple ' Jesus.'[1] Mark

Narrative Designation

employs no other designation in his entire narrative.[2] On the other hand, he places this designation, in its simplicity, in the mouth of no one else.[3] In the heading of his Gospel he sets, it is true, that " solemn designation of the Messianic personality," ' Jesus Christ.' This is a designation not only which occurs nowhere else in this Gospel,[4] but which occurs elsewhere in the four Gospels only rarely and only in similar formal connections. It seems already, here at least, to be

[1] It occurs seventy-three times in Mark. In all these instances it has the article, except the first (1^9), where the article is absent in accordance with the general rule that names of persons occur first without the article, and after that take it.

[2] In 1^1 " Jesus Christ " occurs, but this is not in the narrative but in the *heading* of the book. " Jesus the Nazarene," 10^{47}, is not the language of Mark but of the people, repeated by him. "Lord Jesus," 16^{19}, " Lord," 16^{20}, are in the spurious closing paragraph.

[3] Unless the order in which the words stand in 10^{47}, " Thou Son of David, Jesus," and in 14^{67}, " That Nazarene, Jesus," be thought to constitute an exception. The designation, ' Jesus,' occurs on the lips of others in such *combinations* as: 1^{24}, " Jesus, thou Nazarene "; 5^7, " Jesus, Son of the Most High God "; 10^{47}, " Jesus, the Son of David "; and also again, " Jesus, the Nazarene "; 14^{67}, " Jesus, the Nazarene "; 16^6, " Jesus, the Nazarene."

[4] Cf. Holtzmann, *Hand-Commentar*, p. 37.

employed as a proper name.[5] But in the narrative itself, as we have intimated, Mark uses only the simple ' Jesus,' which nevertheless he never represents as used by others either in speaking of or in speaking to Jesus.

The name by which Jesus was popularly known to His contemporaries, according to Mark, was apparently the fuller descriptive one of ' Jesus of Nazareth ' (10^{47} 16^6 14^{67}).[6] On one occasion He is represented as addressed by this full name (1^{24}), and on two others by the name ' Jesus,' enlarged by a Messianic title (' Jesus, Son of the Most High God ' 5^7, ' Jesus, Son of David ' 10^{47}). The inference would seem to be that ' Jesus ' was too common a name[7] to be sufficiently designatory until our Lord's person had loomed so large, at least in the circles to which the Gospels were addressed, as to put all other Jesuses out of mind when this name was mentioned. The employment of the simple ' Jesus ' as the narrative name in this Gospel is, therefore, an outgrowth of, and a testimony to, the supreme position He occupied in the minds of Christians.

Popular Designation

The formula by which Jesus is represented by Mark as ordinarily addressed is apparently the simple honorific title, ' Rabbi,' by which in that age (Mt 23^7) every professed teacher was courteously greeted.[8] The actual

Formula of Address

---

[5] So, e.g., Meyer, Holtzmann, Wellhausen.

[6] On the form Ναζαρηνός see Swete, on Mark 1^{24}.

[7] See Delitzsch, *Der Jesusname* in "Zeitschr. f. d. luth. Theol.," 1876, 209*seq.*, or *Talmud. Stud.*, xv.; and cf. Keim, *Geschichte Jesu*, 1, 384 *seq.*

[8] Cf. Westcott, on John 3^2.

Aramaic form 'Rabbi' occurs, however, but seldom in his narrative, and only on the lips of Jesus' disciples (9^5 11^{21}; 14^{45}, Judas in betraying Him); although the parallel form 'Rabboni' occurs once on the lips of a petitioner for healing (10^{51}). In its place stands customarily its simplest and most usual Greek rendering, 'Teacher' ($διδάσκαλε$).[9] The general synonomy of the forms of address, 'Teacher,' 'Master,' 'Lord' ($διδάσκαλε$, $ἐπιστάτα$, $κύριε$), as all alike Greek representatives of 'Rabbi,' is fully established by a comparison of the parallel passages in the Synoptics, as well as by such defining passages as Jno 1^{38} 20^{16}.[10]

What is to be noted here is that in his report of the forms of address employed by those conversing with Jesus, Mark confines himself among Greek formulas to 'Teacher' ($διδάσκαλε$) as his standing representation of 'Rabbi.' The use of 'Lord' ($κύριε$) in 7^{28} is not strictly an exception to this, since the speaker on that occasion was a heathen, and 'Lord' ($κύριε$) may be best viewed as indicative of this fact. It is the common Greek honorific address, equivalent in significance to the Jewish 'Rabbi' or 'Teacher.'[11]

The address 'Teacher'[12] is used by Mark broadly, and is put upon the lips both of our Lord's disciples

[9] See esp. Dalman, *The Words of Jesus*, XIV., E. T., pp. 331 *seq.*

[10] Cf. Swete, on Mark 4^{38}; Dalman, 327, 336.

[11] Cf. Wellhausen, *in loc.*: "The address $κύριε$ is found in Mark only in this passage, in the mouth of a heathen woman." Swete goes astray here in paraphrasing, "True, Rabbi,"—"Rabbi" is out of place.

[12] The rendering of $διδάσκαλος$ (after the Vulgate, *Magister*) by "Master" is, as Westcott remarks (on John 3^2), "apt to suggest

in their ordinary colloquy (4^{38} 9^{38} 10^{35} 13^{1}), obviously as their customary form of addressing Him; and of others who approached Him for every variety of reason (5^{35} 9^{17} $10^{17,20}$ $12^{14,19,32}$).

Significance of 'Teacher'

There does not necessarily lie in this mode of address, therefore, anything more than a general polite recognition of our Lord's claim to be a teacher and leader of men, although of course this recognition may rise on occasion above mere courtesy and become the expression of real reverence and dependence and a recognition of His authority and sovereignty. When something like this was insincerely or frivolously expressed, our Lord was offended by it, as in the case of the rich young ruler who addressed Him flatteringly as 'Good Teacher' (10^{17}).[13] But when the expression was sincere it was received by Jesus in good part and the recognition of His authority involved in it welcomed and responded to, even when the authority suggested far exceeded that of an ordinary Rabbi and involved at least Messianic claims (10^{35} 9^{38} 4^{38}). Not only does He accept this designation; He even adopts it, instructing His disciples to speak of Him to others as 'the Teacher' (14^{14}),— and there is involved perhaps in this adoption of the title all that is expressed in the declarations of Mt 23^{1-12}. Although not necessarily recognized as all that He was by every one who approached Him saying 'Teacher,' yet under this designation He certainly is

false associations." Yet the implication of authority is present in it; and that might be missed in rendering it 'Teacher'; cf. Schoettgen, *Hor. Hebr.* on Mt 10^{40}, Jno 15^{14}, Gal 4^{19}.

[13] Dalman, p. 337: "This address was at variance with actual usage, and moreover in the mouth of the speaker, it was mere insolent flattery." Cf. Swete *in loc.*: but see also Alexander and Weiss-Meyer.

recognized as claiming and certainly does claim an authority above that of those who shared the title of 'Teacher' with Him ($1^{22,27}$ etc.).

Similarly we are not quite at the end of the matter when we say that the heathen woman in addressing
Significance of 'Lord'
Him as 'Lord' (7^{28}) only makes use of the common Greek honorific address. When one comes to a religious teacher petitioning so great a benefit, the honorific title which is employed is apt to be charged with a far richer meaning than mere courtesy or respect. And Jesus received it in this case at its full value; in a sense bearing some relation to His own appellative use of the same term, 'Lord' ($\varkappa \acute{u}\rho\iota o\varsigma$), when He declared Himself 'Lord of the Sabbath' and 'David's Lord' as well as his 'Son' (2^{28} $12^{36,37}$). It is in this appellative use of the term 'Lord' by Jesus indeed that we may discover the deepest significance of the application of that title to Him (1^3 2^{28} 11^3 $12^{36,37}$ [12^9 13^{35}]). It is no doubt sometimes very difficult to determine whether in a given instance it refers to God or to Jesus[14], a fact which has its significance. But the certain cases will themselves carry us very far. When, for example, Jesus is quoted as declaring that "the Son of Man is Lord even of the Sabbath" (or, perhaps, "of the Sabbath, too"), the implication is that He is Lord of much more than the Sabbath, and that this His Lordship is an appanage of His Messianic dignity.[15] And

[14] This matter is carefully investigated by Sven Herner, *Die An-wendung des Wortes* $\varkappa \acute{u}\rho\iota o\varsigma$ *im N. T.*, 1903, pp. 7-9, with the result that he assigns 1^3 2^{28} 7^{28} 11^3 $12^{36,37}$, and also possibly but not probably 5^{19}, to Jesus.

[15] So Weiss-Meyer: "The conclusion rests . . . on the vocation of the Son of Man, as bringing the highest blessing to man, to control

when He is represented as arguing with the scribes
over the significance of the title 'Son of David'
($12^{36,37}$), it cannot be doubted that He had Himself
as the Messiah in mind; and, whatever else His words
suggest, they certainly intimate that He held Himself
as the Messiah to be greater than David as truly as
He was greater than Solomon (Mt 12^{42}); that, in
a word, David (as that prophetic monarch himself
recognized) was no more His father by virtue of His
descent from him, than he was His servant by virtue
of his essential relation to Him.[16] He was at the very
least, and was predicted by David himself as, David's
sovereign.

Such being the conception of His lordship which
was in His mind, we must assume it was this lofty
dignity which He claimed for Himself when He
instructed His disciples, whom He sent to bring Him
the ass's colt which was to bear Him into Jerusalem,
to tell those who might dispute their right to it, that
" the Lord hath need of him " (11^3); and this is
borne out by the strongly Messianic character of the
whole transaction (verses 9, 10, cf. Mt $21^{4,5}$, Jno
$12^{14,15}$).[17] And surely some such implications attend

everything that has been arranged for man's blessedness, and therefore also the Sabbath." Wellhausen perceives that the passage as it
stands imports that such authority can be exercised only by the Messiah. Cf. Holtzmann.

[16] Cf. Alexander, *in loc.*: " The person thus described, as the superior and sovereign of David and his house and of all Israel, could not
possibly be David himself, nor any of his sons and successors except
one who by virtue of his twofold nature was at once his sovereign
and his son . . .": also Meyer, *in loc.*, whom, however, Weiss seeks
to correct (cf. Holtzmann, *Hand-Commentar,* 249, and *N. T. Theologie,* I. 243).

[17] Wellhausen remarks *in loc.*: " ὁ κύριος is purposely meant to
sound mysterious; Jesus does not elsewhere so designate Himself, nor

also the semi-parabolic designation of Himself as the
' Lord of the House ' whose coming is to be watched
for (13^{35}). And at least as much as this is involved
when the evangelist identifies Him with ' the Lord '
whose way was to be made ready for Him by the
ministry of John the Baptist in fulfillment of the
prophetic declarations of Isaiah and Malachi (1^3) ;
for the alterations in the language of the declarations
introduced by the evangelist make clear his purpose to
apply these phrases directly to Jesus.[18]

It is not necessary to presuppose that ' Rabbi ' un-
derlies this appellative use of ' Lord ' ($\varkappa\acute{\nu}\rho\iota\sigma\varsigma$). In
Mark 12^{37} (and probably also 1^3) the underlying term
is *Adhoni*, and elsewhere it is doubtless *Maran*, or
Marana (or *Mara'a*).[19] In other words the implications of the term in this application of it are those of
supremacy and sovereignty. Whence it emerges that
Jesus is represented as claiming for Himself (2^{28} $12^{36,37}$
13^{35} 11^3), and as being recognized within His own
circle as possessing (11^3), supreme sovereignty,—a
sovereignty superior to that of the typical king himself

is He so named by His disciples or by the narrator." But this is surely
hypercritical in the presence of 2^{28} and $12^{36,37}$.

[18] Cf. Holtzmann, *Hand-Commentar*, p. 55: " Instead of $a\dot{\nu}\tau o\tilde{\nu}$ at the
end there stands $\tau o\tilde{\nu}\;\theta\epsilon o\tilde{\nu}\;\dot{\eta}\mu\tilde{\omega}\nu$ in the LXX. The change shows that
the evangelist, by the $\varkappa\acute{\nu}\rho\iota o\varsigma$ of the first member, wished not God but
the Messiah to be understood." See also Sven Herner, *Die Anwen-
dung des Wortes $\varkappa\acute{\nu}\rho\iota o\varsigma$ im N. T.*, p. 7: " Nor can there be any doubt
that the citation, already known from Mt. 3^3—' Prepare ye the way
of the Lord '—refers to Christ." Mark has, he tells us, quoted, immediately before, the words found also in Mt 11^{10} with alterations from
the O. T. text such as show they are intended by him to refer to
Christ: and the connection necessarily demands that these now before
us should also be referred to Christ (cf., p. 4).

[19] Cf. Dalman, *Words*, 328, and cf. 326. It must not be supposed,
however, that ' Rabbi ' might not be charged with a high significance
(cf. Dalman, p. 334).

($12^{36,37}$), extending over the divinely ordained religious enactments of the chosen people (7^{28}, cf. 7^{15-19}), and entitling Him to dispose of the possessions (11^3) and the very destinies of men (13^{35}). There is here asserted not only Messianic dignity and authority, but dignity and authority which transcend those ordinarily attributed even to the Messiah ($12^{36,37}$), and are comparable only to those of God Himself (1^3).

The transition from such a designation of Jesus as 'Lord' to the designation of Him as 'Messiah,' is only a passage from the general to the particular. What is noteworthy is, therefore, not that specifically Messianic titles are freely assigned to Jesus in the narrative, but that no other titles than Messianic ones seem to be employed of Him. There is indication indeed that our Lord was recognized as a prophet (6^{15} 8^{28}); in point of fact, that He recognized Himself as a prophet (6^4). It is clear indeed that He was widely spoken of as a prophet and that He Himself accepted the designation as appropriate.[20] But this is little emphasized in this Gospel, and would form no exception to the rule that no designations are suggested for Jesus except Messianic titles. Neither can we consider the designations 'Bridegroom' ($2^{19,19,20}$) and 'Shepherd' (14^{27}), which Jesus seems to have applied incidentally to Himself, exceptions. In the former of these Jesus, discoursing of John the Baptist (2^{18}) doubtless with intentional reference to a saying of his which is re-

Messianic Designations

[20] See Swete's note on 6^4: "The Lord here assumes the *rôle* of the Prophet, which was generally conceded to Him (6^{15} 8^{28}, Mt $21^{11,46}$, Lk 24^{19}, Jno 4^{19} 6^{14} 7^{40} 9^{17}, Acts 3^{22} 7^{37})." And compare Hastings' *Dictionary of Christ and the Gospels*, I, art. "Foresight," where the matter is examined.

corded for us only in John (3^{29}), identified Himself
on the one hand with the 'Bridegroom' of Old Testament prophecy (cf. Hos 2^{19}), and set Himself forth
on the other as the Head of the people of God now to
be gathered into the promised kingdom: in other
words, the designation is Messianic to the core.[21] And
certainly not less is to be said of His identification of
Himself with the mysterious 'Shepherd' of Zech 13^{7},
who is the fellow of the Lord of Hosts (14^{27} ‖ Mt
26^{31}; and cf. 6^{34} ‖ Mt 9^{36}; and see Mt 25^{32}, eschato-
logically; and Jno 10^{2}). By the side of these it may
also be necessary to recognize as a Messianic designation, the epithet 'Beloved,' which is applied to Him
in the divine commendations of the Son—" Thou art
my Son, the Beloved, in whom I am well pleased,"
" This is my Son, the Beloved " (1^{11} 9^{7}).[22] But apart
from these more unusual designations none are applied
to Jesus in the whole course of the narrative by any
of the characters introduced, including Jesus in His
own person, but familiar Messianic titles. These occur
in considerable variety, and include not only the simple
' Christ' with its equivalents, ' the King of Israel' or
' of the Jews,' and ' the Son of David,' but also the

[21] Cf. Swete, *in loc.:* " So the Lord identifies Himself with the Bridegroom of O. T. prophecy (Hos. 2^{20}, etc.), i.e. God in His covenant
relation to Israel, a metaphor in the N. T. applied to the Christ (Mt
25^{1}, Jno $3^{18,29}$, Eph 5^{28} *sq*, Apoc 19^{7}, etc.)." Christ is set forth Mes-
sianically under the name of the Bridegroom in N. T. only in Mk
$2^{19,19,20}$, Mt 9^{15}, Lk 5^{34}, Jno 3^{29}; and in the Parable of the Ten Virgins, Mt $25^{1,5,6,10}$. The *thing* occurs oftener.

[22] Cf. J. Armitage Robinson, in Hastings' *Dictionary of the Bible*, II,
501 (art. " Isaiah, Ascension of," cf. Charles, *The Ascension of
Isaiah*, I. 4), and *St. Paul's Epistle to the Ephesians*, 229-247 (Note on
" ' The Beloved ' as a Messianic title "). Dr. Robinson, however, does
not assert that the title occurs in Mark, though he finds it in the parallel passages in the other Synoptics.

more significant ones of 'the Holy One of God' and 'the Son of God,'—varied to 'the Son of the Most High God,' and 'the Son of the Blessed,'—and Jesus' own chosen self-designation, 'the Son of Man.'

The evangelist himself nowhere in the course of his narrative speaks of Jesus by one of these titles. As we have seen, his narrative name of our Lord is exclusively the simple 'Jesus.' No reader will doubt, however, that he considered all of them applicable to Jesus; and he announces his book, in the heading he has prefixed to it, as intended to recount the origins of "the Gospel of Jesus Christ"—possibly adding also the further Messianic designation of "the Son of God." This compound name 'Jesus Christ' occurs extremely rarely in the Gospels, 'Jesus Christ' and never except in the most formal and ceremonious circumstances.[23] It appears, indeed, to be reserved as an august name, weighted with the implication of the entire content of Jesus' claims, and therefore suitable only for setting at the head of documents designed to exhibit His life and work, or at the opening of accounts of significant periods or acts of His career. It is very fairly described by Holtzmann, therefore, as "the solemn designation of the Messianic personality."[24] Although in it the

[23] It appears only in the headings of Mt (1^1) and Mk (1^1) and at the starting point of the narrative of Mt (1^{18}) and the new beginning made at Mt 16^{21}: and similarly in John only at the first mention of Jesus (1^{17}), which may be accounted the beginning of his narrative, and at the opening of the great sacerdotal prayer (17^3). It begins to be frequent in Acts (2^{38} 3^6 4^{10} $8^{12,[37]}$ 10^{36} 10^{48} 11^{17} 15^{26} 16^{18} 20^{21} 28^{31}) ; and in Paul it is very frequent. The contrary combination, 'Christ Jesus,' does not occur at all in the Gospels: but appears occasionally in Acts (3^{20} 5^{42} [17^3 $18^{5,28}$] 24^{24}) and in Paul very often.

[24] *Hand-Com.,* p. 37.

term 'Christ' has ceased to be an appellation and become a portion of a proper name,[25] its use as such bears all the stronger testimony to the ascription of the Messiahship to Jesus. Other Messiah than He had ceased to be contemplated as conceivable, and the very appellation 'Messiah' had become His distinguishing name.

Although this compound name occurs nowhere else in Mark, and the reverse combination, 'Christ Jesus,' which is also in use in Acts and

'The Christ' Paul, never, the simple 'Christ' appears in his narrative with sufficient frequency to evince that it was a favorite designation of the Messiah (8^{29} 12^{35} 13^{21} 14^{61} 15^{32}), applied as such to Jesus (8^{29} 14^{61} 15^{32}) in order to mark Him out as the Messiah; and accepted as such by Jesus, who thus asserts Himself to be the Messiah (8^{30} 14^{62}, cf. 9^{41} 12^{35} 13^{21}). Its significance, as the simplest of all Messianic titles, is well brought out by the synonyms with which it is coupled. When Peter assigned it to our Lord in his great confession (8^{29}), our Lord at once takes it up as the equivalent of His own favorite self-designation of 'the Son of Man.'[26] When our Lord would instruct the scribes with respect to the real dignity of the Messiah, He asks them how they can speak of the Christ as 'the Son of David,' when David himself

[25] Wellhausen, on Mk 1^1: "But in 'Jesus Christ,' [Christ] has already become a part of a personal name and has therefore lost the article,—like Adam, Gen 5^1." Holtzmann, as cited: "The *nomen proprium* Ἰησοῦς Χριστός . . . in which the personal name Jesus . . . appears as the fore-name, the official name Χριστός as the second personal name."

[26] Cf. also the parallels, Lk 9^{20}, "the Christ of God"; Mt 16^{16}, "the Christ, the Son of the living God."

calls Him his 'Lord' ($12^{35,37}$). When the high-priest at His trial adjured Him to say whether He was 'the Christ, the Son of the Blessed,' in His assenting reply He calls Himself the 'Son of Man' ($14^{62,63}$). And in like manner the scoffing Jews mockingly addressed Him as He hung on the cross as 'the Christ, the King of Israel' (15^{32}). In all these instances the term is obviously used as an appellation, and has no different content from the general one common to all the designations which impute Messiahship. It is the complete synonym of 'the King of Israel' (15^{32}), 'the Son of David' (12^{35}), 'the Son of the Blessed' (14^{61}), 'the Son of Man' (8^{31} 14^{62}). In a word it is the general title of the Messianic Sovereign, whom Jesus claims to be in His acceptance of this designation, and whom He is asserted to be by its application to Him by His followers.

In the remarkable passage, 9^{41}, alone does 'Christ' appear without the article. And therefore it has been frequently supposed to be employed

Anarthrous 'Christ'

there not as an appellation but as a proper name, and therefore again to be out of place on Jesus' lips and to be accordingly an intrusion into the text from the later point of view of His followers.[27] There seems to be no reason, however, why 'Christ' (χριστός) even without the article may not be taken appellatively[28] (cf. Lk 23^2);

[27] Dalman, *Words*, 305-6, explains the words "that ye are Christ's" as an intrusion; on the ground that they are an unnecessary explanation of a μου *which is not genuine*. Even Swete, *in loc.*, following Hawkins, *Hor. Syn.*, p. 122, is inclined to see here "a later writer's hand," and Keil, like Dalman, affirms boldly that " ὅτι χριστοῦ ἐστέ is an explanatory statement adjoined by Mark to ἐν ὀνόματι μου."

[28] It is so understood here e.g. by Fritzsche and Meyer; and Delitzsch points out that sometimes 'Messiah' is used among the Jews them-

and in that case, no reason why our Lord may not have told His followers that no one who should do them a benefit "in the name that they are the Christ's," i. e., on the ground that they are the servants of the Messiah, should lose his appropriate reward. In this view our Lord would no doubt be once again claiming for Himself the Messianic dignity; but He would not be doing it in language inappropriate upon His lips, especially at a period in His ministry subsequent to the great confession of Peter at Cæsarea Philippi (8^{29}), after which, we are expressly told ($8^{31,32}$), Jesus began to teach both formally and quite openly what and who He was and what was to befall Him in the prosecution of His mission. The thought thus brought out differs in nothing from that of Mt 10^{42} and the mode of expressing the thought is equally appropriate with that recorded there, on the lips of One who knew Himself to be Teacher and Lord only because He was the Christ. At the same time it must not be too easily assumed that our Lord could not speak of Himself as 'Christ' taken even as a proper, or quasi-proper, name, although we need not dwell upon this at this point.[29]

It was because He announced Himself as the 'Christ' and was widely understood to possess claims

Royal Titles

upon that dignity that, when He was arraigned before Pilate, it was precisely upon His pretensions to be 'the King of the Jews' that He was interrogated ($15^{2,26}$). On Jewish lips this title naturally was corrected to 'the

selves without the article—according to Dalman, however, only in the Babylonian Talmud (*Words*, p. 292). Dalman, *loc. cit.*, says that anarthrous Χριστός occurs in the Synoptics only in the phrases 'Jesus Christ' (Mt $1^{1,18}$, Mk 1^1), 'Jesus surnamed Christ' (Mt 1^{16} $27^{17,22}$), 'Lord Christ' (Lk 2^{11}), 'King Christ' (Lk 23^2), and here.

[29] Cf. below, pp. 59*seq.*

King of Israel' (15^{32}), which again is identified with the appellation ' the Christ ' (15^{32}). In this form also Jesus was far from repelling the Messianic ascription, but on the contrary expressly allows it (15^{2}). To all appearance, however, neither ' the Christ,' nor ' the King of Israel,' was more current as a Messianic designation than the kindred form ' the Son of David' (12^{35}, cf. 11^{10}),[30] though this title appears in Mark's narrative only once as actually applied to Jesus (10^{47,48}). The blind man at the gates of Jericho, hearing that Jesus of Nazareth was passing by, and wishing to ask a favor at His hands as the expected King of Israel, knew no better name by which to address Him than ' Son of David.' It was the faith thus expressed which Jesus commended in him when He responded to his appeal,—thus accepting this Messianic title also (10^{49,51,52}, cf. 11^{10}). It is quite untenable, therefore, to suppose that Jesus wished to repel this designation[31] in the question He put as He taught in the temple (12^{35}), " How say the scribes that the Christ is the son of David," when " David himself " (and speaking " in the Holy Spirit ") " calls Him rather Lord ? " He does not deny that He is David's

[30] Holtzmann, *N. T. Theologie*, I. 243, speaks of it as " the most popular and comprehensive of all the Messianic titles," and supposes that the underlying Jewish feeling of Matthew shows itself in the important *rôle* which he makes this folk-cry play in his Gospel (Mt 9^{27} 12^{23} 15^{22} 20^{30,31} 21^{9,15} 22^{42,45}).

[31] So e.g. Wellhausen (as before him Strauss, Schenkel and others) : " Jesus represents it as merely a notion of the scribes that the Messiah is the son of David, and refutes it by a statement of David's own which proves the contrary. An incitement to enter upon this question He had only in case it concerned Himself. He held Himself for the Messiah, though He was not the son of David," etc. Cf. on the contrary the remarks in Dalman, *Words*, p. 286: also Meyer's good note.

son; He asserts that He is David's Lord. It seems, therefore, not quite exact even to say that He wishes to suggest that His sonship derives from a higher source than David: that He is, in a word, the Son of God rather than of David.[32] But it seems clear that He desires to intimate that as Lord of David He was something far more than was conveyed by the accustomed—and so far acceptable[33]—title of 'Son of David':[34] and something of this higher dignity than mere kingship belonging to Him is doubtless inherent in this, therefore, higher Messianic title of 'Son of God.'

This higher title, if it is not applied to Jesus by Mark himself in the heading of his Gospel (1^1), is at least in the course of the narrative repeatedly represented as applied to Him by others, and is expressly approved as so applied not only by the evangelist (3^{11}), but by our Lord Himself (14^{62}). The form of the title varies from the simple 'Son of God' ($[1^1]$ 3^{11}, cf. 15^{39}) to the 'Son of the Blessed' (14^{61}) and the 'Son of the Most High God' (5^7). It is, in the instances recited by Mark, found chiefly on the lips of the unclean spirits whom Jesus cast out (3^{11} 5^7); though it is employed also, apparently as a culminating Messianic title, by the high priest at His trial,

'Son of God'

[32] See Dalman, *Words,* 286.

[33] Cf. Meyer's good note E. T. *Mark and Luke,* 1. 194 note.

[34] Dalman, arguing that what Jesus wished to suggest was that He was Son of God, not of David, goes on to urge that this implies a supernatural birth, and (though not the doctrine of the two natures) a nature which though "appearing in human weakness, is yet a perfect revelation of God," and fits Him for future rulership over the world. Swete remarks: "The title does not involve divine sovereignty; yet it was a natural inference that a descendant who was David's Lord was also David's God."

seeking to obtain from Jesus an acknowledgment of
His great pretensions (14[62]), and was frankly accepted
by our Lord as fairly setting these pretensions forth
(14[63]). As a Messianic title it differs from those
which have been heretofore engaging our attention, in
emphasizing, as they do not, the supernatural side of
the office and functions of the Messiah: He comes as
the representative of God to do God's will in the world.
From this point of view another Messianic title applied to Him by a demoniac—' the Holy One of God '
(1[24]),[35]—ranges with it: and the employment by
the unclean spirits of this class of titles only (cf. 3[11] and
1[34]) may be due to the fact that they were voices
from the spiritual world and were as such less
concerned than the people of the land with national
hopes or earthly developments.[36]

[35] Westcott (on Jno 6[69]) remarks: "The knowledge of the demoniacs reached to the essential nature of the Lord" (comparing Rev
3[7], 1 Jno 2[20]; and Jno 10[36] and 6[27]). The expression, however, (which
occurs only in Mk 1[24], Lk 4[34], Jno 6[69]) need not in itself, as Hahn
(Lk 4[34]) puts it, "refer to the moral purity of Jesus (Keil); but may
express rather His Messianic dignity, designating Him as God's consecrated, dedicated One (cf. Jno 10[36])." Hahn adds that though the
demon knows of the humble human origin of Jesus (Ναζαρηνέ) he
nevertheless knows also of His divine appointment. Holtzmann (p.
76) accords in general with Hahn, and points out that the demon
speaks for his class ("us"). Wellhausen supposes this title to have
been formed by transference to the Messiah of epithets at first appropriated to Israel: "Israel originally is both the Son of God and the
Holy One of the Highest" (on Mk 1[24]). It seems, however, a little
difficult to understand how the demons were supposed to recognize at
sight ("as soon as ever they saw him") an official appointment. Does
it not seem that there must have been supposed to be something about
Jesus which betrayed to an eye which saw beneath the surface His
superhuman nature—whether this were thought of as His supreme holiness or as His unapproachable majesty?

[36] From his own point of view Wellhausen speaks (on 1[25,26]) of
"the popular belief that the spirits have for the supersensual other-

By the side of the passages in which the precise title 'Son of God' is employed, there stands another series in which Jesus speaks of Himself, or **'The Son'** is represented as spoken of by God, simply as 'the Son' (13^{32}, cf. 12^6; 1^{11} 9^7), used obviously in a very pregnant sense:[37] and these naturally suggest their correlatives in which He speaks of God as His 'Father' in the same pregnant manner (8^{38}, cf. 13^{32} 14^{36}). The uniqueness of the relation intended to be intimated by this mode of speech is sharply thrust forward in the parable recorded in Mark 12. There were many slaves who were sent

eyes than flesh and blood," and that these eyes were sharpened in the present case by their danger. This remark seems to imply that in the popular view " the Holy One of God " imported something more than divine appointment—something of superhuman nature or character. The sharpest eyes could scarcely discern appointment.

[37] On the strength of the difference between the precise phrase 'the Son of God' and these phrases where Jesus is called God's 'Son' or speaks of Himself as 'Son,' it has become common to say Jesus does not use the title 'Son of God.' Thus e.g. Shailer Mathews, *The Messianic Hope in the N. T.*, 1905, pp. 106-7: " Jesus Himself does not use the expression, although others use it with reference to Him. It is of course true that Jesus frequently speaks of God as 'Father' and of Himself as 'the Son,' but this is quite another matter from speaking of Himself as ὁ υἱὸς τοῦ θεοῦ. . . . That Jesus spoke of God as His Father in some unique sense cannot be denied, but such sayings as imply this do not employ either ὁ υἱὸς τοῦ θεοῦ or υἱὸς θεοῦ." Dr. Mathews in a note refers to Jno 10^{36} 11^4, but hesitates to speak of these as exceptions because of the possibility that John may have substituted here " a term expressive of his own estimate of Jesus for the word which Jesus used Himself." He might have pointed also not only to the general implication of Jesus' acceptance of the title when applied to Him by the demons and others, but to His express acceptance of it at Mk 14^{62}, and we may add at Mt 16^{16}, though Dr. Mathews would not allow this instance. Nor is it so very clear that the 'Son of God,' 'God's Son,' 'the Son,' are not closely related to one another as Messianic titles.

one after the other to the rebellious husbandmen; but only one son—who is called " the beloved one," a term which is not so much designatory of affection as of that on which special affection is grounded, and is therefore practically equivalent to " only begotten," or " unique."[38] It is possible that it is by this epithet that God designates this His Son on both of the occasions when He spoke from heaven in order to point Him out and mark Him as His own (1^{11} 9^7)—" This is my beloved Son." The meaning is that the Son stands out among all others who may be called sons as in a unique and unapproached sense the Son of God. Of course it is possible to represent this as importing nothing more than that the person so designated is the Messiah, singled out to be the vice-gerent of God on earth; and it is noticeable that it is as the Messiah that Jesus calls God appropriatingly ' His Father ' when He declares that the Son of Man is to come in the glory of His Father with the holy angels (8^{38}), and certainly it was in lowly subjection to the will of God that He prayed at Gethsemane, " Abba, Father, remove this cup from me " (14^{36}). But this explanation seems scarcely adequate; in any case there is intimated in this usage a closeness as well as a uniqueness of rela-

[38] Cf. Swete on Mk 12^6 and also Wellhausen on these passages. " 'O υἱός μου ὁ ἀγαπητός," says the latter on 1^{11}, " for the Semites means, not 'my dear Son,' but 'my unique Son.'" For a careful discussion of all the involved conceptions see J. Armitage Robinson, *St. Paul's Epistle to the Ephesians,* 1903, pp. 229-233, on "'The Beloved' as a Messianic Title." Dr. Robinson seems to suppose that " beloved Son " in Mark—not elsewhere—means simply " dear Son." But this is scarcely conceivable. In point of fact, in 12^6 the meaning seems to be, " sole, unique, Son "; while 1^{11} 9^7 either bear that same meaning or else must be taken, like their parallels, as uniting to the ascription of Sonship an additional Messianic title—" the Beloved."

tion existing between Jesus and God, which raises Jesus far beyond comparison with any other son of man. And that remarkable passage, 13^{32}, in which Jesus declares His ignorance, though He be the Son, of the day of His advent, exalts Him apparently above not men only, but angels as well, next to the Father Himself, with whom rather than with the angels He seems to be classed.[39]

All these Messianic designations are represented as not only ascribed to Jesus but accepted by Him. They **Our Lord's own** are not, however, currently employed by **Testimony to** Him; as reported in this narrative, He **His Messiahship** does indeed make occasional use of them—'the Christ' (9^{41}, cf. 8^{29} 12^{35} 13^{21}), the 'Son of David' (12^{35}), the 'Son [of God]' (13^{32}, cf. 12^6) —but only exceptionally. The Messianic designation which He is represented as constantly applying to Him-

---

[39] "Note," says Meyer, "the climax—the angels, the Son, the Father." A. J. Mason (*Conditions of our Lord's Life on Earth*, 120), on the other hand, thinks "there is no express triple ascent, from men to angels, from angels to the Son "—but the οὐδὲ—οὐδέ is in a sort parenthetical: " None knoweth—no not the angels in heaven, nor yet the Son—except the Father." " All the same," he adds, " the sentence *is* a climax, and a pointed one. Our Lord does not say (what would have been good Greek) οὐδὲ οἱ ἄγγελοι οὔτε ὁ υἱός, as if the Son were in the same class of beings with the angels in heaven, only the highest of them. He says οὐδὲ—οὐδέ; as if to say, ' You might suppose that the secret was only a secret from those on earth; but it is kept a secret even from those in heaven. You might suppose that the secret was only a secret for created beings, but it is a secret for the uncreated Son Himself. The Father alone knows it.'" Cf. Swete: " No one . . . not even . . . nor yet." Dalman, *Words*, p. 194, arbitrarily supposes that the closing words, " nor the Son but the Father only," may be an accretion, while Zeller (*Z. für w. Th.*, 1865, p. 308), on the ground of this ascription to Christ of a superangelic nature wishes to assign Mark to the second century (see Meyer's reply, *Mk. and Lk.*, E. T., I, 205 note). From all which it is at least clear that the passage confessedly assigns a superhuman nature to Jesus.

self is also one peculiar to Himself—'the Son of Man.'[40] That this designation is actually employed as a Messianic title, is apparent not only from its obvious origin in the vision of Daniel 7[13], to which reference is repeatedly made (8[38] 13[26] 14[62]),[41] but also from the easy passage which is made, in the course of the conversations reported, from one of the other designations to this, whereby they are evinced as its synonyms. Thus in 8[31] in sequence to Peter's confession of Him as 'the Christ,' we are told that Jesus began to teach that "the Son of Man must suffer many things." Similarly in 13[26] our Lord notifies us that although many "false Christs" shall arise who may deceive men, yet when certain signs occur, "then shall they see the Son of Man coming." Again when exhorted to declare whether He is "the Christ, the Son of the Blessed" (14[61]), He responds in the affirmative and adds: "And ye shall see the Son of Man sitting at the right hand of power." Evidently if we are to ask, 'Who is this Son of Man,' we must give answer,

---

[40] 2[10,28] 8[31,38] 9[9,12,31] 10[33,45] 13[26] 14[21,41,62].

[41] The reference to Daniel 7[13] seems indisputable. But it is in somewhat wide circles not allowed. Even conservative writers are occasionally found seeking another explanation of the phrase, although this involves treating the passages mentioned as unhistorical. Examples may be found in Volkmar Fritzsche, *Das Berufsbewusstsein Jesu,* 1905, pp. 17 *sq.;* Siegfried Goebel, *Die Reden unseres Herrn nach Johannes,* 1906, (following his note on Jno 1[51]); and Zahn in his Commentary on Matthew. (Zahn is directly refuted by Fritz Tillmann in the *Biblische Zeitschrift,* 1907, vol. I., 348 *seq.*). Critics like Wellhausen and N. Schmidt, of course, assume that 'Son of Man' is merely Aramaic for "Man," and deny all reference to Daniel. What may be made of the term, and of the Danielic passage itself, from this point of view may be conveniently read in Dr. Cheyne's *Bible Problems,* 1904; or with a great display of hypothetical learning in Hugo Gressmann's *Der Ursprung der israelitisch-jüdischen Eschatologie,* 1905.

shortly, 'The Christ of God.' And it lies in the evidence not only that this was the underlying conception of our Lord as reported in this Gospel but also that it was—however dimly—apprehended by those He addressed. There is perhaps no single passage in Mark so clear to this effect as John 12[34], where the multitude are represented as puzzled by our Lord's teaching that the " Son of Man must be lifted up," in view of their conviction that "the Christ abideth forever." "We have heard out of the law," they say, "that the Christ abideth forever: and how sayest thou that the Son of Man must be lifted up? Who is this Son of Man?" This is as much as to say that that 'Son of Man' who is the Messiah is known to them and is known to them as the eternal King: but no other 'Son of Man' is known to them—who is to be "lifted up" from the earth that He may draw all men unto Him. The same implication is latent, however, in the instances reported by Mark, the conversations recorded in which would have been unintelligible had there not been in the hearers' minds some intelligence of the phrase 'Son of Man' as a Messianic title, although it was apparently not a Messianic title either in such current use that it came naturally to their lips or so unambiguous as to be easily comprehended by them in all the implications which our Lord compressed into it.

The difficulty created by our Lord's use of this phrase seems, indeed, as represented by Mark, not so much to have lain in apprehending

'Son of Man'

that it involved a claim to Messianic dignity, as in comprehending the character of the Messianic conception which He expressed by it. The constant employment of this designation of Himself by our Lord[42] in preference to the more current ones, such as, say, 'Son of David' or 'King of Israel,' appears to mark in effect an attempt on our Lord's part, in claiming for Himself the Messianic dignity, at the same time to fill the conception itself with a new import. The nature of the revolution which He would work in the Messianic ideal current among the people, in other words, is signalized by His avoidance of the current designations of the Messiah and His choice for His constant use of a more or less unwonted one which would direct their attention to a different region of Old Testament prophecy. He says, in effect, In the conception you are cherishing of the Messianic king, you are neglecting whole regions of prophecy, and are forming most mistaken expectations regarding Him: it is from the Son of Man of Daniel rather than from the Son of David of the Psalms and Samuel that you should take your starting point. No single title, of course, sums up the entirety of our Lord's conception of the Messianic function: there are elements of it adumbrated in very different sections of Old Testament prediction.   But

---

[42] Cf. Dalman, *Words,* p. 259: "As for the evangelists themselves they take the view that Jesus called Himself the 'Son of Man' at all times and before any company." Nevertheless Dalman himself supposes He probably did not actually use the title before Peter's confession (Mk 8[38]); and Bousset (*Jesus,* 194) is sure that it was only towards the close of His life as death loomed before Him that He applied the Danielic prophecy of the Son of Man to Himself, and that He never adopted the title in its full content, including the ideas of preëxistence and of His own judgeship of the world—the ascription of these to Him by the evangelists being only an instance of the faith of the community working on the tradition ("it is inconceivable that Jesus should have arrogated to Himself the judgeship of the world in place of God," pp. 203-5).

He elected, apparently, to point to the picture which Daniel draws of the establishment of the Kingdom of God on earth as furnishing a starting point for a revision of the Messianic ideal current among those to whom His preaching was in the first instance addressed.

It may be difficult, in view of the varied elements which entered into His Messianic conception, to infer with confidence from the substance of the sayings in which Jesus refers to Himself as the ' Son of Man,' precisely the Messianic conception He understood to be covered by that designation.[43] And much less can we suppose that His whole Messianic idea is embedded in these sayings. He refers to Himself by this designation in only a portion of the sayings which must be utilized in an attempt to determine His Messianic conception; and there is no reason to suppose that He always uses this designation when giving utterance to conceptions which He subsumed under it. Nevertheless, having guarded ourselves against rashness of inference and undue narrowness of view by reminding ourselves of these obvious facts, we must certainly, in an attempt to discover the significance of the designation ' Son of Man ' in the Gospel of Mark, begin by observing the actual connections in which Jesus is represented in that Gospel as employing it, with a view to discovering, as far as possible, from the substance of these sayings the actual implications which it embodied for Him, and through Him for the writer of this Gospel who reports just these sayings from His lips.

[43] Cf. the opening sentence of Dalman in his discussion of this subject (*Words*, 256).

From these sayings, then, we learn that the life of
the 'Son of Man' on earth is essentially a lowly one:

Usage of
'Son of Man'

He came not to be ministered unto, but
to minister (10^{45}). Suffering belongs
therefore to the very essence of His
mission (8^{31} $9^{12,31}$ 10^{33} $14^{21,41}$) and has accordingly
been pre-announced for Him in the Scriptures (9^{12}
14^{21}). But this suffering is not in His own behalf,
but for others, the form of His ministry to whom is
"to give His life a ransom for many" (10^{45}). But
just because His death is a sufficing ransom, death
cannot be all: having given His life as a ransom for
many the 'Son of Man' shall rise again (8^{31} $9^{9,31}$ 10^{34}).
Nor is this vindication by resurrection all. He is
to "rise again" after three days (8^{31} 9^{31} 10^{34}), but
is to "come" again "in clouds with great glory and
power" (13^{26}, cf. 14^{62}) at some more remote, undes-
ignated time (13^{32}), to establish the Kingdom in which
He shall sit at the right hand of power (14^{62}). At
this His coming He "shall send forth the angels and
gather together His elect from the four winds, from
the uttermost part of the earth to the uttermost part
of heaven" (13^{27}); and shall show Himself ashamed
of all who shall have been ashamed of Him and of
His words in the adulterous generation with which He
dwelt on earth (8^{38}). It is clearly the judgment scene
that is here brought before us, and the eternal destinies
of men are represented as lying in the hands of the
'Son of Man.' "His elect," "those whom He has
chosen," are gathered into the Kingdom; His enemies,
those who have rejected Him, are left without. Accordingly it is not surprising that He who came to
give His life a ransom for many (10^{45}) and who is

to come again in order to distribute to men their final destinies should have authority given Him even while on earth to order the religious observances by which men are trained in the life which looks beyond the limits of earth (2^{28}) and even to forgive sins (2^{10}). Perhaps in the light of 8^{38} 13^{27}, in the phrase " on earth " we may see a contrast not so much with the " power " of God to forgive sins " in heaven " (cf. verse 7), as with the authority to award the destinies of all flesh (13^{27} " His elect "; 8^{38} those that are ashamed of Him) hereafter to be exercised in the heavenly kingdom by the 'Son of Man' Himself.

What perhaps most strikes us in this series of utterances is its prevailing soteriological, or perhaps we should say soteriologico-eschatological, rather than christological bearing. To Mark the 'Son of Man,' as reflected in the sayings he cites from the lips of the Lord, is the divinely sent Redeemer, come to minister to men and to give His life a ransom for many, who as Redeemer brings His chosen ones to glory and, holding the destinies of men in His hands, casts out those who have rejected Him—even while yet on earth preadumbrating the final issue by exercising His authority over religious ordinances and the forgiveness of sins. Little is said directly of the person of this Redeemer. It is a human figure, ministering, suffering, dying,—though clothed already with authority in the midst of its humility (or should we not rather say, its humiliation?)—which moves before us in its earthly career: it is a superhuman figure which is to return, clothed in glory—" sitting at the right hand of power " and

Meaning of 'Son of Man'

coming with the clouds of heaven (14^{62}), or " coming
in clouds with great power and glory " (13^{26})—" in
the glory of His Father with the holy angels " (8^{38}),
those holy angels who are sent forth by Him to do
His bidding, that they may gather to Him His chosen
ones (13^{27}). Although there are intermingled traits
derived from other lines of prophecy, the reference
to the great vision of Daniel $7^{13,14}$ in these utterances
is express and pervasive, and we cannot go astray in
assuming that Jesus is represented as, in adopting the
title of ' Son of Man ' for His constant designation of
Himself, intending to identify Himself with that
heavenly figure of Daniel's vision, who is described as
" like to a son of man " in contrast with the bestial
figures of the preceding context, and as having committed to Him by God a universal and eternal dominion.   Primarily His purpose seems to have been
to represent Himself as the introducer of the Kingdom
of God; and in doing so, to emphasize on the one
hand the humiliation of His earthly lot as the founder
of the kingdom in His blood, and on the other the
glory of His real station as exhibited in His consummation of the kingdom with power.   So conceived, this
designation takes its place at the head of all the Messianic designations, and involves a conception of the
Messianic function and personality alike which re-
moves it as far as possible from that of a purely
earthly monarchy, administered by an earth-born king.
Under this conception the Messianic person is conceived as a heavenly being, who comes to earth with
a divinely given mission; His work on earth is conceived as purely spiritual and as carried out in a state
of humiliation; while His glory is postponed to a fu-

ture manifestation which is identified with the judgment day and the end of the world. In the figure of the 'Son of Man,' in a word, we have the spiritual and supernatural Messiah by way of eminence.[44]

[44] The whole subject has recently been excellently reviewed by a Roman Catholic scholar, F. Tillmann, *Der Menschensohn,* 1907. He sums up as follows: " The result of our investigation is in brief this: The designation 'the Son of Man' is a title of the Messiah just as truly as the designation 'Son of David,' 'the Anointed,' and the like. Jesus adopted this designation because it corresponded best to His nature and His purposes, and gave least occasion for the political, national hopes which His people connected with the person of the Messiah. If we inquire further into the specific content of this Messianic designation, the key is supplied by the reference embodied in it to the prophecy of Daniel: the Son of Man is the Divine-human inaugurator of the Messianic salvation predicted by the prophets, He with whom the reign of God on earth takes its start" (pp. 175-6).

MARK'S CONCEPTION OF OUR LORD

If, now, we review the series of designations applied to our Lord in the Gospel of Mark, as a whole, we shall, we think, be led by them into the heart of Mark's representation of Jesus.

What Mark undertook in his Gospel was obviously to give an account of how that great religious move-

A Divine Intervention in Christ ment originated which we call Christianity, but which he calls " the Gospel of Jesus Christ "—the glad tidings, that is, concerning Jesus Christ which were being proclaimed throughout the world. To put it in his own words, he undertook to set forth " the *beginning* of the Gospel of Jesus Christ " (1^1). The account which he gives of the beginning of this great religious movement, by means of his ' Gospel,' is briefly that it originated in a divine intervention; and that this divine intervention was manifested in the ministry of the divinely promised and divinely sent Messiah who was no other than the man Jesus. This man is represented as coming, endowed with ample authority for His task; and as prosecuting this task by the aid of supernatural powers by which He was at once marked out as God's delegate on earth and enabled, in the face of all difficulties and oppositions, to accomplish to its end what He had set His hand to do.

It is idle to speak of Mark presenting us in his

account of Jesus with the picture of a purely human
Christ's Life life.   It belongs to the very essence of
Thoroughly his undertaking to portray this life as
Supernatural supernatural;   and, from beginning to
end, he sets it forth as thoroughly supernatural.   The
Gospel opens, therefore, by introducing Jesus to us
as the divinely given Messiah, in whom God had from
the ages past promised to visit His people;   heralded
as such by the promised messenger making ready the
way of the Lord;   and witnessed by this messenger
as the "mightiest" of men, who bore in His hands
the real potencies of a new life (1^8);   and by God
Himself from heaven as His Son, His beloved, in
whom He was well pleased (1^{11}).   Anointed and
tested for His task, Jesus is then presented as entering
upon and prosecuting His work as God's representative, endowed with all authority and endued with all
miraculous powers.   His authority was manifested
alike in His teaching (1^{22}), in His control of demonic
personalities (1^{27}), in the forgiveness of sins (2^{10}),
in His sovereignty over the religious ordinances of
Israel (2^{28}), in His relations to nature and nature's
laws (4^{41}), in His dominion over death itself (5^{42}).
As each of these typical exercises of authority is signalized in turn and copiously illustrated by instances,
the picture of a miraculous life becomes ever more
striking, and indeed stupendous.   Even the failure of
His friends to comprehend Him and the malice of
His enemies in assaulting Him, are made by the evangelist contributory to the impression of an utterly
supernatural life which he wishes to make on his
readers.   So little was it a normal human life that
Jesus lived that His uncomprehending friends were

tempted to think Him beside Himself, and His enemies proclaimed Him obviously suffering from " possession " ($3^{20\text{-}30}$). Whatever else this life was, it certainly was not, in view of any observer, a " natural "
one. The " unnaturalness " of it is not denied: it is
only pointed out that this " unnaturalness " was systematic, and that it was systematically in the interests
of holiness. What is manifested in it, therefore, is
neither the vagaries of lunacy nor the wickedness of
demonism. What is exhibited is the binding of Satan
and the destruction of satanic powers (cf. 1^{27} *et saepe*).
To ascribe these manifestations to Satan is therefore
to blaspheme the Spirit of God. Nobody, it appears,
dreamed of doubting in any interest the abnormality
of this career: and we should not misrepresent Mark
if we said that his whole Gospel is devoted to making
the impression that Jesus' life and manifestation were
supernatural through and through.

This is, of course, however, not quite the same as
saying that Mark has set himself to portray in Jesus

Jesus
the
Messiah

the life of a supernatural person.
Whether the supernatural life he de-
picts is supernatural because it is the
life on earth of a supernatural person, or because it is the
life of a man with whom God dwelt and through whom
God wrought, may yet remain a question. Certainly
very much in Mark's narrative would fall in readily
with the latter hypothesis. To him Jesus is primarily
the Messiah, and the Messiah is primarily the agent
of God in bringing in the new order of things. Undoubtedly Mark's fundamental thought of Jesus is that
He is the man of God's appointment, with whom

God is. Designating Him currently merely by His personal name of ' Jesus,' and representing Him as currently spoken of by His contemporaries merely as ' Jesus of Nazareth ' and addressed by the simple honorific titles of ' Rabbi,' ' Teacher,' ' Lord '—His fundamental manifestation is to him plainly that of a man among men. That this man was the Messiah need not in itself import more than that He was the subject of divine influences beyond all other men, and the vehicle of divine operations surpassing all other human experience. It may fairly be asked, therefore, what requires us to go beyond the divine office to explain this supernaturally filled life? Will not the assumption of the Messiahship of Jesus fully account for the abounding supernaturalism of His activity as portrayed by Mark? Questions like these are in point of fact constantly raised around us and very variously answered. But it behooves us to be on our guard respecting them that we be not led into a false antithesis, as if we must explain Mark's presentation of the supernatural life of Jesus either on the basis of His office as Messiah or on the basis of His superhuman personality.

There is no necessary contradiction between these two hypotheses; and we must not introduce here a factitious " either—or." What it behooves us to do is simply to inquire how the matter lay in Mark's mind; what the real significance of the Messiahship he attributed to Jesus, and represented Jesus as claiming for Himself, is; and whether he posits for Jesus and represents Him as asserting for Himself something more than a human personality.

We cannot have failed to note in reviewing the designations applied in the course of Mark's narrative to our Lord, a tendency of them all when applied to Him to grow in richness of content. The term ' Lord ' is merely an honorific address, equivalent to our ' Sir ' : but when applied to Jesus it seems to expand in significance until it ends by implying supreme authority. The term ' Messiah ' is a mere term of office and might be applied to anyone solemnly set apart for a service : but when applied to Jesus it takes on fuller and fuller significance until it ends by assimilating Him to the Divine Being Himself. He who simply reads over Mark's narrative, noting the designations he applies to our Lord, accordingly, will not be able to doubt that Mark conceived of Jesus not merely as officially the representative of God but as Himself a superhuman person, or that Mark means to present Jesus as Himself so conceiving of His nature and personality. The evidence of this is very copious, but also often rather subtle; and, in endeavoring to collect and appreciate it, we might as well commence with some of the plainest items, although this method involves a somewhat unordered presentation of it.

Jesus' Person Enhances His Designations

Let us look, then, first at that remarkable passage (13^{32}) in which Jesus acknowledges ignorance of the time of His (second) coming.[1] Here, in the very act of admitting limitations to His knowledge, in themselves astonishing, He yet asserts for Himself not merely a super-

Jesus a Superangelic Person

[1] On account of this profession of ignorance, Prof. Schmiedel (*Encyc. Biblica,* 1881) gives this passage a place among those nine " absolutely credible passages " which he calls " the foundation pillars for a truly

human but even a superangelic rank in the scale of being.

In any possible interpretation of the passage, He separates Himself from the " angels in heaven " (note the enhancing definition of locality, carrying with it the sense of the exaltation of these angels above all that is earthly) as belonging to a different class from them, and that a superior class. To Jesus as He is reported, and presumably to Mark reporting Him, we see, Jesus " the Son " stands as definitely and as incomparably above the category of angels, the highest of God's creatures, as to the author of the Epistle to the Hebrews, whose argument may be taken as a commentary upon this passage (Heb 1^4 2^8). Nor is this passage singular in Mark in exalting Jesus in dignity and authority above the angels. Already in the account of the temptation at the opening of His ministry we find the angels signalized as ministering to Him (1^{13}), and elsewhere they appear as His subordinates swelling His train (8^{38}) or His servants obeying His behests (13^{27}, " He shall send the angels "). Clearly, therefore, to Mark Jesus is not merely a superhuman but a superangelic personality: and the question at once obtrudes itself whether a superangelic person is not by that very fact removed from the category of creatures.

scientific life of Jesus." If so, a " truly scientific life of Jesus " must allow that He asserted for Himself a superangelic, that is, a more than creaturely dignity of person. Others, just for this reason, would deny the words to Jesus (e.g. Martineau, *Seat of Authority in Religion,* 590; N. Schmidt, *The Prophet of Nazareth,* 147, 231 note), and even Dalman is not superior to the temptation arbitrarily to apportion them partly to Jesus and partly to His followers (*Words,* p. 194). But all this is purely subjective criticism.

A similar implication, as has already been pointed out, is embedded in the title 'Son of Man,' which

Mark represents as our Lord's stated self-designation. The appeal involved in it to Daniel $7^{13,14}$ is a definite assertion for the Messiah of a heavenly as distinguished from an earthly origin, with all the suggestions of preëxistence, divine exaltation and authority, and endless sovereignty necessarily connected with a heavenly origin. It would be impossible to frame a Messianic conception on the basis of this vision of Daniel and to suppose the Messiah to be in His person a mere man deriving His origin from the earth.[2] This is sufficiently illustrated indeed by the history of the Messianic ideal among the Jews. There is very little evidence among the Jews before or contemporary with our Lord, of resort to Daniel $7^{13,14}$ as a basis for Messianic hopes: but wherever this occurs it is the conception of a preexistent, heavenly monarch who is to judge the world in righteousness which is derived from this passage.[3] No other conception, in fact, could be derived from Daniel, where the heavenly origin of the eternal King is thrown into the sharpest contrast with the lower

[2] Cf. Dalman, *Words,* 242: "The destined possessor of the universal dominion comes not from the earth, far less from the sea, but from heaven. He is a being standing in a near relation to God . . ."

[3] The Similitudes of Enoch and the Second Book of Esdras (more commonly called 4 Esdras). Cf. Dalman, *Words,* pp. 242 and 131: "From the first Christian century there are only two writings known which deal with Dan 7^{13}, the Similitudes of the Book of Enoch, and the Second Book of Esdras" . . . "After the Similitudes of Enoch the only representatives of the idea [of the heavenly preëxistence of the Messiah] independent of Enoch, are 2 Esdras in the first Christian century and the Appendix to Pesikta Rabbati in the seventh or eighth century."

source of the preceding bestial rulers. Judaism may
not have known how to reconcile this heavenly origin
of the Messiah with His birth as a human being, and
may have, therefore, when so conceiving the Messiah, sacrificed His human condition entirely to His
heavenly nature and supposed Him to appear upon the
earth as a developed personality.[4]   That our Lord does
not feel this difficulty or share this notion manifests,
in the matter of His adoption of the title 'Son of
Man' as His favorite Messianic self-designation, His
independence of whatever Jewish tradition may be
supposed to have formed itself.   But His adoption of
the title at all, with its obvious reference to the vision
of Daniel,[5] necessarily carried with it the assertion of
heavenly origination and nature.

This in turn carried with it, we may add, the conception that He had "come" to earth upon a mission,
Jesus' a conception which does not fail to find
Earthly Life independent expression in such passages,
a Mission as 1^{38} 2^{17} 10^{45}.   For, that the assertions
in these passages that He "came forth" to preach,
that He "came" not to save the righteous but sinners,
that He "came" not to be ministered unto but to
minister and to give His life as a ransom for many,
refer to His divine mission (cf. also $11^{9,10}$), lies on
their face.   It is suggested by the pregnancy of the

[4] Cf. Dalman, 131: "Judaism has never known anything of a pre-
existence peculiar to the Messiah, *antecedent to His birth as a human
being.*"   "He is to make His appearance on earth as a fully developed
personality."   See p. 301: "The celestial preëxistence of Messiah, as
stated in the Similitudes of Enoch and in 2 [4] Esdr 13, 14, excluding—
so at least it seems—an earthly origin, implies, apart from the incen-
tive contributed by Dan 7^{13}, his miraculous superhuman appearance."
Cf. p. 257 *et seq.*

[5] Cf. Dalman, pp. 257 *et seq.*

expressions themselves, and the connections in which they are employed; and it is supported by the even more direct language of some of the parallels.[6]   In themselves these expressions may not necessarily involve the idea of preëxistence (cf. 9^{11} and Jno 1^7 of John the Baptist); but they fall readily in with it, and so far suggest it that when supported by other forms of statement implying it, they cannot well be taken in any other sense.[7]

[6] Cf. Swete, on Mk 1^{38}: "'For to this end came I forth' (Mark), is interpreted for us by Luke, 'Because to this end was I sent.' 'Came I forth' does not refer to His departure from Capernaum ($v.$ 35), but to His mission from the Father (Jno 8^{42} 13^{20})"; and on Mk 10^{45}: "For $\check{\eta}\lambda\theta o\nu$ in reference to our Lord's entrance into the world, cf. 1^{38} 2^{17}; it is used also of the Baptist ($9^{11\ seq.}$, Jno 1^7) regarded as a divine messenger"—whence we observe that it does not of itself imply preëxistence. Meyer, on 1^{38}, notes that this view is held by Euthymius Zigabenus, Maldonatus, Grotius, Bengel, Lange and others,—conf. Baumgarten-Crusius; he himself does not hold it. Cf. Meyer, on Mt 3^{11}: "His *coming* as such is always brought forward with great emphasis by Mark and Luke." Holtzmann on 1^{38} thinks the reference is to the departure from Capernaum, while Luke's phrase (4^{43}) is a transition to the Johannine form of expression (e.g. 8^{42}).

[7] Cf. G. S. Streatfeild, *The Self-Interpretation of Jesus Christ*, 1906, pp. 81-83. Mr. Streatfeild connects these sayings with those in which our Lord refers to His return in glory. "Thus to describe Himself as *coming* into the world," he remarks, "suggests, if it does no more, a consciousness of personal vocation, a conviction, if not a consciousness, of preëxistence." "The word 'come,'" he adds, "is never, so far as the present writer recollects, used of or by the prophets in the sense in which our Lord applies it to Himself. Apparent exceptions are shown to be only apparent by the context. On the other hand, the term is constantly used in the O. T. of God and the Messianic theophany." Perhaps Mr. Streatfeild slightly overstates the matter, but what he says is essentially true. His use of these phrases certainly testifies to our Lord's deep consciousness of being intrusted with a great mission which He had come into the world to fulfil—as the use of them of John the Baptist testifies to his mission: and the pregnancy of the use He makes of them, and the connections in which He uses them, strongly suggest a

It is, however, above all in the picture which Jesus Himself draws for us of the 'Son of Man' that we

Jesus' Functions Divine

see His superhuman nature portrayed. For the figure thus brought before us is distinctly a superhuman one; one which is not only in the future to be seen sitting at the right hand of power and coming with the clouds of heaven (14^{62})—in clouds with great power and glory (13^{26}), even in the glory of His Father with the holy angels (8^{38}) who do His bidding as the Judge of all the earth, gathering His elect for Him (13^{26}) while He punishes His enemies (8^{38}); but which in the present world itself exercises functions which are truly divine,—for who is Lord of the Sabbath but the God who instituted it in commemoration of His own rest (2^{28}), and who can forgive sins but God only ($2^{10,}$ cf. verse 7)? The assignment to the Son of Man of the function of Judge of the world and the ascription to Him of the right to forgive sins are, in each case, but another way of saying that He is a divine person; for these are divine acts.[8]

conviction on His part of preëxistence, though they do not in themselves unsupportedly avail to prove it. The language might be employed consistently of a divine mission without preëxistence; but it seems to be employed here with deeper implications.

[8] On the forgiveness of sins as a divine act, cf. Dalman, *Words,* 262 and 314, 315. As against J. Weiss, Dalman notes that it is a fact "that Judaism never from O. T. times to the present day, has ventured to make any such assertion in regard to the Messiah" as that the "Lord hath power to forgive sins." Cf. Briggs, *The Messiah of the Gospels,* 83, 84. On the judgment of the world as a divine act, cf. Bousset, *Jesus,* 203-205. Dr. Stanton, *Jewish and Christian Messiah,* 291, says: "The Judge in that last judgment is on Jewish ground nowhere the Messiah. The assignment of this office to Him is the most significant new feature in the Christian doctrine of the Messiah." But this is because Dr. Stanton considers the Similitudes of Enoch post-Christian (cf. pp. 61,

We have already had occasion to point out the uniqueness and closeness of the relation to God which The Uniqueness is indicated by the designation ' Son of of God ' as ascribed to Jesus. In the Jesus' Sonship parable of Mark 12 not only is it emphasized that God has but one such son (verse 6), but He is as such expressly contrasted with all God's " servants " (verses 2 and 4) and expressly signalized as God's " heir " (verse 7). As we read this parable

140). There, but apparently there only, in pre-Christian Jewish literature the Messiah appears as Judge of the world to whom all judgment has been committed (see Charles, *The Book of Enoch*, 128, 129). Hence Dr. Stanton in Hastings' *B. D.* III. 356 *et seq.* says more exactly: " In this document, . . . He is to be the Judge in the universal judgment, . . . a function never assigned to the Messiah, but always ascribed to the Most High in other Jewish writings." Cf. Salmond (Hastings' *B. D.*, I, 751) : " In the O. T. the final arbitrament of men's lives is not committed to the Messiah . . . Only in the late section of the Book of Enoch does the Messiah appear in any certain or definite form as the Judge at the last day." Perhaps, however, it is not perfectly accurate with respect to this particular point to sum up as Dr. Salmond does, thus: " Christ's doctrine of a universal, individual judgment, at the end of things, in which judgment He Himself is arbiter of human destinies, carried the O. T. conception to its proper issue, while it gave a new certainty, consistency and spirituality to the developed idea which had arisen in Judaism in the period following the last of the Jewish prophets." Though Jesus had a forerunner in Enoch in conceiving the Messiah as the Judge of the world, He does not seem at all dependent on Enoch in this conception, any more than in others connected with it and growing out of the common reference of both to Dan $7^{13,14}$. Salmond, *Christian Doct. of Immortality*, 4 ed., 282-284, treats the whole subject judiciously: cf. further Charles, *Encyc. Biblica*, 1362, §66, and *Expositor*, VI. v. 251, 258; also Briggs, *Messianic Prophecy*, 154, 487. What is to be noted is that in the Similitudes of Enoch, where alone in pre-Christian sources the judgment is attributed to the Messiah, the Messiah is conceived as a superhuman Being, the Revealer of all things, and the Messianic Lord of the earth, i.e. the attribution of judgment to Him is connected with the attribution of other divine prerogatives to Him also, so that the implication of divinity inherent in this attribution is not obscured.

the mind inevitably reverts again to the representation of the Epistle to the Hebrews, which in its doctrine of the Son (cf. Heb 1^4 3^6 etc.), might almost appear a thetical exposition of it. And in the immediate recognition of Jesus as the ' Son of God ' by the evil spirits—" as soon as ever they caught sight of Him "[9] —we can scarcely fail to see a testimony from the spiritual world to a sonship in Jesus surpassing that of mere appointment to an earthly office and function and rooted in what lies beyond this temporal sphere. It is noteworthy also that when responding to the adjuration of the high priest to declare whether He were ' the Christ, the Son of the Blessed,' Jesus points apparently to His exaltation at the right hand of power and His coming with the clouds of heaven, which they were to see, as the warranty for His acceptance of the designation: as much as to say that to be ' the Christ, the Son of the Blessed,' involves session at the right hand of God and the eternal dominion promised in Daniel (Mk 14^{62}). And it is noticeable farther that immediately upon our Lord's acceptance of the ascription the high priest accused Him of blasphemy (14^{63}), which appears to be an open indication that to claim to be ' the Son of the Blessed ' was all one with claiming to be a divine person.[10] Even the heathen cen-

[9] Cf. Meyer and Swete on Mk 3^{11}.

[10] W. C. Allen, on Mt 26^{63}, remarks: " Wellhausen argues that the claim to be the Messiah could not, according to Jewish conceptions, have been regarded as a blasphemous claim. But quite apart from the exact meaning of the relationship of the Messiah to God which is implied in such terms as ' Son of God,' ' Son of the Blessed,' the nature of the Messiah as depicted in the literature of the period as of earthly and heavenly origin (cf. Volz, *Jüd. Eschat.,* pp. 214 f.) is such that claims to be the Messiah might quite well be regarded as blasphemous, if they were untrue." This, however, seems scarcely well founded. Zahn

turion's enforced conviction, as he witnessed the circumstances of Jesus' death, that this man certainly was 'a Son of God,' appears to be recorded for no other reason (15^{39}) than to make plain that the supernaturalness of Jesus' person was such as necessarily to impress any observer. No doubt a heathen centurion is but a poor witness to Jesus' essential nature; and no doubt his designation of Him as "a son of God" must needs be taken in a sense consonant with his standpoint as a heathen.[11] But it manifests how from his own standpoint Jesus' death impressed him—as the death, to wit, of one of superhuman dignity. And its record seems to round out the total impression which Mark appears to wish to make in his use of the phrase, viz., that the superhuman dignity of Jesus was perforce recognized and testified to by all classes and by every variety of witness. The spiritual denizens of another world (1^{24} 1^{34} 3^{11} 5^{7}), the appointed guardians of the spiritual life of Israel (14^{61}), Jesus Himself (12^{6} 13^{32} 14^{62}), God in Heaven (1^{11} 9^{7}), and even the heathen man who gazed upon Him as He hung on the cross, alike certify to His elevation, as the Son

(on Mt, pp. 694-5) is better: "The high priest demands an answer not to the simple question whether Jesus gave Himself out for the Messiah, but whether He was the Messiah, the Son of God. . . . The mere affirmative of the question whether He were the Messiah, could not be understood by the whole Sanhedrin as an unambiguous blasphemy. It was only a liar or a fanatic that Jesus could have been called on that ground by those who did not believe in Him. Jesus affirmed, however, also the other question, whether He was the Son of God; and indeed on oath, since he was sworn by the Living God (I Kings 2^{24}) . . ."

[11] Wellhausen's remark need not be disputed: "The centurion uses the expression 'Son of God' not, like the high priest (14^{61}), as an epithet of the Jewish Messiah, but in the heathen sense; he says also not 'the Son' but 'a son' of God" (on 15^{39}).

of God, in the supernatural dignity of His person, above all that is earthly, all " servants " and " ministers " of God whatever, including the very angels. Certainly this designation, ' Son of God,' is colored so deeply with supernatural implications that even apart from such a passage as 13[32] where the superangelic nature of the Son is openly expressed, we cannot avoid concluding (cf. especially 12[6] 14[62] 15[39]) that a supernatural personality as well as a supernatural office is intended to be understood by it. And if so, in view of the nature of the term itself, it is difficult to doubt that this supernaturalness of personality is intended to be taken at the height of the Divine. What can the Son, the unique and " beloved " Son of God, who also is God's heir, in contradistinction from all His servants, even the angels, be—but God Himself?

It has already been suggested that something of this implication is embedded in the employment of the designation ' Bridegroom ' (2[19,20]) of our Lord. For there is certainly involved in it not merely the representation, afterwards copiously developed in the New Testament, of our Lord as the Bridegroom of the people of God, by virtue of which His Church is His bride (Mt 22[2] 25[1], Jno 3[29], Rom 7[4], 2 Cor 11[2], Eph 5[29], Rev 19[7] 21[2,9]), but also a reminiscence of those Old Testament passages, of which Hos 2[19] may be taken as the type (cf. Ex 20[5], Jer 2[20], Ezek 16[38,60,63]), in which Jehovah's relation to His people is set forth under the figure of that of a loving husband to his wife. In other words, the use of ' the Bridegroom ' as a designation of our Lord assimilates His relation to the people of God to that which in the Old Testament is exclu-

Jesus Assimilated to Jehovah

sively, even jealously, occupied by Jehovah Himself, and raises the question whether Jesus is not thereby, in some sense, at any rate, identified with Jehovah.[12] This question once clearly raised, other phenomena obtrude themselves at once upon our attention. We are impelled, for example, to ask afresh what sense our Lord put upon the words of the 110th Psalm, " The Lord said unto my Lord, ' Sit Thou on my right hand till I make Thine enemies the footstool of Thy feet,' " when (Mk 12[35 et seq.]) He adduced them to rebuke the Jews for conceiving the Christ as only the son of David, whereas David himself in this passage, and that speaking in the Spirit, expressly calls Him his Lord? It is not merely the term ' Lord ' which comes into consideration here; but the exaltation which the application of the term in this connection to Him assigns to the Messiah. The scribes would have had no difficulty in understanding that the Messiah should be David's " greater son," who should—nay, must— because Messiah, occupy a higher place in the Kingdom of God than even His great father.[13] The point of the argument turns on the supreme exaltation of the Lordship ascribed to Him, implying something superhuman in the Messiah's personality and therefore in His origin. Who is this ' Lord ' who is to sit at

[12] Cf. Streatfeild, *The Self-Interpretation of Jesus Christ*, pp. 92, 93: " What that term meant to the mind of the Jew may be gathered from a study of the prophetic writings, which frequently portray God as the Husband of His people, and denounce the disobedience and idolatry of Israel as spiritual adultery. For any one to speak of Himself as the Bridegroom of the Kingdom was little short of a claim to Deity: the title was an impossible one for man."

[13] Dalman, p. 285: " There would indeed be nothing remarkable in the fact that a son should attain a higher rank than his father, and for the scribes it would not in the least be strange that the Messiah should be greater than David."

the right hand of the ' Lord ' who is Jehovah, and to whom David himself therefore does reverence? It is hard to believe that our Lord intended—or was understood by Mark to intend—by such a designation of the Messiah, who He Himself was, to attribute to Him less than a superhuman—or shall we not even say a divine—dignity, by virtue of which He should be recognized as rightfully occupying the throne of God.[14] To sit at the right hand of God is to participate in the divine dominion,[15] which, as it is a greater than human dignity, would seem to require a greater than human nature. To be in this sense David's Lord falls little if anything short of being David's God.[16]

In estimating the significance of such a passage, we must not permit to fall out of sight the constant use of the term ' Lord ' in the LXX version of the Old Testament for God.[17] There it is " practically equivalent to God ($\theta\varepsilon\delta\varsigma$) and is the rendering of the solemn name of Jehovah."[18] The writers of the New Testament, and

Jesus Identified with Jehovah

[14] So Dalman (*Words*, 214) says shortly: " He whom David called 'Lord' was no mere man" (cf. pp. 385-7). Dalman thinks there is no hint of "the two natures" in the passage: this may be doubted (cf. Meyer on Mt 22[45], and Alexander *in loc.*, also Delitzsch on Ps 110, p. 185) ; but this need not be pressed here.

[15] Cf. Delitzsch, *Psalms*, III. p. 189. Stanton, *Jewish and Christian Messiah*, 101-2, points out that there is no difficulty in supposing that David himself may have anticipated a greater son: " Knowing how far he had himself fallen below the standard of the true covenant king, and how the glory and prosperity of his reign had been marred through the consequences of his own sins, he might thus in spirit pay homage to a greater descendant."

[16] Cf. Swete's note on Mk 12[37].

[17] Cf. D. Somerville, *St. Paul's Conception of Christ*, pp. 295 *et seq.*

[18] Somerville, p. 143. The supplanting of Jehovah by ' Lord ' in the LXX of course rests upon the *K^eri perpetuum* by which Adhonai was substituted for the " ineffable name " in the reading of the Hebrew

Mark among them, must be understood to have been
thoroughly familiar with this use of the term, and could
scarcely fail to see in its appellative application to
Christ a suggestion of His deity, when the implications
of the context were, as we have seen them repeatedly
to be, of His superhuman dignity and nature.   Particularly when they apply to Him Old Testament
passages in which the term 'Lord' refers to God, we
can scarcely suppose they do so without a consciousness
of the implications involved, and without a distinct
intention to convey them.[19] When, for example, in the
opening verses of Mark, we read: " Even as it is written in Isaiah the prophet, Behold I send my messenger
before thy face, who shall prepare thy way; The voice
of one crying in the wilderness, make ye ready the way
of the Lord, make His paths straight,—[so] John
came," etc., we cannot easily rid ourselves of the impression that the term 'Lord' is applied to Jesus. The
former of the two prophetic citations here brought

text. This in turn, however, rests upon the connection of the idea of
'Lord' with 'Jehovah.' "Jehovah," says Oehler (*Theology of the
O. T.*, E. T., ed. Day, 1883, p. 101), "is the *Lord* . . . That the idea
of אדני is immediately connected with the idea of Jehovah is clear
from the fact that the two names are frequently associated, and that
אדני would in later times be substituted in reading for יהוה . . ."
When our Lord is called 'Lord,' therefore, in the divine sense, it is
to Jehovah specifically that the suggestion points.

19 Cf. Stanton, *Jewish and Christian Messiah,* 197, 198 and Note on
the latter page. Speaking of passages like these he says: " Deut 33[2]
appears to be alluded to in various places in the Synoptists. It is a
passage which speaks in the clearest terms of Jehovah coming to judgment, and the attribution of the language in the Synoptists to the
second coming of the Christ is an indication of the existence, even in
the body of tradition which they record, of a belief in the oneness of
Christ with God." *Mutatis mutandis,* this remark applies to the passage
immediately to be adduced.

together is distinctly made to refer to Christ, by a change in the pronouns from the form they bear in the original—though the reference in the original is to Jehovah: and this by an inevitable consequence carries with it the reference of the latter also to Christ.[20] But in the original of Isaiah 40[3] again the reference of the term 'Lord' is to Jehovah. Here we see Jesus then identified by means of the common term 'Lord' with Jehovah.[21] Of course it may be said that it is not Jesus who is identified with Jehovah, but the coming of Jesus which is identified with the "advent of Jehovah" to redeem His people predicted so frequently in the Old Testament.[22] And this explanation might

[20] So Sven Herner (*op. cit.*, pp. 7 *et seq.*, cf. pp. 4, 5) solidly argues.

[21] Cf. A. B. Davidson, *The Theology of the O. T.*, p. 262: "That splendid passage, Is 40[1-11], which speaks of Jehovah coming in strength, that is, in His fulness, and feeding His flock like a shepherd, is interpreted in the Gospels of the Son. It was in the Son, or as the Son, that Jehovah so manifested Himself. By the Old Testament prophet a distinction in the Godhead was not thought of; but subsequent revelation casts light on the preceding. The Lord, the Redeemer and Judge, is God in the Son."

[22] According to Dr. A. B. Davidson's representation this is as far as the Old Testament writers themselves go with regard to the Messiah. They came to look upon the coming of the Messianic King as the coming of Jehovah; but not as if the Messiah were Jehovah, but only as if in the Messiah Jehovah came to His people. Cf. e.g. *The Theology of the O. T.*, p. 385: "It may be doubtful if the O. T. went so far as to identify the Messiah with Jehovah or to represent the Messiah as divine. It went the length of saying, however, that Jehovah would be present in His fulness in the Messiah, so that the Messiah might fitly be named 'God with us' and 'Mighty God.'" He adds: "It was not a difficult step to take, to infer that the Messiah was Himself God, and that because He was God He was Saviour; and then to apply even those passages which speak of Jehovah's coming in person to His coming as Messiah." It was this step that (if it remained to be taken) was taken by our Lord and the evangelists.

serve very well in the absence of other indications in
this Gospel that Jesus was viewed as a superhuman
being. In the presence of such indications, however,—
especially so clear an instance as is afforded by the
saying of Jesus in 13^{32}—and in the presence of other suggestions of the identification of Jesus with the Jehovah
of the Old Testament,—such as is afforded by His adoption of the title of ' Bridegroom,'—the natural implication of joining this prediction to its fellow in which
we hear of the " messenger " coming " before the
face " of Jesus (" thy ") and " preparing His way "
(" thy "), must be permitted to determine the question in favor of the application of the term ' Lord '
to Jesus Himself. And in that case it is the person
of Jesus which is identified with Jehovah.

It cannot be doubted, therefore, that Mark sees in
Jesus a supernatural person,—not merely a person
endowed with supernatural powers, but
a person in His own personality superior to angels and therefore standing
outside the category of creatures. He does not, however, dwell upon this. It emerges in his narrative, almost, we may say, by accident. This is in accordance
with the character of his undertaking, which is illustrated by many kindred phenomena. His is not the
Gospel of reflection: it is the Gospel of action. This
evangelist is not accustomed to stop to muse upon the
events he records or to develop all their significance.
He does not attempt to give even a full record of the
teaching of Jesus. He has set himself to exhibit " the
beginning of the Gospel of Jesus Christ "; and he
exhibits this " beginning " in a vivid picture of the
wonderful career of the divine Messiah, preserving

Mark's
Method

only casually certain of our Lord's sayings as substantial elements in his presentation of His career and
only incidentally suggesting what our Lord was in describing what He did. His concern is to portray fully
the supernatural life which Jesus lived, at the beginning of the Gospel, as the fountain from which has
flowed the great movement in which he was himself
an actor. In doing this his method is of a piece
throughout. He does not record for us, for example,
the great saying in which Jesus declares: "All authority has been given unto me in heaven and in earth"
(Mt 28[18]). He simply exhibits the exercise of this
authority by Jesus in detail ($1^{22,27}$ $2^{10,28}$ 3^{27} 4^{41} 5^{42}, etc.);
leaving it to the reader to infer the gift. Similarly he
does not stop in his rapidly moving narrative to say,
"Lo, here is a supernatural person": much less does
he pause to develop that conception into its implications. He does not even charge himself to cite from
Jesus' lips His own claims to divine origin and His
own conception of His unique relations with the Father.
What he gives us on these themes is incidental to the
narrative and falls out in it almost by accident.

What he gives us is ample, nevertheless, to make it
clear that Mark was not ignorant of these things.

**Mark's
Silence**

How can it be said that Mark knows
nothing of the preëxistence of Christ
when he records Jesus' constant application to Himself of the title 'Son of Man'? How
can it be said that he knows nothing of the supernatural birth of Jesus when he records Jesus' assertion of
a superangelic nature for Himself? How should one
above angels enter into the sphere of human life except by a supernatural birth? Unless we consider it

more credible that Mark claimed for Him an even
more supernatural descent as an adult from heaven?
Mark, in a word, leaves the exposition of these things
to others. It is Matthew and Luke who complete the
story by the record of the supernatural birth. It is
John who develops all the implications of Jesus' pre-
existence. But all that these bring to expression in
their fuller accounts is implied in Mark's narrative, in
which he incidentally tells us of the dignity of that
person's nature whose wonderful career he has undertaken to describe. And there is no reason why we
should suppose him ignorant of the implications of his
own facts, especially when his purpose in writing did
not call for the explication of these implications. In
a word, it seems clear enough that there lies behind
the narrative of Mark not an undeveloped christology,
but only an unexpressed one. To give expression to
his christology did not lie within the limits of the
task he had undertaken.[23]

[23] Cf. a careful *précis* of *Mark's Conception of the Person and Office
of Christ* in a section of Dr. Swete's Introduction to his commentary on
Mark: pp. xc-xcv. If we should put together, simply, the elements of
Mark's christology, perhaps it might be expressed as follows: Jesus
was a man, appointed by God Messiah, and endowed for His Messianic
tasks; but not a mere man, but a superhuman being, in rank and dignity above angels (13^{35}), who "came" to earth for a mission. This
mission was not to be ministered unto, but to minister, and accordingly
involved humiliation and suffering: but a humiliation and suffering
not for Himself but vicarious (10^{45}, cf. 2^{17}). He prosecuted this ministry by a career of preaching (1^{38}), and in the end died and rose
again that He might give His life a ransom for many (10^{45}). Mean-
time, being God's beloved Son, the heavenly King of God's own Kingdom predicted in Daniel, the Lord of the House (13^{35}, cf. 11^3) and
no servant (12^6, cf. 1^{11} 9^7), not merely David's son but David's Lord
(12^{35}) who is Jehovah Himself (1^3), He had in His hands all author-
ity (1^{22} 1^{27} 2^{10} 2^{28} 4^{41} 5^{43}, cf. 1^{41} 2^{11} 9^{25}), and exercised all divine
prerogatives—controlling evil spirits, the laws of nature, death itself,—

We must guard ourselves especially from imagining that the recognition found in Mark of the deity of

Mark's Conception of the Messiahship Jesus is in any way clouded by the emphasis he places on the Messiahship of Jesus as the fundamental fact of His mission. We have already had occasion to point out that the Messiahship and the deity of Jesus are not mutually exclusive conceptions. Even on the purely Jewish plane it was possible to conceive the Messiah a supernatural person: and He is so conceived, for example, in the Similitudes of Enoch and the Visions of 4 Esdras. The recognition of the deity of Jesus by Mark—and by Jesus as reported by Mark—in no way interferes with the central place taken in Mark's narrative—and in Jesus' thought of Himself as reported by Mark,—by our Lord's Messianic claims. It only deepens the conception of the Messiahship which is presented as the conception which Jesus fulfilled. The result is merely that the Christian movement becomes, from the point of view of the history of the Messianic ideal, an attempt to work a change in the current conception of the Messianic office—a change which involved its broadening to cover a wider area of Old Testament prophecy and its deepening to embody spiritual rather than prevailingly external aspirations.[24] We have already noted that our Lord's

reading the heart and the future (9^{31} 10^{33}), and forgiving sin on earth, and after His dying rose again and in His own proper time will return in the clouds of heaven with the angels to establish the Kingdom and judge the world.

[24] Cf. Wellhausen, *Mark,* p. 71: " I can find this at least not incredible, that Jesus was pleased with the name of the Jewish ideal, and yet changed its contents, and that not merely with respect to the Messiah, but analogously also with respect to the Kingdom of God." How

preference for His self-designation of the title 'Son of Man' over other more current titles is indicatory of His enlarged and enriched conception of the Messiahship: and we have already hinted that even the title 'Son of Man' only partly suggests the contents of His conception, elements of which found their adumbration in yet other portions of Old Testament prediction. Among these further elements of Old Testament prophecy taken up into and given validity in His conception, there are especially notable those that portray the Righteous Servant of Jehovah, culminating in the 53d chapter of Isaiah, and those that set forth what has appropriately been called the "Advent of Jehovah,"—the promises, in a word, of the intervention of Jehovah Himself to redeem His people.

Wellhausen would have such a remark understood, however, may be commodiously learned from his section on "the Jewish and the Christian Messiah" in the closing pages of his *Einleitung in die drei ersten Evangelien* (1905). The Christian conception of the Messiah, such as lies on the pages of Mark, for example—that paradoxical contradiction of the gallows-Messiah, formed on the basis of the actual crucifixion of Jesus—is of course the product of the time subsequent to the death of Jesus; but its existence would be inexplicable without the assumption that Jesus was supposed by His followers to be the Messiah, although of course in His life-time it was not this Christian conception but the ordinary Jewish conception of the Messiah which they attributed to Him. The attitude of Jesus Himself to this ascription of Messiahship to Him Wellhausen finds it somewhat difficult to determine (p. 92). He is certain that Jesus did not follow the method of the Pseudochrists and openly proclaim Himself Messiah; but he thinks that there are indications that He did not repel the notion when applied to Him— though, of course, this involved an "accommodation," as He was by no means prepared to meet the expectations connected with the title. It was no doubt, then, as a religious regenerator, not as a political restorer, that He accepted the title; but this remained at least so far within Jewish limits as not to involve that complete renunciation of Judaism which "lies in the conception of the gallows-Messiah, of the Messiah rejected by the Jews," of the writers of the New Testament.

It may be very easy to do less than justice to the Messianic ideal current among the Jewish people at the time of our Lord, centering as it did in the hope of the establishment of an external kingdom endowed with the irresistible might of God. Of course this Kingdom of God was conceived as a kingdom of righteousness; and it may be possible to show that most of the items that enter into the Old Testament predictions, including that of redemption from sin, were not wholly neglected in one or another form of its expression. The difference between it and the Messianic conception developed by Jesus and His followers may thus almost be represented as merely a difference of emphasis.[25] But a difference of emphasis may be far from a small difference; and the effect of the difference in this case certainly amounted to a difference in kind. This new Messianic ideal is unmistakably apparent in Mark's conception and in the conception of Jesus as represented by Mark's record of His sayings. We can trace in Mark's record the influence of factors recalling the Righteous Servant (10^{45} 9^{12} 14^{21} 1^{24}) and the Divine Redeemer (1^3) as well as the Danielic Son of Man.[26] But these fac-

[25] On this general subject see two or three very strong pages in Dalman, *Words*, pp. 295-299: cf. Stanton, 134.

[26] Speaking of the conception embodied in the title 'Son of Man' by our Lord as reported in the Gospels, Charles (*The Book of Enoch*, pp. 312-317) argues that it included in it all the ideas suggested by the Servant of Jehovah of Isaiah, and therefore so far commends Bartlet's construction (*Expositor*, Dec. 1892). Says Charles (p. 316): "This transformed conception of the Son of Man is thus permeated throughout by the Isaian conception of the Servant of Jehovah; but though the Enochic conception is fundamentally transformed, the transcendent claims underlying it are not for a moment forgotten." If we may be permitted to find the preadumbration of the "transcendent" element of

tors attain fuller expression in the records of the other evangelists. So that here too we find them bringing out into clearness what already lies in Mark rather than adding anything really new to his presentation.

this conception, not in Enoch but in the O. T. representation of the Advent of Jehovah, Charles' conception of the Messianic ideal of our Lord, for the expression of which He chose the term 'Son of Man,' seems to us generally just. It is—for whatever reason—essentially a synthesis of the three lines of prediction embodied in the Isaianic "Servant of Jehovah," the Danielic "Son of Man," and the general O. T. "Advent of Jehovah," along with which the other lines of prophecy—such as those embodied in the "Davidic King"—also find their place.

THE DESIGNATIONS OF OUR LORD IN MATTHEW

When we turn to Matthew's Gospel, and observe the designations applied in it to our Lord, what chiefly strikes us is that it runs in this matter on precisely the same lines with Mark, with only this difference, that what is more or less latent in Mark becomes fully patent in Matthew.

The narrative name of our Lord is in Matthew (as in Mark) the simple ' Jesus '; which (as in Mark) **The Narrative** never occurs as other than the narra-**Name, and** tive name, with the single exception **Exceptions** (which is no exception) that in announcing His birth the Angel of the Lord is reported as commanding, " Thou shalt call His name Jesus " (1^{21}). And not only does Matthew, like Mark, reserve the simple ' Jesus ' for his narrative name, but, also like Mark, he practically confines himself to it. The only outstanding exceptions to this are that Matthew sets (like Mark) the solemn Messianic designation ' Jesus Christ ' in the heading of his Gospel (1^1), and follows this up (unlike Mark) by repeating it both at the opening of his formal narrative (1^{18}), and at an important new starting point in his narrative ($16^{21 \text{ v. r.}}$) ;[1] and that he employs a certain fulness of des-

---

[1] In all these three places Ἰησοῦς Χριστός seems to be used as a proper name. Meyer (1^1, p. 51) says: " In the Gospels Χριστός stands as a proper name only in Mt $1^{1,16,17,18}$, Mk 1^1, Jno 1^{17}, . . . here also

ignation throughout the formal genealogy with which
the Gospel begins, by which he places the ' Jesus ' of
whom he is to speak clearly before the readers and
clearly as the Messiah. " The book of the generation
of Jesus Christ, the Son of David, the Son of Abraham " (1^1) is the phraseology with which he opens
this genealogy: he closes it with the words, " Mary
of whom was born Jesus surnamed Christ " (1^{16}) ;
and in the summary which he adjoins he calculates the
generations " unto Christ " (1^{17})—a designation which
meets us again at 11^2. Thus Matthew in beginning
his Gospel leaves no room for doubting that he purposes to present the story of Jesus' life as the life of
the Messiah; but as soon as he has given that formal
emphatic enunciation, he takes up the narrative with
the simple ' Jesus ' and with only the two breaks at
11^2 and $16^{21 \text{ v.r.}}$ carries it on with the simple ' Jesus '
to the end.[2] The simple ' Jesus ' occurs thus in his

(cf. Mk 1^1), in the superscription, the whole of the great name Ἰησοῦς
Χριστός is highly appropriate, nay, necessary."

[2] The name ' Jesus ' occurs in Matthew about 149 times. Of these,
on nine occasions it is used in combination with additional designa-
tions (' Jesus Christ,' 1^1 1^{18} 16^{21}; ' Jesus surnamed Christ,' 1^{16} $27^{17,22}$;
' Jesus the Nazarene,' 26^{71}; ' Jesus the Galilean,' 26^{69}; ' the prophet
Jesus who is from Nazareth of Galilee,' 21^{11}; ' Jesus the King of the
Jews,' 27^{37}). The simple ' Jesus ' occurs therefore about 140 times;
and always is Matthew's own except 1^{21}. It is according to Moulton
and Geden anarthrous in the following passages: (1^1) $1^{16,21,25}$ 14^1
(16^{21}) 17^8 $20^{17,30}$ $21^{1,12}$ $26^{51,69,71,75}$ $27^{17,22,37}$ $28^{5,9}$ ($18[20]$ in all).
Two of these instances (17^8 and 20^{17}) may, however, be eliminated as
probably false readings. ' Jesus Christ,' 1^1, is properly without the
article, both because that is the regular usage with proper names in
headings, and because that is the regular usage with the first mention
of a proper name; 16^{21} is to be looked upon in accordance with this
as a new beginning; while at 1^{18} the article is present because it takes
up the ' Jesus Christ ' of 1^1 again, further explained at 1^{16} as the
" Jesus surnamed Christ," and hence is almost equivalent to "*this* Jesus
Christ." In 1^{16} $27^{17,22}$ $26^{69,71}$ 27^{37}, the article is properly absent on

narrative about 139 times, and is replaced only by the compound 'Jesus Christ' ($1^{1,18}$ $16^{21 \text{ v. r.}}$, cf. 1^{16}), and by the simple 'Christ' (1^{17} 11^2, cf. 1^{16}), each, at most three times.

In this sparing use of 'Jesus Christ' and 'Christ' by Matthew himself, the term 'Christ' appears to be employed not as an appellative but as a proper name. In 2^4, no doubt, "the Christ" is used in the general

'Christ' as a Proper Name

sense of "the Messiah": Herod did not inquire of "the chief priests and scribes of the people" where Jesus was born, but where, according to prophecy, "the Messiah should be born": but just on that account there is no direct reference to Jesus at all here. The commentators are very generally inclined to look upon the use of "the Christ" in 11^2 as a similar instance, as if what John had heard in the prison was that "the works of the Messiah"—such works, that is, as were expected of the Messiah,—were occurring abroad; and accordingly sent and asked Jesus whether He was indeed "the Coming One."[3] Attractive as this explana-

---

the general rule that it is always omitted as superfluous in the presence of a defining appositional phrase with the article (Blass, p. 152; Moulton-Winer, 140-1). Perhaps even 28^5 may be classed here. Blass (152) supposes the omission of the article at 28^9 regular, on the ground that no anaphora is conceivable there. In 20^{30} the article seems wanting because (present, '*passeth*') the clause is a quotation from the popular mouth, and the use of 'Jesus' does not range anaphorically with preceding instances; possibly 28^5 may be so explained. In $1^{21,25}$ certainly an article would be out of place. There remain 14^1 $21^{1,12}$ $26^{51,75}$, an explanation of which does not readily present itself. The use of the article with personal names seems to have been capricious in the Greek of all ages (cf. J. H. Moulton, *Grammar*, p. 83; Moulton's Winer, 140; Schmiedel-Winer, 153; Blass, 152).

[3] "John the Baptist," says Holtzmann (*Hand-Com.*, **133**), "was almost persuaded that Jesus could fulfil the Messianic purpose, that His works were therefore of the Messianic variety (ἔργα τοῦ Χριστοῦ)."

tion is, however, it scarcely seems to fit in with the connection. Jesus' exhibition of His works to the messengers would hardly in these circumstances have been an answer to John's inquiry, so much as rather a refusal to give an answer. And the connection of the pronoun " Him " in verse 3 with its antecedent " Christ " of verse 2 appears to require us to take that term not as a general but as a particular one: John surely is not said to have sent to " the Messiah " and inquired of " Him " whether He was the Messiah. In other words if " the Christ " (ὁ Χριστός) can be taken as a proper name, designating Jesus, surely it must be so taken here. And that it can be so taken and is so taken by Matthew, its use in 1^{17} appears to show.

" The Christ " in 1^{17} also has sometimes, to be

" The works which Jesus does," says Wellhausen *in loc.,* " rouse doubts in John whether He is really the Christ; for he had expected from the Christ something wholly different. Just on this account Matthew calls them the works of the Christ; . . . the Baptist turns, however, with his doubts to Jesus Himself and leaves the decision to Him." " *The works,*" comments J. A. Alexander, " i.e. the miracles (Lk 7^{18}) *of Christ,* not of Jesus as a private person, but *of the Messiah,* which He claimed to be, . . . The meaning then is that John heard in prison of miraculous performances appearing and purporting to be wrought by the Messiah." These commentators seem to suppose that Mt 11^2 is to be rendered somewhat like this: " But John, because he heard in his prison through the medium of his disciples of [talk about] the works of the Messiah, sent through the medium of his disciples to ask Him, Art thou the Coming One, or are we to look for another? " The query arises, however, to whom John sent this inquiry? To " the Messiah "? Or to Jesus? What, then, is the antecedent of the αὐτῷ? As the αὐτῷ is Jesus, so its antecedent τοῦ Χριστοῦ is Jesus: and the concrete rather than the abstract seems more natural. Why not then translate: " Having heard of the works of Christ he sent and asked Him "? The solution seems to depend on whether ὁ Χριστός is used always as a pure appellative in Mat., or sometimes as a *nomen proprium,* or at least as a *quasi nomen proprium.* But the answer to that is scarcely doubtful (e.g. 1^{17}).

sure, been understood as the general term, " the Messiah."[4] But this throws it out of range not only with the other names in this simple summary, wherein the corresponding terms in the accounting are most simply given—Abraham, David, the Babylonian deportation; but also with the precedent phrase, ' Jesus, surnamed Christ,' of verse 16 to which it refers back and which it takes up and repeats. For that the ' Christ ' in this phrase is a simple proper name is not only suggested by the absence of the article with it, but is indicated by the currency of a similar mode of speech in the case of like instances of double names.[5] It appears then that the addition, " surnamed Christ," is intended in this passage as a formal identification of the par-

---

[4] So, for example, Weiss, in his reworking of Meyer. He supposes that the summary here is not merely a mnemonic device, but rests on a deeply-laid symbolism. There were fourteen generations from Abraham to the establishment of the kingdom; and fourteen more from its establishment to its loss: should there not be just fourteen more from its destruction to its re-establishment in the Messiah? " It is accordingly," he says, " also beyond dispute that we should translate—' up to the Messiah.' " Similarly (he says) Kübel and Nösgen. This carries with it the appellative sense in 1^{17} and 27^{17}.

[5] Cf. Dalman (*Words*, 303): " In Mt $27^{17,22}$ Pilate uses the expression Ἰησοῦς ὁ λεγόμενος Χριστός. That is not intended to mean ' Jesus, who is supposed to be the Messiah,' but with the usual sense of this idiom, ' Jesus surnamed Christ.' " The same form is seen in Mt 1^{16}, and in Σίμων ὁ λεγόμενος Πέτρος 4^{18} 10^2. Cf. Meyer's note on 1^{16}, where he remarks that ὁ λεγόμενος expresses neither doubt, nor assurance, but means simply " *who bears the name of Christ* (4^{18} 10^2 27^{17}); for this *name,* which became His from the official designation, was the *distinctive* name of *this* Jesus." Exact parallels to " Jesus surnamed Christ " (Mt 1^{16} $27^{17,22}$) occur in N. T. only at Mt 4^{18} 10^2, " Simon surnamed Peter "; Jno 11^{16} 20^{24} 21^2, " Thomas surnamed Didymus "; Col 4^{11}, " Jesus surnamed Justus." Its equivalent in such forms as " a man named " (Mt 9^9 $26^{3,14}$ 27^{16}, Mk 15^7, Lk 22^{47}), or a " city called " (Mt 2^{23}, Jno 4^5 11^{54} 19^{13}), or " a place called " (Mt 26^{36} 27^{33}, Jno 5^2. Acts 3^2 6^9) are not infrequent.

ticular Jesus in question;[6] and the employment of
" Christ " instead of " Jesus " in the subsequent summary (verse 17) is perhaps best explained in the interests of this clearness of designation, the article
accompanying it having the force of " the aforesaid
Christ."

Matthew thus notifies us at the beginning of his
narrative that the ' Jesus ' with whom he is to deal
has another name, to wit, ' Christ '
Why so Seldom Used (1^{16}), and so prepares the way for an
occasional employment of this other
name (1^{17} 11^2). Our only surprise is that he employs
it so seldom. The account to be given of this is probably that, after all, in the circles for which Matthew
wrote, this ' Jesus ' had become so unapproachably the
only ' Jesus ' who would come to mind on the mention
of the name, that the more distinctive surname ' Christ '
was not needed in speaking of Him to secure His
identification; it is employed, therefore, only when
some suggestion of His Messiahship was intruding
itself upon the mind, as is the case certainly at $11^{2\,7}$
and no doubt also at 1^{17}; and we may add equally so

---

[6] So also Fritzsche, *in loc.,* who translates: " Jesus, whose cognomen
is Christ." " Thus," he continues, " Jesus is by these words discrimi-
nated from other men of the same name, and $X\rho\iota\sigma\tau\acute{o}\varsigma$ does not declare
Him Messiah, but as in verse 1^1 is His name." According to this interpretation, he would have passages of similar character explained,
e.g. Mt 27^{17} [and 22] " *Jesus quem Christi nomine ornant* "—and so
Mk 15^7, Mt 26^{14} 9^9 $26^{3,36}$ 27^{33}, Jno $19^{13,17}$, Acts 3^2, Eph 2^{11}. Similarly Keil, on 1^{16}.

[7] Cf. Zahn, *in loc.:* " That Matthew, who elsewhere in the narra-
tive statedly speaks of Jesus by His proper name, writes $\tau o\tilde{v}$ $X\rho\iota\sigma\tauo\tilde{v}$
here instead, is explained just as in 1^{18} from his purpose to give brief
and emphatic expression to the fact that the deeds which are spoken of
indicate Him as the Messiah."

in 1^1 (cf. "the Son of David"), 1^{18} and 16^{21} (cf. v. 20), where the compound 'Jesus Christ' occurs. This is to recognize, of course, that the surname 'Christ' was the name of dignity as distinguished from the simple name of designation, and preserved, even when employed as a proper name, its implications of Messiahship; but this is in any event a matter of course and should not be confounded with the question of its appellative use. The employment of the term 'Christ' as a proper name of Jesus so far from losing sight of His claim to Messiahship, accordingly, bears witness to so complete an acquiescence in that claim on the part of the community in which this usage of the term was current, that the very official designation was conceived as His peculiar property and His proper designation (cf. 27^{17-22}).[8] The sparingness of Matthew's employment of it, on the other hand, manifests how little our Lord's dignity as Messiah needed to be insisted on in the circles for which Matthew wrote, and how fully the simple name 'Jesus' could convey to the readers all that was wrapped up in His personality.

Besides this sparing use of 'Jesus Christ' and 'Christ,' then, Matthew makes use in his own person **Jesus' Popular Name** of no other designation in speaking of our Lord than the simple 'Jesus,' although on three occasions he adduces with reference to Him designations which he finds in the prophets: 'Immanuel' (1^{23}), 'Lord' (3^3), 'the Nazarene' (2^{23}). The implications of the first two

[8] The climax of this development was reached, of course, when the followers of Jesus were called simply "Christians"—which occurred first, we are told, at Antioch (Acts 11^{26}). Cf. art. "Christian" in Hastings' *Dict. of the Bible*.

of these we may leave for later reference. The last
bears witness to the fact that Jesus was currently
known by His contemporaries as " a Nazarene," that
is to say, that His ordinary distinctive designation
among the people in the midst of whom His ministry
was passed would be, ' Jesus the Nazarene,' as the
maid, indeed, is recorded to have spoken of Him in
the court of the high priest (26^{71}). This exact designation, however, does not elsewhere occur in Matthew's
narrative, although its broader equivalent, from the
standpoint of a Jerusalemite, ' Jesus the Galilean,' is
represented as employed by the companion maid (26^{69}),
and the multitude seeking to do Him honor is represented as describing Him with great fulness as " the
prophet Jesus from Nazareth of Galilee " (21^{11}). The
simple ' Jesus,' as has been already pointed out, He
is not represented as called, except by the angel announcing His birth (1^{21}), but Pilate is quoted as designating Him by His full name, " Jesus, surnamed
Christ " ($27^{17,22}$), and we are told that there was set
over His head on the cross the legend, " This is Jesus,
the King of the Jews " (27^{37}). In both instances the
adjunct is, no doubt, scornful, though it is less obviously so on Pilate's lips than in the inscription on
the cross.

The employment by Pilate of the full name, ' Jesus,
surnamed Christ,' seems to bear witness that already
Early Use of   before Jesus' death He had been so pre-
' Christ ' as a   vailingly spoken of as the Messiah that
Proper Name   this official designation might seem to
have become part of His proper name. The alternatives are to suppose that Matthew does not report the
exact words of Pilate, who may be thought rather to

have used the phrase appearing in the parallel passage in Mark—" the King of the Jews ";[9] or else that the term Christ is employed here in its full official sense as an appellative,—" Jesus who is commonly called the Christ."[10] The former, however, is a purely gratuitous suggestion; Mark and Matthew do not contradict but supplement one another. And the latter seems not quite consonant with the language used. There seems, moreover, really no reason why we may not suppose Pilate to have caught the term " Christ " as applied to Jesus, and to have understood it as a proper name, especially when we are expressly told by Luke (23^2) that the accusation which was lodged against Him took the form that He had proclaimed Himself to be " Christ, a King." Nor, indeed, does there seem any compelling reason why it may not already have been employed of Jesus by His followers sufficiently constantly to have begun to be attached to Him as at least a quasi-proper name (cf. 11^2). On heathen ears, as we know, the term " Christ " was apt to strike as a proper name;[11] and, in any event, the title 'Christ' began very early, at least in Christian circles, to be appropriated to Jesus in much the connotation of a proper name, because men did not wait for His death before they began to hope it would be He who should deliver Israel.[12] If we may suppose, as in any event we must, that even as a proper name, or as a quasi-proper name, there clung to the term 'Christ' a sense of its honorific character, it would appear quite possible

[9] So Dalman.
[10] So e.g. Alexander and Weiss.
[11] Suetonius, " *Chresto impulsore,*" and note Acts 11^{26}.
[12] Lk 24^{21}.

that Pilate, " knowing that it was from envy that they had delivered Him up," meant by giving Jesus His full and evidently honorific name, to play upon the multitude, that they should demand " Jesus, surnamed Christ," rather than Barabbas.[13]

Like Mark, Matthew represents Jesus as customarily addressed by the simple current honorific titles. The

Simple Honorific Addresses

actual Aramaic form, ' Rabbi,' how‑ ever, oddly enough, is retained only in repeating the only two remarks recorded in Matthew's narrative as made to the Lord by Judas Iscariot ($26^{25,49}$).[14] Its usual Greek rendering, ' Teacher ' ($\delta\iota\delta\acute{a}\sigma\varkappa\alpha\lambda\varepsilon$), also takes a relatively infe‑ rior place in Matthew, being largely supplanted by the more Greek ' Lord ' ($\varkappa\acute{v}\rho\iota\varepsilon$), perhaps as the representative of the Aramaic *Mâri*.[15] A tendency seems even observable to reserve ' Teacher ' ($\delta\iota\delta\acute{a}\sigma\varkappa\alpha\lambda\varepsilon$) for the non-committal, respectful address of those who were not followers of Jesus (12^{38} $22^{16,24,36}$; 9^{11} 17^{24}, cf. 19^{16}). It is employed, however, in

[13] If the reading ' Jesus Barabbas ' in Mt 27^{16-17} could be accepted, it would supply a reason why Pilate should have employed the full name ' Jesus surnamed Christ.' He would have wished to ascertain which Jesus the people wanted. But see A. Plummer in Hastings' *Dict. of the Bible,* art. ' Barabbas ' (1. 245).

[14] The contrast between the address of the other disciples, " Is it I, Lord ($\varkappa\acute{v}\rho\iota\varepsilon$) ? " (verse 22), and that of Judas, " Is it I, Rabbi? " is marked. It imports that Judas, though among our Lord's closest fol‑ lowers, was not of them: they recognize Him as their Lord, he only as his teacher. But it remains obscure why in the case of Judas only Matthew uses the Aramaic " Rabbi," rather than, as in other cases of similar contrast, the current Greek form, $\delta\iota\delta\acute{a}\sigma\varkappa\alpha\lambda\varepsilon$.

[15] Wellhausen on Mt 23^{7-10} (p. 117) remarks: " We observe that the address $\dot{\rho}\alpha\beta\beta\acute{\iota}$ or $\delta\iota\delta\acute{a}\sigma\varkappa\alpha\lambda\varepsilon$ is claimed here for Jesus and for Him alone, whereas elsewhere in Matthew and Luke it is too low for Him and is replaced by $\varkappa\acute{v}\rho\iota\varepsilon$ (mâri)."

the case of a scribe who came to Jesus and declared his purpose to become His constant follower (8^{19}, cf. 19^{16}). And our Lord places it on His disciples' lips when He instructs them to " go into the city to such a man, and say unto him, The Teacher says, My time is at hand; I keep the passover with my disciples at thy house " (26^{18}). Similarly in didactic statements He refers ($10^{24.25}$) to the relation between Him and His followers as well under the terms of ' Teacher and disciple ' as under those of ' servant and Lord,' ' the Householder and the household ': and forbids His followers to be called ' Rabbi,' because He alone is their ' Teacher,' as pointedly as He forbids them to be called ' guides,' because He, the Christ, alone is their ' Guide ' (23^{7-10}).

Two new terms are brought before us in these last-quoted declarations,—' House-master ' ($οἰκοδεσπότης$, Mt 10^{25} 24^{43}; cf. Mk 13^{25}) and ' Guide ' ($καθηγητής$, 23^{10} only in N. T.) ; both of which seem to have higher implications than ' Teacher ' ($διδάσκαλος$), although both are placed in the closest connection with it as its practical synonyms ($10^{24,25}$ $23^{8,10}$). ' Guide ' ($καθηγητής$) occurs indeed nowhere else :[16] and we can say of it only that our Lord chose it as one of

[16] The source of the term $καθηγητής$ has been much discussed. It seems to have been in use in the Greek philosophical schools in the sense of Master, Teacher (see Wettstein *in loc.*). The Hebraists (Wünsche, Delitzsch, Salkinson) are inclined to seek for it an Aramaic original, מוֹרה (cf. Holtzmann, *Hand-Com.*, 251) : but on this see Dalman, *Words*, pp. 335-340. It is a deeper question whether it may not be a Messianic title in accordance with the preservation of such a designation—' Hathab,' ' the Guide '—among the Samaritans : see Stanton, *Jewish and Christian Messiah*, 127. There is no rational ground for simply casting the verse out of Matthew (Blass, Wellhausen, Holtzmann, even Dalman).

the designations which expressed His exclusive relation to His disciples. He was their only Teacher,
Guide, Master and Lord. But 'House-master'
(οἰκοδεσπότης) seems to have been rather a favorite

**Master of
the House**

figurative expression with Him, to set
forth His relation to His disciples,
whether in didactic or in parabolic statement. In one of His parables, indeed, it is not
He who is the 'House-master' (οἰκοδεσπότης), but
God,[17] while He is God's Son and Heir (21^{33} et seq.)
in distinction from the slaves which make up otherwise the household; and the uniqueness of His relation to the Father as His Son is thrown up into the
strongest light, and is further emphasized in the
application, where Jesus speaks of Himself as the
chief cornerstone on which the Kingdom of God
is built (verse 42) and on their relation to which
the destinies of men hang (verse 44). In other
parables, however (13^{24} et seq., 20^1 et seq.), the 'House-
master' (οἰκοδεσπότης) is Jesus Himself, and the functions that are ascribed to Him as such have especial
reference to the destinies of men. As the 'House-
master' (οἰκοδεσπότης) He distributes to men the rewards
of their labors in accordance with His own will, doing
as He will with His own (20^{15}) : and bears with the
tares in the field in which He has sown good corn until
the time of harvest shall come, when He will send the
reapers—who are "His Angels"—to gather them out
and burn them with fire (13^{24} et seq., 36 et seq.). In a
word, to the 'House-master' (οἰκοδεσπότης), who is ex-

[17] In 13^{52} the οἰκοδεσπότης is "every scribe who has been made
a disciple in the kingdom of heaven." And in 24^{43} the οἰκοδεσπότης
is the watching follower on earth who waits for His coming.

pressly identified with 'the Son of Man' (13^{38}) the inalienably divine function of Judge of the earth is assigned, and it is with this high connotation in His mind that He speaks of Himself as such, over against His " domestics," when He warns them not to expect better treatment at the hands of men than He has received (10^{25}). The implications of sovereignty inherent in the term run up in its application therefore into the sovereignty of God: as 'House-master' (οἰχοδεσπότης), Jesus is pictured as our divine Lord.[18]

If 'Teacher' (διδάσχαλε) somewhat sinks in value as an honorific form of address in Matthew as

'Lord' as an Address

compared with Mark, its more Greek equivalent, 'Lord' (χύριε), on the other hand, is more frequently and variously employed by Matthew than by Mark.[19] It

---

[18] On the meaning of οἰχοδεσπότης see T. D. Woolsey, *Bibliotheca Sacra,* July, 1861, p. 599. Δεσπότης means "the *absolute* owner of things . . . as . . . δεσπότης οἰχίας, the master of a house or household; whence the οἰχοδεσπότης of the sacred writers." Cf. Trench, *Synonyms of N. T.,* xxviii., p. 91.

[19] On the use of χύριε in Matthew and its relations to other forms of address, cf. Zahn, on Mt. 7^{21} (p. 315, note 235). *Κύριε,* he tells us, is employed " as an address to Jesus on the part of people who still stood at a distance from Jesus, commonly in seeking help from Him, in Mt $8^{2,6,8}$ 9^{28} (v. 27, Son of David), $15^{22,27}$ (the first time along with Son of David), 17^{15} $20^{30,33}$, Jno $4^{11,15,19,49}$ 5^7 6^{34} $9^{36,38}$; on the part of male and female disciples at Mt $8^{21,25}$ $14^{28,30}$ 16^{22} 17^4 18^{21} 26^{22}, Jno 6^{68} $11^{3,12,21,27,32,34,39}$ $13^{6,9,25,36}$ $14^{5,8,22}$. Although the disciples of Jesus also address Him by διδάσχαλε (Jno 13^{13-16}, cf. Mt 10^{24}; examples: Mk 4^{38} 9^{38} 13^1; ῥαββί, Mk 9^5 11^{21}, Jno $1^{38,49}$ 4^{31} 9^2 11^8), the distinction is, however, to be noted that this address is used also by His opponents, and especially by the scribes (in Mt 8^{19} no doubt by a friendly scribe in approaching Him, but still one who did not become a disciple, in clear distinction from 8^{21}, cf. 12^{38} 19^{16} $22^{16,24,36}$ Jno 3^2: and by Judas, Mt $26^{25,49}$), while on the other hand χύριε is never so used, since from the very nature of the case it is the address

appears upon the lips alike of applicants for our Lord's mercy, whether Jewish (8^2 9^{28} 17^{15} $20^{30,31,33}$) or heathen ($8^{6,8}$ $15^{22,25}$ 15^{27}), and of His disciples ($8^{21,25}$ $14^{28,30}$ 16^{22} 17^4 18^{21} 26^{22}) ; but never on the lips of one who is not in some sense a follower of Jesus, either as suitor for His grace or as His professed disciple. ' Lord ' (κύριε) is accordingly a higher mode of designation in Matthew than ' Teacher ' (διδάσκαλε), and imports a closer bond of connection with Jesus and a more profound and operative recognition of His authority. It occurs some twenty-one times[20] as a form of address to Jesus, and, besides once as an address to God (11^{25}), only a single time (to Pilate, 27^{63}), outside of parables, as an address to anyone else. Even in its parabolic use, indeed, its reference is always (except 21^{30} only) either to God ($18^{25,[26],27,31}$ $18^{32,34}$ 21^{42}, cf. 6^{24}) or to Jesus pictured in positions of supreme authority ([13^{27}] 20^8 $24^{45,46,48,50}$ $25^{[11],[11],18,19,}$

of the servant to his master and ruler, among the Orientals and later the Hellenists and after Domitian also the Romans the address of subjects to governors, occasionally also of the son to the father (e.g. Berlin *Aegypt. Urkund.* 816, 1. 28, 821, 1) and always an honorific expression of subjection to those addressed (cf. Mt 22^{44} ˢᵉ𐞥·), or at least of dependence upon them at the moment. Thus Pilate is so addressed by the Sanhedrin (Mt 27^{63}), but also Philip by the Greeks (Jno 12^{21}), the gardener by the Magdalen (Jno 20^{15}), in each case in preferring a request." When Zahn says (on the same page) that "it was only after Jesus' death " that κύριε "took on in the Christian community a more precise and richer content," he seems not to be bearing in mind the implications of such passages as 21^3 24^{42} 22^{43-45}, and even 7^{21} itself, though Zahn explains that passage otherwise. It is clear from even 21^3 alone that Jesus was constantly called ' Lord ' and that in a very high connotation.

[20] $8^{2,6,8,21,25}$ 9^{28} $14^{28,30}$ $15^{25,27}$ 16^{22} $17^{4,15}$ 18^{21} $20^{30,33}$ 26^{22}, cf. $25^{37,44}$ $7^{21,21}$. Also 15^{22} 20^{31}.

[20],21,21,[22],23,23,[24],26, cf. $10^{24,25}$). It cannot be said, of course, that this supreme authority is explicit in every case of the actual use of the term: in a number of instances the term may express no more than high respect and a general recognition of authority, and in several instances it is represented in parallel passages in the other evangelists by one or another of its lower synonyms.[21] But its tendency is distinctly upwards; and no reader can fail to catch a very high note in its repeated use, or can feel surprise when it is observed to be connected usually with at least Messianic implications (15^{22} $20^{30,31}$ $7^{21,21}$) and is found occasionally to be suggestive of something even higher ($25^{37,44}$). Nor will he be surprised to perceive that in its highest connotation it appears characteristically upon the lips of our Lord Himself, who represents men as seeking to enter the Kingdom of Heaven by crying to Him ' Lord, Lord ' (7^{21}), and as addressing Him on the Day of Judgment as He sits King on the throne of His glory by the appropriate title of ' Lord ' ($25^{37,44}$). In the latter case, of course, nothing is lacking of recognition of divine majesty itself: this ' Lord ' is not only " the Son of Man " come in His glory with all the angels with Him (verse 31), ' the King ' (verses 34, 40) seated on the throne of His majesty (verse 31), but ' the Judge of all the earth,' distributing to each man his eternal destiny, according to the relation in which each stands to His own person.

It is clear enough from passages like these that

---

[21] ῥαββεί Mk 9^5 (17^4); ῥαββουνί Mk 10^{51} ($20^{31,33}$); διδάσκαλε Lk 4^{38} (8^{25}), Mk 9^{17}, Lk 9^{38} (17^{15}); ἐπιστάτα Lk 8^{24} (8^{25}) 9^{33} (17^4).

our Lord is represented by Matthew as conceiving

'Lord' as an Appellation

His relation to His followers as very properly expressed by the term 'Lord.' But the appellative use of the term of Jesus is nevertheless not common in Matthew. No more in Matthew than in Mark is Jesus spoken of by the evangelist himself or represented as freely spoken of by others as ' the Lord.' Even in the words of the angel at the tomb, " Come, see the place where the Lord lay " (28⁶), the words " the Lord " are probably not genuine. Nevertheless, on the lips of our Lord Himself the appellative use of the term does occur, and that in no low significance. He declares Himself as ' the Son of Man ' to be ' Lord of the Sabbath ' (12⁸). He instructs His disciples in requisitioning the ass and her colt for His formal entry into Jerusalem to reply to all challengers with the simple words, " The Lord has need of them " (21³),—and the narrator connects this instruction with the fulfillment of the prophecy that the King of Zion shall enter it " riding upon an ass, and upon a colt, the foal of an ass " (verse 5). He warns His followers that as they know not on what day ' their Lord ' cometh (24⁴²),—that Lord who is the Son of Man, who is to come in glory for the judgment of the world (verse 44),—they are to preserve a constant attitude of watchfulness. And in accordance with these declarations He explains that though David's son, He, the Christ, is much more than David's son,—as David himself in the Spirit recognized,—even David's ' Lord ' (22⁴³⁻⁴⁵), and that, a Lord who sits on the right hand of the Lord who is Jehovah. It is in full harmony with these definitions of His Lordship cited from the Lord's own lips that

the evangelist himself (3^3) applies to Him the term
'Lord' in that prophecy of Isaiah, in which there is
promised "a voice of one crying in the wilderness,
Make ye ready the way of the Lord," Jehovah; thus
identifying His coming with the promised advent of
Jehovah and His person with Jehovah who was to
come. However little therefore the mere form of
address 'Lord' as applied to Christ may necessarily
imply in Him a superhuman dignity, it is clear that
the actual Lordship accredited to Him by Matthew,
and by Himself as reported by Matthew, stretches
above all human claims.

We cannot fail to have observed, as we have contemplated these honorific addresses and titles accorded
to our Lord, that it is His Messianic
dignity which proximately underlies
them all. And we shall be prepared by
this observation to note that with Matthew as with
Mark, the presentation of Him as the promised Messiah belongs among the primary ends of the evangelist, and that in the process of this presentation a
considerable number of Messianic titles are ascribed
to Him. Matthew bears witness, like Mark, to be
sure, that the people recognized in Him a prophet
(21^{46} 21^{11} 16^{14}) and that Jesus Himself was far from
repelling this attribution (13^{57}); but little stress is
laid upon this and it may be easily understood that
prophetic powers were conceived by Matthew, as by
Mark, to be included in His Messianic endowment. We
have seen that he himself calls Jesus in the formal
opening of his Gospel (1^1), at the beginning of the
narrative proper (1^{18}), and at the new beginning
marked by His open proclamation of His dignity

*Messianic
Titles*

(16^{21}), by the solemn compound name of 'Jesus Christ,' thus carefully announcing His Messianic claims as governing the very frame-work of his Gospel. And we have seen him following up this ceremonious use of the full name 'Jesus Christ' in the opening of the Gospel, by explaining the term 'Christ,' which forms a part of it, as a surname of Jesus due to the recognition of Him as the Messiah (1^{16}), on which account He forms the natural termination of the genealogy begun in Abraham (1^{17}); and by implying that His works marked Him out as the Messiah (11^{2}), so that the imprisoned John, hearing of them, was impelled to inquire into their meaning. How widespread the knowledge of His Messianic claims was is witnessed by the adjuration of the high priest at His trial, "I adjure thee by the living God, that thou tell us whether thou be the Christ" (26^{93}), and the bitter sport His judges made of Him (26^{68}) as they smote Him and demanded, "Tell us, Christ, who smote thee."

Evidently our Lord's claim to the Messianic dignity is intended to be represented as having been **Our Lord's** clear, constant and emphatic: so a part **Own Messianic** of Himself in the popular understand- **Claims** ing that His heathen judge already conceived the title 'Christ' as only His surname ($27^{17,22}$, cf. 11^{2}). And indeed Matthew's narrative leaves us in no uncertainty that Jesus had claimed this title for Himself from His earliest ministry. When the Baptist, having heard of the works He did, sent from his prison to ask Him whether He was 'the Coming One' (11^{3}), He replied with no doubtful indication that He was indeed 'the Christ.' When Peter (16^{16}) in his

great confession declared Him " the Christ, the Son
of the living God," Jesus pronounced the declaration
a revelation from heaven (16^{17}), and only charged
His disciples not as yet to reveal the fact that He was
" the Christ " (16^{20}). It was evidently to elevate the
conception current as to the Christ whom He represented Himself as being that He put to His opponents
the searching question, how could the Christ be merely
David's son, when David himself, in the Spirit, spoke
of Him as his Lord—a Lord seated on the right hand
of God (22^{41-46}). Because He was, as ' the Christ,'
the sole ' Guide ' to His followers, He would not have
them be called guides, even as they should put no
earthly person in the place of their one Father in
heaven (23^{10}). The name ' the Christ,' He explained
(24^{5}), was exclusively His own, and it would be a
usurpation, therefore, which could only lead astray, if
others should come " in the strength of His name, saying "—therefore falsely,—" I am the Christ." When
the high priest adjured Him to tell whether He were
" the Christ, the Son of God " (26^{63}) He, accordingly,
solemnly accepted the title and explained that in accepting it He took it in its highest connotation (26^{64})
—in so high a connotation indeed that His judges
promptly pronounced what He had spoken blasphemy.
It is, therefore, only in imitation of Jesus Himself that
Matthew treats the designation of ' the Christ ' as
Jesus' peculiar property and—though of course without emptying it of its lofty connotation—deals with it as
His proper name by which He might be currently designated.

The ascription of the title ' Christ ' to Jesus carries
with it naturally certain other Messianic titles which

are involved in it. The simplest of these is 'the Coming One,' based apparently on Mal 3^1 or Ps 40^7 or 118^{26}, and itself the basis of a customary method of pregnant speech of the Messiah as "coming."[22] This designation is applied to Jesus in the question of the Baptist—"Art thou the Coming One, or do we look for another?" (11^3), which Matthew records as having been called out by the report brought the Baptist of the "works of Christ"—using the name of 'Christ' here instead of 'Jesus,' contrary to his custom, apparently under the influence of this train of thought. And the evangelist records in accordance with this designation a series of sayings of our Lord in which He speaks pregnantly of having "come" (5^{17} 9^{13} 10^{34} 20^{28}, cf.

The Simple Messianic Designations

[22] See the passages carefully enumerated in Thayer-Grimm, *sub voc.* ἔρχομαι, I. 1 a. β. (pp. 250-1 near top). Dr. Edersheim, *Life,* etc., I. 668, says: "The designation, 'the Coming One' (*habba*), though a most truthful expression of Jewish expectations, was not one ordinarily used of the Messiah. But it was invariably used with reference to the Messianic age . . ." Dr. Edersheim is speaking, of course, of what is to be garnered from extant Jewish writings. The employment of the phrase in Mt 11^3 and Lk 7^{19} is sufficient proof that it bore among the Jews of the day "a technical sense" as a title of the Messiah (cf. Westcott on Jno 1^{11}). With reference to the appearance of this designation precisely here, Zahn (*in loc.*) remarks: "While Matthew expresses the dignity, as the possessor of which Jesus has manifested Himself by means of His works heretofore described, by the long established title of ὁ Χριστός (cf. esp. 2^4), he makes the Baptist (who also in his public preaching seems to have avoided this title) give expression to the same conception, consonantly with the manner in which he had spoken of the future founder and King of the Kingdom of Heaven (3^{11}, Mk 1^7, Lk 3^{16}, Jno 1^{27}) by the term ὁ ἐρχόμενος, the Coming One, the Great Expected. No doubt other expected personalities might be similarly spoken of (Mt 11^{14} $17^{10\ seq.}$, Jno 6^{14}), but in the mouth of the Baptist the expression was without ambiguity: for he had spoken of One only who was already on the way, which John was to prepare for Him."

10⁴⁰), as well as certain popular ascriptions to the same effect (21⁹ 23³⁹).²³

Even more directly connected with the title, ' Christ,' however, is that of ' King ': and we find Matthew accordingly recording the ascription of that title to Him in the heathen form of ' the King of the Jews,' alike by the wise men of the east who came to worship Him in His cradle (2²) and by the Roman governor at His trial (27¹¹, cf. 27³⁷) and the mocking soldiery (27²⁹). Jesus accepts it at Pilate's hands, despite the heathen form which he gives it, and which the priests (27⁴²) correct to the more acceptable ' King of Israel.' Of more significance is Matthew's application to Him, when He entered Jerusalem in triumph, of the prophecy of Zechariah, " Behold thy King cometh unto thee," etc. (21⁵). But, of course, the deepest significance of all attaches to our Lord's own use of the title ' King ' with reference to Himself in the great judgment scene of Mt 25³¹ ˢᵉ𐞥· (verses 34 and 40). Here, calling Himself the ' Son of Man,' He ascends the throne of His glory, and as King, not of Israel, but of all flesh, dispenses their final awards to all, according to their several relations to Himself. Such a King certainly was something more than a ' Son of David ' (22⁴³ ˢᵉ𐞥·). But that designation also belongs to Him as the ' Christ,' God's Anointed, who was to occupy the Davidic throne, and accordingly it is represented that the sight of His Messianic works led Him to be recognized no more as ' the Coming One ' (11³) than

²³ Cf. W. C. Allen on Mt 11²⁷. Commenting on the aorist, $\pi\alpha\rho\epsilon\delta\delta\theta\eta$, he remarks: " The idea involved is of a pre-temporal act, and carries with it the conception of the preëxistence of the Messiah. The same thought probably underlies $\tilde{\eta}\lambda\theta o\nu$ of 5¹⁷ 10³⁴, and the $\dot{\alpha}\pi o\sigma\tau\epsilon\ \lambda\alpha\nu\tau\alpha$ of 10⁴⁰."

as 'the Son of David' (12^{23} 9^{27} 15^{22} $20^{30,31}$ $21^{9,15}$, cf. 1^1)—and that He by no means refused the ascription (esp. $21^{9,15}$).

Obviously, however, no lower title would suit the state of this Messianic King than that highest con-

Meaning of the 'Son of God' ceivable one, 'the Son of God.' It is likely that there were supernatural implications in the mind of the evangelist even when he applied to the persecuted infant Jesus the prophetic summary of Israelitish history, " Out of Egypt did I call my Son " (2^{15}), although at first sight we might seem to be moving here in the atmosphere of a merely official sonship.[24] In every other instance of the adduction of this designation in Matthew these supernatural implications are thrust prominently forward. The very point of Satan's temptation of our Lord was that He should exercise the supernatural powers which necessarily belonged to Him— if He were indeed really 'a Son of God' ($4^{3,6}$, cf. 8^{29}).[25] Similarly the confession wrung from the dis-

---

[24] Cf. Zahn *in loc.:* "According to the connection of the narrative up to this point, Jesus can be called the Son of God for no other reason than that He was born of the Virgin apart from any aid of man (cf. Lk 1^{35}). The divine sonship of Israel, which was grounded in God's calling this people into being for a particular purpose, and, as it were, begetting it (Deut 32^{18})—an idea which was so vividly conceived that God's fatherhood is set excludingly over against that of Abraham and Jacob (Is 63^{16})—appears as a type of the divine Sonship of Jesus, which actually excludes the bodily fatherhood of the son of David."

[25] Cf. Zahn, *in loc.* (p. 152): "He is by a word of power to create for Himself the food for which He hungers. This is an echo out of the abyss corresponding to the voice from heaven (3^{17}). What God declares of Jesus, the devil brings into question (Gen 3^1, Job $1^{8\ seq.}$), demanding from Jesus that He should offer him proof of it. We must not overlook, however, that he does not say, as might have been expected from the undeniable connection with 3^{17}, εἰ ὁ υἱὸς but εἰ υἱὸς

ciples by the spectacle of His control of the forces of nature, emphasizes as strongly as possible the supernaturalness of the Being who is capable of such works (14^{33}).[26] In Peter's great confession (16^{16})[27] the adjunction of ' the Son of the Living God ' to the simple ' Christ ' is no more without its high significance than the similar adjunction in the high priest's adjuration (26^{63})[28] of ' the Son of God ' to the simple ' Christ.'

εἰ τοῦ θεοῦ. He is to prove not that He is the unique Son of God whom God just on that account has chosen as the Messiah, but that He is a being more closely related than other men to God (cf. Mt 14^{33} 27^{40}). If it cannot be unknown to the evil spirit, who is acquainted with the voice from heaven, that Jesus has been chosen to be the Messiah, nevertheless what he demands of Him has nothing directly to do with this vocation. It is, however, surely to be expected of One who as a Son of God must have power over nature, that He should rescue Himself from the unsuitable condition of a hungry man by the use of His power."

[26] Cf. Zahn, *in loc.* (p. 513): "Neither the absence of the article from the predicate (cf. on the other hand, 3^{17} 16^{16} even 11^{27}), nor the position of θεοῦ before υἱός is to be overlooked. Even if divine Sonship and Messianic dignity were synonyms (see to the contrary p. 145 *seq.*), and what had cast the disciples into adoring wonder had had anything to do with the office of the Messiah, the absence of the article nevertheless would forbid us to think of that here (cf. on the contrary, 12^{23} 16^{16} 21^9 26^{63}). What is said and what there was occasion to say is not who but what kind of a man Jesus was. The question elicited by a similar occasion, ποταπός ἐστιν οὗτος (8^{27}) is here answered; though, naturally, not after the fashion of a scholastic dictum, but in the direct expression of an overwhelming experience. Not a son of man, but a Son of God He is, who exhibits such supernatural power over the elements, and shows Himself so exalted over the hesitancies between the power of faith and the feebleness of the flesh which accompany human weakness even when the spirit is willing, —as was to be seen in Peter."

[27] Cf. Zahn *in loc.* pp. 534-5: goes above 14^{33} in confessing Jesus as *the* Son of God, and of the living God; that is, Jesus had manifested the works of the Son of a God who exists and acts, etc.

[28] Cf. Zahn *in loc.,* pp. 694-5.

In both instances the intention is to go beyond the mere designation of our Lord as the Messiah, and to bring into relief the supernaturalness of His person. Even when the Jews railed at Him as He hung on the cross that He had proclaimed Himself 'the Son of God' ($27^{40,43}$), the point of their scoff was that He had laid claim to a supernatural relationship which implied supernatural powers. Nevertheless, the deepest connotations of the Sonship to God come out most plainly in connection with the less technical forms of this designation. At the apex of these stands, of course, the double attestation which, it is recorded, was given to Jesus from heaven itself as God's 'Son,' who because His 'Son' was also His 'Beloved,' His chosen, in whom He was well pleased (3^{17} 17^5).[29] But quite worthy of a place by the side of these supreme attestations is the allusion which our Lord makes to Himself in one or two of His parables, as the 'Son,' in differentiation from all " servants " of God whatsoever; as God's Son and unique Heir, who, despite what those to whom He was sent should do unto Him, shall be constituted by God's marvelous working the stone

---

[29] Cf. Zahn *in loc.*, pp. 145 *seq.*, where the question is fully discussed and solidly argued: " As at 2^{15} so here the divine Sonship is to be explained from 1^{18-25}. It expresses not an official, but a personal relation; it is not identical with the Messianic office, but its presupposition." One of the arguments on which Zahn lays stress, however, scarcely serves: " The idea that God, out of the many sons which He has, has chosen one and that for the Messiahship, is excluded by the attribute ἀγαπητός; for in this connection ἀγαπητός bears the established sense of only son=μονογενής." It appears to be probable, on the contrary, that, as W. C. Allen, *in loc.*, puts it " ὁ ἀγαπητός is not an attribute of ὁ υἱός μου, but an independent title—' the Beloved '—the Messiah." The matter is discussed by Dr. J. Armitage Robinson in Hastings' *Dict. Bib.* II. 501, and in his commentary on Ephesians, pp. 229ff.

which is the head of the corner ($21^{37\text{-}38}$) ;[30] and as the King's Son, all those unworthy of a place at whose marriage feast should have their part in the outer darkness where is the weeping and the gnashing of teeth (22^2). This 'Son' obviously is no less in origin and nature divine than in His working in the earth the Lord of the destinies of men.

But perhaps the most illuminating passages in this reference remain yet to be adduced. These are those **Culminating Assertions** three remarkable utterances of our Lord which are recorded at 24^{36}, 11^{27} and $28^{18\text{-}20}$. The first of these we have already met with in Mark. It is that difficult saying in which our Lord declares that " concerning the day and hour " of His coming " no one knows, not even the angels of heaven, nor yet the Son, but the Father only "—which differs from the parallel in Mark significantly only in the added emphasis placed on the exclusion of all others whatsoever from this knowledge by the adjunction to the exception of the Father of the emphatic word " only." The elevation of the Son here to superangelic dignity, as the climax of the enumeration of those excluded from the knowledge in question is reached in His name—no one at all, not even the angels of heaven, nor yet even the Son—is what it particularly concerns us to note, implying as it does the exaltation of the Son above the highest of creatures, " the angels of heaven."[31] The second of

[30] Cf. Zahn, *in loc.*, pp. 620, 621.

[31] The words " nor yet the Son " are, to be sure, lacking in a few somewhat unimportant witnesses to the text, but can scarcely be adjudged of doubtful genuineness. W. C. Allen rejects them in sequence to a theory of his own of the relation of Matthew to Mark, and Matthew's habit of dealing with Mark's christological statements. Zahn

the utterances in question (11^{27}) is in some respects
the most remarkable in the whole compass of the four
Gospels. Even the Gospel of John contains nothing
which penetrates more deeply into the essential relation of the·Son to the Father. Indeed, as Dr. Sanday
suggests, " we might describe the teaching of the
Fourth Gospel " as only " a series of variations upon
the one theme, which has its classical expression in "
this " verse of the Synoptics ":[32] " All things were delivered unto me by my Father; and no one knoweth
the Son save the Father; neither doth any know the
Father save the Son, and he to whomsoever the Son
willeth to reveal Him." The point of the utterance,
it will be seen, is that in it our Lord asserts for Himself
a relation of practical equality with the Father, here
described in most elevated terms as the " Lord of
heaven and earth " (v. 25).[33] As the Father only can
know the Son, so the Son only can know the Father:
and others may know the Father only as He is revealed
by the Son. That is, not merely is the Son the exclusive revealer of God, but the mutual knowledge of
Father and Son is put on what seems very much a par.
The Son can be known only by the Father in all that
He is, as if His being were infinite and as such in-

more wisely retains them, as do all the editors. " The documentary
evidence in their favor," says Hort justly, " is overwhelming."

[32] *Criticism of the New Testament,*—by a company of scholars,—
p. 17.

[33] Cf. Zahn on Mt 11^{25-30} (p. 440) : " As Jesus here names Him
whom He has just called ' His Father,' in the second and third clauses
simply 'the Father '—which is not to be paralleled with the address of
vv. 25, 26—so He names Himself three times simply ' the Son,' in
order to designate Himself as the only one who stood to God in the
full sense of that name in the relation of a Son to a Father."

scrutable to the finite intelligence; and His knowledge alone—again as if He were infinite in His attributes— is competent to compass the depths of the Father's infinite being. He who holds this relation to the Father cannot conceivably be a creature, and we ought not to be surprised, therefore, to find in the third of these great utterances ($28^{18\text{-}20}$) the Son made openly a sharer with the Father (and with the Holy Spirit) in the single Name of God: "All authority was given me[34] in heaven and in earth. Go ye therefore and make disciples of all the nations, baptizing them into the Name of the Father and of the Son and of the Holy Spirit; teaching them to observe all things whatsoever I commanded you; and lo, I am with you alway, even unto the end of the world." Having in the former passage (11^{27}) declared His intercommunion with the Father, who is the Lord of heaven and earth, Jesus here asserts that all authority in heaven and earth has been given Him, and asserts a place for Himself in the precincts of the ineffable Name. Here is a claim not merely to a deity in some sense equivalent to and as it were alongside of the deity of the Father, but to a deity in some high sense one with the deity of the Father.

Alongside of these more usual Messianic titles, there are found in Matthew, as in Mark, traces of the use **Less Common** of others of our Lord, apparently less **Messianic** current among the people. In Mat- **Titles** thew, too, for example, we find Jesus represented as designated from heaven 'the Beloved,' who has been chosen out by God as His rep-

[34] Note the aorist, which as in 11^{27} (cf. W. C. Allen, *in loc.*) appears to refer to a pre-temporal act.

resentative (3^{17} 17^5),[35] and as identifying Himself
with the mysterious Shepherd of Zechariah who is
Jehovah's fellow (26^{31}). And we find Him here also
not only designating Himself the 'Bridegroom'
(9^{15}), but elucidating the designation in a couple of
striking parables (the parable of the Ten Virgins,
$25^{1 \text{ seq.},5,6,10}$: and the parable of the Marriage of the
King's Son, $22^{1 \text{ seq.}}$), the suggestion of which is that
the fate of men hangs on their relation to Him; that
men all live with reference to Him; and it is He that
opens and shuts the door of life for them. The high
significance of these designations as applied to Jesus
has already been pointed out when we met with them
in Mark. It is more important, therefore, to observe
here that the implicit reference in Mark to the 'Servant of Jehovah' as a designation of Jesus is made
explicit in Matthew by the formal application to Him
of the prophecy in Isaiah $40^{1 \text{ seq.}}$ ($12^{18 \text{ seq.}}$) as a divine
prediction of the unostentatiousness of His ministry,
in its striking contrast with the expectations which had
been formed of the Messiah's work on the basis of the
predictions centering around the Anointed King, the
Son of David.

This unostentatiousness entered also into the conception of the Messiah expressed in our Lord's favorite
self-designation of 'Son of Man,'—
The 'Son of Man' which in Matthew's representation, too,
appears as the standing Messianic designation which our Lord employs of Himself, occurring as such about thirty times. The Messianic
character of this designation is placed beyond all doubt

[35] Cf. W. C. Allen on 3^{17} and J. A. Robinson, *Ephesians* 229 *seq.* and
Hastings' *Dict. of the Bible,* II., p. 501; also Charles, *Ascension of
Isaiah,* p. 3 *et passim,* and E. Daplyn *sub voc.* Hastings' *D. C. G.*

by its interchange with other Messianic titles (16^{13}, cf. verses 16, 20; 17^9, cf. verse 10 [the forerunner of Messiah]; 24^{27}, cf. verse 23; 26^{64}, cf. verse 63) : and the conception suggested by it of the Messiah, as judged by the substance of the passages in which it occurs, differs in nothing from that derived from the passages in Mark except that it is illuminated by more details. Here, too, we learn that the ' Son of Man ' came to minister,—or more specifically for the purpose of redemption: "the Son of Man came not to be ministered unto, but to minister, and to give His life a ransom for many " (20^{28}). Suffering and death were, therefore, His appointed portion (17^{12} 17^{22} 20^{18} $26^{2,24,45}$), as indeed Scripture had foretold (12^{40}). But after death is the resurrection ($17^{9,22}$ 20^{19} 12^{40}), and after the resurrection the " coming " in great glory to judge the world (10^{23} $24^{27,30,39,44}$ 26^{64}). There is nothing here which we had not already in Mark, but everywhere details are filled in. The fortunes of the earthly life of the ' Son of Man ' are traced. We learn that He lived like other men, without asceticism,—" eating and drinking " (11^{19}) ; but lived a hard and suffering life,—He had not where to lay His head (8^{20}). His task was to sow the good seed of the word (13^{37}). As part of His lowliness, it emerges that blasphemy against Him is forgivable, as it is not against the Holy Ghost (12^{32}). And the suffering He is called on to endure runs out into death ($17^{12,22}$). It would not be easy to give a more itemized account of the sufferings He endured at the end than Mark gives, but they are all set down here, too (20^{18}), as also is the promise of the resurrection (12^{40} $17^{9,23}$ 20^{18}). When He shall come again is left here, too, in the indefinite future

(24^{36}, cf. 10^{23}), but the suddenness of its eventuation is emphasized ($24^{27,37,39,44}$).

The details become notably numerous again, however, when the purpose and accompaniment of this coming are adverted to (13^{41} 16^{27} 19^{28} 24^{31} 25^{31} 26^{64}). The 'Son of Man' is "henceforth to be seen sitting at the right hand of power and coming in the clouds of heaven" (26^{64} 24^{30}). He is to come in the glory of His Father with His angels (16^{27}), for all the angels are to be with Him (25^{31}). The end of His coming is to pass judgment on men and to consummate the Kingdom. "For the Son of Man shall come in the glory of His Father with His angels, and then shall He render unto every man according to his deeds" (16^{27})—and this is "to come in His kingdom" (16^{28}). There is naturally a punitive side to this judgment and a side of reward. Of the punitive side we are told that "when the sign of the Son of Man coming in the clouds of heaven with power and great glory shall appear," "all the tribes of the earth shall mourn" (24^{30}); and that He "shall send forth His angels, and they shall gather out of His kingdom all things that cause stumbling and them that do iniquity, and shall cast them into the furnace of fire: there shall be the weeping and the gnashing of teeth" (13^{41}). On the side of reward we are told that "those who have followed Him, in the regeneration when the 'Son of Man' shall sit on the throne of His glory" "also shall sit upon twelve thrones judging the twelve tribes of Israel" (19^{28}). For "He shall send forth His angels with a great sound of trumpets, and they shall gather together His elect from the four winds; from one end of heaven to the other" (24^{31}), and "then shall the righteous shine forth as the sun in the Kingdom of their Father" (13^{43}). It is obviously the universal judgment that is here brought before us; and the consummation of the Kingdom, when by this judgment all that is impure is drafted out of it and the chosen are made sharers in the universal regeneration. The whole scene of the judgment is pictured for us with great vividness in the remarkable passage, $25^{31\text{-}46}$, where all the nations are depicted as summoned before the throne of the 'Son of Man's' glory and separated according to their deeds done in the body—interpreted as relating to Him—to the eternal inheritance of the kingdom prepared for them from the foundation of the world or to the eternal fire prepared for the devil and his angels. The 'Son of Man' appears here accordingly as the King on His throne apportioning to men their eternal destinies.

Clearly, according to Matthew's account of our Lord's declarations, the 'Son of Man' has His period The High of humiliation on earth, living as other Meaning of men (11^{19}), sowing the seed (13^{37}), 'Son of Man' having not where to lay His head (8^{20}) as He ministers to men (20^{28}), forgiving even blasphemy against Himself (12^{32}) and all indignities ($17^{12,22}$), down to death itself (17^{22} 20^{18})—and yet even while on earth having authority to forgive sins (9^{6}) and to regulate religious ordinances (12^{8}), and dying only that He may ransom others (20^{28}). And He has also His period of exaltation, when having risen from the dead (12^{40} $17^{9,23}$ 20^{18}) He in due time comes in His glory, surrounded by His servants the angels (16^{27} 25^{31} 24^{31}), and gathers to Himself His chosen ones whom He has ransomed by His death (24^{31} 13^{43}) and, cleansing His Kingdom of all that is unclean, sets it up in its destined perfection (16^{28}).

The picture that is drawn is clearly, then, a picture of
voluntary humiliation for a high end, with the ac-
complishment of the end and return to the original
glory.   In order to bring all its implications out in
their completeness we have only to recall what Matthew tells us, on the one hand, of the ' Son ' who is
superior to angels (24^{36}), who is God's adequate and
exclusive Revelation, knowing Him even as He is
known (11^{27}), who is sharer with the Father in the
one ineffable Name (28^{18-20}) ; and, on the other, in
the opening chapter of his Gospel, of the supernatural
birth of this heavenly Being, breaking His way to earth
through a virgin's womb in fulfillment of the prophecy
that He should be called " Immanuel," " God with
us."   For it can scarcely be doubted that Matthew
means this name ' Immanuel ' (1^{23}) to be interpreted
metaphysically of Jesus, and therefore adduces the
prophecy as a testimony to the essential deity of the
virgin-born child,—and indeed the angel messenger
himself is recorded as not obscurely indicating this
when he explains that the child whose birth he announces shall be called Jesus " because it is He that
shall save His people from their sins "—thus applying
to the promised infant the words spoken in Ps 130^8
of Jehovah Himself: " And He shall redeem Israel
from all his iniquities."[36]   The very name ' Jesus '
for Matthew, as truly as that of ' Immanuel ' itself, is
thus freighted with an implication of the deity of its
bearer: and this is only a symbol of the saturation of
his Gospel with the sense of the supreme majesty of the
great personality whose life-history as the promised
Messiah he has undertaken to portray.

[36] So Dalman, strikingly, *Words,* 297.

MATTHEW'S CONCEPTION OF OUR LORD

In seeking to form an estimate of the significance of this list of designations ascribed to Jesus in Matthew, it does not seem necessary to attempt to draw out separately, as we attempted to do in the case of Mark, the evidence they supply to the primary emphasis laid in Matthew upon the Messianic dignity of Jesus and that they supply to the recognition of the divine majesty of His person. It lies on the very face of these designations that by Matthew, as truly as by Mark, Jesus is conceived in the first instance as the promised Messiah, and His career and work as fundamentally the career and work of the Messiah, at last come to introduce the promised Kingdom. And it lies equally on their very face that this Messiah whom Jesus is represented as being is conceived by Matthew, and is represented by Matthew as having been conceived by Jesus Himself, as a "transcendent" figure, as the current mode of speech puts it, i. e., as far transcending in His nature and dignity human conditions.

Profundity of Matthew's Suggestiveness

So clear is this in fact that our interest as we read instinctively takes hold in Matthew of matters quite other than those which naturally occupy it in Mark. In Mark the attention of the reader is attracted particularly to the implications of the superangelic dignity ascribed to the Messiah; and he finds himself unpre-

meditatingly noting the evidence of the presupposition
of His heavenly origin and relations, of His pre-
existence, of His more than human majesty, of His
divine powers and functions. These things are so
much a matter of course with Matthew that the attention of the reader is drawn insensibly off from them
to profounder problems. This Gospel opens with an
account of the supernatural birth of Jesus, which is
so told as to imply that the birth is supernatural only
because the person so born is not of this world, but
in descending to it fulfills the prophecies that Jehovah
shall come to His people to dwell among them and to
save them from their sins. From the very outset,
therefore, there can be no question in the mind of the
reader that he has to deal not merely with a supernatural life but with a supernatural person, all whose
life on earth is a concession to a necessity arising solely
from His purpose to save.[1] No wonder rises in him,
therefore, when he reads of the supramundane powers
of this person, of His superhuman insight, of His
supernatural deeds. That He is superior to the angels,
who appear constantly as His servants, and is in some
profound sense divine, clothed with all divine qualities,
strikes him as in no sense strange. The matters on
which he finds his mind keenly alert rise above these

[1]Cf. W. C. Allen, Hastings' *D. C. G.*, I., 308: " In the thought of
the evangelist, Jesus, born of the Virgin by the Holy Spirit, was the
preëxistent Messiah (= the Beloved) or Son (11^{27}), who had been
forechosen by God (3^{17} 17^5), and who, when born into the world as
Jesus, was ' God-with-us ' (1^{23}). In this respect the writer of the
First Gospel shows himself to be under the influence of the same conception of the Person of Christ that dominates the Johannine theology,
though this conception under the categories of the *Logos* and the Divine
Son is worked out much more fully in the Fourth than in the First
Gospel."

things, and concern the precise relations in which this superangelic, and therefore uncreated, Being is conceived to stand to the Deity Himself.

It is not possible to avoid noting that all the designations applied to Jesus in this narrative tend to run

Richness of His Implications

up at once on being applied to Him into their highest implications. Even the simple name ' Jesus ' is no exception to this. For here it is represented as itself a gift from heaven, designed to indicate that in this person is fulfilled the promise that Jehovah shall visit His people, —for it is He who, in accordance with the prediction of the Psalmist (130^8), shall save His people—*His* people, although, in accordance with that prediction, they are Jehovah's people—from their sins (1^{21}). Similarly the simple honorifics ' Master ' and ' Lord ' rise in Matthew's hands to their highest value; ' Master ' becomes transformed into the more absolute " Master of the House " with His despotic power, governing all things in accordance with His will (20^{15}) and disposing of the destinies of men in supreme sovereignty (10^{25} $13^{24 \text{ seq.},36 \text{ seq.}}$) ; and ' Lord ' becomes the proper designation of the universal King and Judge ($25^{37,44}$) whose coming is the coming of Jehovah (3^3). As the ' Christ ' He is pictured as sitting less on David's throne than on God's ($22^{43,44}$) ; as ' King,' less as the ruler of the nation for Israel than as Judge of all the world for God ($25^{31 \text{ seq.}}$) ; as ' Bridegroom ' as holding in His own hands the issues of life (22^1 25^1) ; as ' the Son of Man ' as passing through humiliation only to His own proper glory (16^{27} 24^{30} 26^{64}) ; as ' the Son of God ' less as God's representative and the vehicle of His grace than as God's fellow (11^{27}) and

the sharer with the Father in the one ineffable Name
(28^{18-20}). Thus the reader is brought steadily upwards
to the great passages in which Matthew records Jesus'
supreme self-testimony to His essential relations with
His Father, and his attention is quite insistently focused
upon them.

" All things were delivered unto me of my Father,"
says Jesus, as reported in one of them (11^{27}) : " and

Assimilation
of Jesus
With God

no one knoweth the Son save the
Father; neither doth any know the
Father save the Son, and he to whom-

soever the Son willeth to reveal Him.   Come unto
me, all ye that labor and are heavy laden, and I will
give you rest."   Thus our Lord solemnly presents Himself to men as the exclusive source of all knowledge of
God, and the exclusive channel of divine grace.   No
one can know the Father save through Him, and
through Him alone can rest be found for weary souls.
And this His exclusive mediation of saving knowledge
He makes to rest upon His unique relation to the
Father, by virtue of which the Father and Son, and
all that is in the Father and Son, lie mutually open to
each other's gaze.   Attention has been called to the
fact, and it is important to observe it, that the whole
passage is cast in the present tense, and the relation
announced to exist between the Father and Son is,
therefore, represented not as a past relation but as a
continuous and unbroken one.   What our Lord asserts
is thus not that He once was with the Father and knew
His mind, and is therefore fitted to mediate it as His
representative on earth: it is that He, though on
earth, still is with the Father and knows His mind—
yea, and will know it unchangeably forever.   The rela-

tions of time do not enter into the representation. Our Lord presents Himself as the sole source of the knowledge of God and of the divine grace, because this is the relation in which He stands essentially to the Father,—a relation of complete and perfect intercommunion. The assertion of the reciprocal knowledge of the Father and Son, in other words, rises far above the merely mediatorial function of the Son, although it underlies His mediatorial mission: it carries us back into the region of metaphysical relations. The Son is a fit and perfect mediator of the divine knowledge and grace because the Son and the Father are mutually intercommunicative. The depths of the Son's being, we are told, can be fathomed by none but a divine knowledge, while the knowledge of the Son compasses all that God is; from both points of view, the Son appears thus as " equal with God."

But even this is far from the whole story. The perfect reciprocal knowledge of each by the other

Identification of Jesus With God

which is affirmed goes far towards suggesting that even equality with God falls short of fully expressing the relation in which the Son actually stands to the Father. Equality is an external relation: here there is indicated an internal relation which suggests rather the term interpenetration. There is a relation with the Father here suggested which transcends all creaturely possibilities, and in which there is no place even for subordination. The man Jesus does indeed represent Himself as exercising a mediatorial function; what He does is to reveal the Father and to mediate His grace; and that because of a delivery over to Him by the Father. But this mediatorial function is rooted in a metaphysical relation in which is suggested no hint of subordination. Rather in this region what the Father is that the Son seems to be also. There is mystery here, no doubt, and nothing is done to relieve the mystery. All that is done is to enunciate in plain words the conception of the relation actually existing between the Father and Son which supplies their suitable account to all those passages in Matthew in which there seems to be suggested a confusion of Jesus with God, whether in function or in person. If this be the relation of Son and Father—if there is a certain mysterious interpenetration to be recognized between them—then it is no longer strange that to Jesus is attributed all the functions of God, including the forgiveness of sins and the universal judgment of men, nor that in Him is seen the coming of Jehovah to save His people, in His presence with men the fulfillment of the prophecy of ' Immanuel,' God-with-us, in the coming of John the Baptist to prepare His way the fulfillment of the prophecy of the messenger to make the way of Jehovah straight, and the like. All things were delivered to Him, in short, because He is none else than God on earth.

Of quite similar import is the great declaration with which the Gospel closes. In this our Lord, announcing 'Participation that all authority was given to Him of Jesus in the in heaven and earth—that is, that uni-Name versal dominion was committed to Him —commands His disciples to advance to the actual conquest of the world, baptizing all the nations into the Name of the Father and of the Son and of the Holy Spirit, and promises to be Himself with them unto the end of the world ($28^{18\text{-}20}$). In the absence of the

former passage, it might conceivably be possible to
look upon the dominion here claimed and the conjunction here asserted of the Son with the Father in the
future government of the Kingdom as having no root-
ing in His essential nature but as constituting merely
a reward consequent upon our Lord's work. In
the presence of that passage we cannot void this, however, of its testimony to essential relations. And the
relation here assigned to the Son with respect to deity
is the same as was suggested there. The significant
point of this passage is the singular " Name." It does
not read, " Into the names "—as of many, but of one,
—" Into the Name " of the Father and of the Son and
of the Holy Spirit. The Father, the Son and the
Spirit are therefore in some ineffable sense one, sharers
in the single Name. Of course it is what we know as
the Christian doctrine of the Trinity which is suggested here, as it was less clearly suggested in the
former passage, and as this doctrine is needed in order
to give consistency and solidity to the pervasive suggestion of Matthew's entire narrative that Jesus, whose
career he is recounting, is in some higher sense than
mere delegation or representation not merely a superhuman or superangelic or supercreaturely person, but
an actually Divine Person, possessed of divine prerogatives, active in divine power, and in multiform ways
manifesting a divine nature. It were impossible for
Matthew to paint Jesus as he has painted Him, and to
attribute to Him what we have seen him attributing
to Him, without some such conception as is enunciated
in these two great passages in his mind to support, sus-
tain and give its justification to his representation. So
far from these passages offending the reader as they

stand in Matthew's Gospel, therefore, and raising doubts of their genuineness, we should have had to postulate something like them for Matthew, had they not stood in his Gospel. Matthew's portrait of Jesus and the self-witness he quotes from Jesus' lips to His estate and dignity, in other words, themselves necessitate a doctrine of His nature and relations with God very much such as is set forth in these passages: and we can feel perfectly assured, therefore, that these passages represent with great exactness what Matthew would tell us of Jesus' deity and what he would report as Jesus' own conception of His divine relations. And what they tell us—we must not balk at it—is just that Jesus is all that God is, and shares in God's nature as truly as in God's majesty and power.

THE DESIGNATIONS OF OUR LORD IN
LUKE AND THEIR IMPLICATIONS

We meet very much the same series of designations applied to our Lord in Luke as in the other Synoptists. But they are applied with some characteristic differences.

In Luke, too, the ordinary narrative designation of our Lord is the simple ' Jesus,' which occurs about seventy-seven times.[1] This simplest of all designations is not so exclusively employed in the narrative of Luke, however, as in those of Matthew and Mark. There is an occasional variation in Luke to the more descriptive designation of ' the Lord ' ($7^{13,19}$ $10^{1,39,41}$ 11^{39} 12^{42} 13^{15} $17^{5,6}$ 18^6 19^8 $22^{61,61}$, fourteen times). No other designation than these two, however, occurs as a narrative designation in Luke, although in three instances Luke makes use of another in his narrative. In two of these instances he is apparently repeating words from the lips of others: he tells us that it had been revealed to Simeon that he should not die until he had seen ' the Lord's Christ ' (2^{26}) and that Bartimæus was told that ' Jesus of Nazareth ' was passing (18^{37}). In the remaining instance he remarks that the evil spirits knew that Jesus was ' the Christ ' (4^{41}); where ' the Christ ' is not strictly a designation of Jesus, but the

The Narrative Designations

---

[1] ' Jesus ' is anarthrous: 1^{31} $2^{21,43,52}$ $3^{21,23}$ 4^1 $5^{8,10}$ 8^{41} $9^{36,50}$ $18^{37,40}$ $22^{48,52}$ 23^{28} $24^{15,19}$.

general term ' the Messiah.' These instances exhibit Luke's willingness to speak of Jesus as the Messiah indeed; but are scarcely exceptions to the general fact that he himself designates Jesus in the course of his narrative only as ' Jesus ' and as ' the Lord.'[2] As in the other Synoptists, the simple ' Jesus ' in Luke is also practically reserved for the narrative designation. Only in the two instances of the annunciation of His name by the angel (1^{31}), which is no exception, and in the address to Jesus on the cross by the dying thief (23^{42})[3] is this rule broken. But, as in the other Synoptists, the name ' Jesus ' occurs in compound forms of address to Him recorded by the evangelist,— ' Jesus, Thou Son of God ' (8^{28}), ' Jesus, Thou Son of David " (18^{38}), ' Jesus, Master ' (17^{13}); and at the hands of the evil spirits (4^{34}), the people (18^{37}) and His disciples (24^{19}) alike, ' Jesus the Nazarene '

---

[2] In 24^{3} the general transmission gives " the Lord Jesus ": but this is one of the instances in which it is scarcely possible not to follow a few " Western " witnesses in omitting a very strongly attested reading. This combination of designations occurs also in the spurious ending of Mark (16^{19}), but not elsewhere in the Gospels. It becomes, however, quite frequent in Acts: 1^{21} 4^{33} 7^{59} 8^{16} $11^{17,20}$ 15^{26} 16^{31} $19^{5,13,17}$ $20^{21,24,35}$ 21^{13} 28^{31}. It might thus have very well been used by Luke in his Gospel also. It is common in the Epistles.

[3] The text is not quite certain here, and there are three ways of rendering it: (1) " And he said to Jesus, Remember me "; (2) " And he said, Jesus, remember me "; (3) " And he said, Lord, remember me." The reading ' Jesus ' seems the preferable one; but it is not altogether clear that anarthrous ᾽Ιησοῦ here may not be the dative after ἔλεγεν. The uniqueness of the ascription of the simple ' Jesus ' as a form of address, to a speaker in the evangelist's narrative, is, of course, favorable to taking it as a dative. In that case κύριε would be an instinctive correction of ᾽Ιησοῦ mistaken for a vocative; as in the other case it would be an instinctive insertion of a vocative "because ᾽Ιησοῦ here was mistaken for the dative " (Plummer).

—whence it emerges that it was by this name that He was popularly identified.[4]

The ordinary forms of address applied to Jesus in Luke are the simple honorifics, ' Teacher,' ' Master,' 'Lord,' employed, however, with a certain discrimination.[5] The Aramaic form ' Rabbi ' does not occur in Luke at all. Its common Greek rendering, ' Teacher ' ($\delta\iota\delta\acute{a}\sigma\varkappa\alpha\lambda\varepsilon$), seems to be treated as the current non-committal honorific, especially appropriate on the lips of those who were not, or at least not yet, His disciples (7^{40} 10^{25} 11^{45} 12^{13} 18^{18} 19^{39} $20^{21,28,39}$; 8^{49} 9^{38}). The only exception to its employment by this rule is supplied by 21^7, where we are told that certain of His disciples " asked Him saying, ' Teacher,' " etc. That it was not thought inappropriate as a form of address from His disciples to Him is also evinced, however, by the report of His own employment of it on two occasions. He instructs His followers, in preparing the last passover meal for Him, to say to the goodman of the house, " The Teacher saith unto thee, where is the guest-chamber, where I shall eat the passover with my disciples " (22^{11}); and He tells them, broadly indeed, but no doubt with some, though certainly remote, reference to Himself and them, that

Ordinary Forms of Address

---

[4] In 4^{34} 24^{19}, the form is $\acute{o}$ $Na\zeta\alpha\rho\eta\nu\acute{o}\varsigma$, as it is in Mark: in 18^{37} $\acute{o}$ $Na\zeta\alpha\rho\alpha\tilde{\iota}o\varsigma$, as in Mt, Jno and Acts. Cf. Plummer on 4^{34}.

[5] There is a tendency, of course, to refer to Jesus where He was present in fact or thought by the simple demonstrative $o\tilde{\upsilon}\tau o\varsigma$ (1^{32} 8^{28} 9^{35} 23^{41} $[20^{14}$ $23^{2,4,14,23}]$, and this is sometimes contemptuous ($[5^{21}]$ $7^{39,49}$ 15^2 19^{14} $[24^{14}]$ $23^{[4,14,22],25,38}$ 23^{18}). So in the other evangelists: Mt 3^{17} 8^{27} 12^{22} 17^5 $21^{10,11,[38]}$ 27^{54}, and contemptuously, 9^3 12^{24} $[13^{54,55,56}]$ 26^{61} $[27^{37}]$ 27^{47}, Mk 4^{41} 9^7 12^7 15^{39} and contemptuously, 2^7 $[6^{2,2,3}]$. On this depreciatory $o\tilde{\upsilon}\tau o\varsigma$ see Meyer on $7^{39,49}$.

" the disciple is not above his teacher; but every one when he is perfected shall be as his teacher " (6⁴⁰). The choice of the term ' Teacher ' (διδάσκαλος) in these two passages appears to be due to the correlative " disciples " occurring in each; and it remains true that ' Teacher ' (διδάσκαλε) as a form of address is characteristic in Luke, of non-followers of our Lord.[6]

The place of ' Teacher ' on the lips of His followers is partly taken by a new term for ' Master,' peculiar to Luke (ἐπιστάτης),[7] which however occurs only six times (5⁵ 8²⁴,⁴⁵ 9³³,⁴⁹ 17¹³), only one of which (17¹³) forms an exception or quasi-exception to the rule that the term indicates that the user of it stands in the closest relation to Jesus, and acknowledges Him as his Superior Officer—Chief, Commander, Master, Leader. This quasi-exception occurs in the case of the ten lepers who, we are told, lifted up their voices and said, " Jesus, Leader, have mercy on us." Perhaps there is an intention to convey the impression that these lepers, formally at least, recognized the authority of Jesus completely. We cannot account 5⁵ another such exception, since the whole tone of the narrative indicates that this was not the first call of Peter to become Jesus' disciple (cf. Jno 1⁴²), but his call to become Jesus' constant companion. There is no such direct use of Jesus in Luke (or in Mk) as in Matthew of the figurative expression ' Master of the House '

'Master'

---

[6] ' Teacher ' is in 3¹² employed as an address to John the Baptist; and the Jewish Rabbis in the temple are called ' Teachers ' in 2⁴⁶.

[7] When Wellhausen on 5⁴,⁵ says " 'Επιστάτα (and κύριε) is used in Luke by the disciples; διδάσκαλε by others," he is thus substantially right. Cf. Plummer on 5⁵, where the meaning of the word is discussed.

(οἰκοδεσπότης), although the term occurs in parables with reference to Him (13²⁵ 14²¹).

The prevailing form of address to Jesus in Luke is, however, the ordinary Greek honorific 'Lord' (κύριε),

'Lord' as an Address

used, however, obviously as an honorific of especially high connotation. It is put upon the lips, indeed, of outsiders, suitors for mercy (5¹² 7⁶ 18⁴¹ 19⁸) and possibly others (9⁵⁹,⁶¹ 13²³) ; and our Lord's own remark to the effect that some called Him 'Lord, Lord,' who did not do the things He said (6⁴⁶) shows that it might be insincerely used of Him. But this very passage also indicates that to address Him as 'Lord' was to acknowledge His authority and involved subjection to His commandments, and accordingly the term is represented as employed chiefly by His professed followers (5⁸ 10¹⁷,⁴⁰ 11¹ 12⁴¹ 17³⁷ 22³³,³⁸,⁴⁹). Something of its high implication, when so used, may be caught from 5⁸ in comparison with 5⁵. When our Lord, having used Simon's boat for a pulpit, commanded him to let down his nets for a draught, Simon responded with the respectful address which implied that he recognized Jesus as his 'Superior Officer' (ἐπιστάτης), "Master, we toiled all night, and took nothing: but at Thy word I will let down the nets." But when he saw the resultant miraculous draught, he fell at Jesus' knees and said: "Depart from me; for I am a sinful man, O Lord"—using now the higher honorific, 'Lord' (κύριε).⁸ Obviously the address

⁸ Streatfeild, *Self-Interpretation of Jesus Christ,* p. 99 note, is clearly in the wrong in supposing that the change from ἐπιστάτα of v. 5 to κύριε of v. 8 has no significance; and the occasional interchange of the terms, noted by Dalman as appealed to by Streatfeild, does not

'Lord' on the lips of Jesus' followers was charged with very high significance, and this is borne out in its entire use.

Such a constant mode of address as 'Lord' by His followers, naturally would beget the habit of speaking

'Lord' as an Appellative

of Jesus among themselves as 'the Lord'; and we can feel no surprise therefore that Jesus, in giving them instructions how to reply to possible objections to their taking the ass He sent them for as He was about to enter Jerusalem, placed this designation on their lips. " Say," He said, " the Lord hath need of him " (19^{31}) ; and accordingly they said (v. 34), " The Lord hath need of him " (cf. $12^{36,42,43 \text{ seq.}}$). This instruction is recorded by all the Synoptists, and the usage which it involves of the term 'Lord' of Jesus as an appellative designation might very well, therefore, have been illustrated in the narratives of them all. The copious designatory employment of the title 'Lord' of Christ, however, is characteristic of Luke.[9] It is placed on the

interpose an obstacle. Cf. Godet on verse 8: " Peter here employs the more religious expression, *Lord,* which answers to his actual feelings "; and Plummer, verse 8: " The change from ἐπιστάτα (see on verse 5) is remarkable and quite in harmony with the change of circumstances. It is the 'Master' whose orders must be obeyed, the 'Lord' whose holiness causes moral agony to the sinner (Dan 10^{16})."

[9] Cf. Sven Herner, *Die Anwendung des Wortes* κύριος *im N. T.,* pp. 12, 13: " In contrast with Matthew and Mark, Luke speaks of Jesus by the designation κύριος comparatively often. Even if $7^{19,31}$ 10^{41} 22^{31} 24^{3} be neglected as more or less uncertain in the reading, and 19^{31} as a parallel to Mt 21^{3}, Mk 11^{3}, there remain nevertheless fourteen passages peculiar to Luke (7^{13} $10^{1,40}$ 11^{39} 12^{42} 13^{15} $17^{5,6}$ 18^{6} $19^{8,34}$ $22^{61,61}$ 24^{34}) which speak of Jesus by the designation of 'Lord': and to these may be added the expressions 'the mother of my Lord' (1^{43}) and 'the Lord Christ' (2^{11})." " It may be further remarked that although one of the uncertain passages enumerated (24^{3}) belongs to

lips of the disciples themselves in this designatory form at 24^{34}, and it occurs in two passages in the opening chapters of the Gospel—in the elevated language of the angelic announcement in the combination, ' Christ the Lord ' or ' the anointed Lord ' (2^{11}), and in the response of Elisabeth (1^{45}) in which she expresses her wondering awe that " the mother of her Lord " should come to her. Obviously in such usages the term connotes a very high dignity, certainly Messianic at the least. It is also employed of Himself by our Lord in the question He is recorded by all the Synoptists as putting to the scribes as to the significance of David's prediction of the Messiah as his ' Lord ' ($20^{41\ seq.}$)—again, obviously with a high connotation. But the particularly significant fact in this connection is its current employment by Luke himself as an alternative narrative designation to the simple ' Jesus ' ($7^{13,19}$ $10^{1,39,41}$ 11^{39} 12^{42} 13^{15} $17^{5,6}$ 18^{6} 19^{8} $22^{61,61}$). It does not seem easy to detect any special significance in the interchange of these designations; the reason for the passage from one to the other seems either purely literary or at least obscure. The meaning of the appearance of this narrative employment of the term in Luke seems, therefore, to be merely that in the usage of Luke in his own person there emerges a reflection of a usage evidently common among the disciples of Jesus from the beginning, but not chancing to be copiously illustrated

the time when Christ was, though resurrected, not yet manifested to His disciples, and one of the certain ones (24^{34}) is a word of the disciples to whom the risen Lord had manifested Himself, yet all the others fall in the time before the resurrection. Although Luke mentions Jesus, however, comparatively often by the designation ' Lord,' this is nevertheless far from his current designation of Him, as the names of ' Jesus ' and ' Christ ' meet us 112 times."

in the personal literary manner of Mark and Matthew: the usage, namely, of currently speaking of Jesus as ' the Lord.'

This implies, naturally, that Jesus stood to His disciples for whatever the title ' Lord ' meant to them.

Significance of 'Lord' There is involved in it certainly the recognition of His Messianic dignity, and there is included, therefore, the recognition in Him of all that they saw in His Messianic dignity. So far, we suppose, we may be sure that, as has been suggested, He was thought of as ' Lord ' in contrast to the earthly potentates who were claiming lordship of men, and especially in contrast with the emperor in Rome, the ' Lord ' by way of eminence in all men's minds.[10] To Jesus, rather than to the emperor, was allegiance due. But we must not forget that the allegiance expressed to Jesus rested on a spiritual basis, while, perhaps, it is going too far to suppose that the divine claims of the imperial monarch were held clearly in mind.[11] The simplest thing to say is that the term ' Lord ' was applied to Jesus by Luke obviously with the deepest reverence and obviously as the expression of that reverence.

[10] Cf. Dalman, *Words,* 330: "When the Christians called Jesus ὁ κύριος, they will have meant that He is the true ' divine Lord ' in opposition to the ' God and Lord ' on the imperial throne of Rome. Luke's frequent use of ὁ κύριος is certainly intended in this sense. The phrase Χριστὸς κύριος used in his Gospel 2[11] (cf. Acts 2[36]) defines the term Χριστός in that sense for the reader." Dalman is probably thinking of "Luke" as representing a *Gentile* Christian usage. It is clear, on the contrary, that his is simply an aboriginal Christian usage—possibly with slightly changing—or enlarging—content, but with no essential alteration of meaning.

[11] On the employment of κύριος of the emperor and its significance see T. D. Woolsey in the *Bibliotheca Sacra* for 1861, pp. 595-608.

The full height of this reverence may be suggested to us by certain passages in which the term ' Lord ' occurs in citations from the Old Testament, where its reference is to Jehovah, though in the citations it seems to be applied to Jesus. Like the other Synoptists, Luke cites, for instance, from Isaiah the promise of a voice crying in the wilderness, " Make ye ready the way of the Lord, make His paths straight " (3^4), and applies it to the coming of John the Baptist whom he represents as preparing the way for Jesus' manifestation. As in the case of the other evangelists, the inference lies close that by ' the Lord ' here Luke means Jesus, whose coming he thus identifies with the advent of Jehovah and whose person he seems to identify with Jehovah.[12] On the other hand, in passages like $1^{17,76}$, although the language is similar, it seems more natural to understand the term ' Lord ' as referring to God Himself, and to conceive the speaker to be thinking of the coming of Jehovah to redemption in Jesus without necessary identification of the person of Jesus with Jehovah.[13] The mere circumstance, however, that the

[12] Cf. Sven Herner, as cited, p. 11: " With a reference to our discussion of the citation in the passages in Matthew and Mark we hold it most probable that Christ is meant, and this view is more easily maintained in the case of Luke than of Matthew because Luke comparatively frequently uses the designation ' Lord ' of Jesus." Proceeding to discuss the parallel passage, 1^{76}, he decides that there ' Lord ' probably refers to God the Father; which appears just. It does not follow, however, that Godet's remark may not also be accepted: " In saying *the Lord* Zacharias can only be thinking of the Messiah: but he could not designate Him by this name, unless, with Malachi, he recognized in His coming the appearing of Jehovah (cf. $1^{17,43}$ 2^{11})"—if this can be read of the advent of Jehovah in His Representative.

[13] Hahn says, rightly as we think, at 1^{16}: " Not to be understood of the Messiah (Ambr., Beda, Euthym., Beng., Cast., Bisp., Schegg, Schanz) but of God "; and at 1^{76}: " Not to be understood of the

reader is led to pause over such passages and to consider whether they may not intend by their 'Lord'—
who is Jehovah—to identify the person of Jesus with
Jehovah, is significant. We should never lose from
sight the outstanding fact that to men familiar with
the LXX and the usage of 'Lord' as the personal
name of the Deity there illustrated, the term 'Lord'
was charged with associations of deity, so that a habit
of speaking of Jesus as 'the Lord,' by way of eminence, such as is illustrated by Luke and certainly was
current from the beginning of the Christian proclamation (19^{31}), was apt to carry with it implications of
deity which, if not rebuked or in some way guarded
against, must be considered as receiving the sanction
of Jesus Himself.

The leading designations of Jesus in Luke, as in the
other Synoptists, however, are, broadly speaking, Messianic. In other words, it is distinc-
The 'Prophet' tively as the Messiah that Luke sets
forth Jesus and represents Him as hav-
ing conceived of Himself and as having been revered
by His followers. We find in Luke, as in the other
Synoptists, to be sure, traces of a widespread recognition of Him as a prophet ($7^{16,39}$ $9^{8,19}$). His followers
set their hopes upon Him in that office (24^{19}); and
indeed with no uncertainty He Himself assumed the

Messiah (Kün., Ols., Bisp., Schanz), but of God"; but, we think,
wrongly at 3^4: "By the κύριος there is here, just as in the Old Test.
passage, to be understood, not the Messiah (Kün., Bl., Haupt) but
God, for Luke wishes to say that in the Messiah God would hold His
own advent." So far as the mere language goes, that might be accepted: but the passage seems to mean otherwise (see Plummer *per
contra*). Meyer has an excellent note on $1^{16,17}$ and decides rightly
also at 1^{76}: whom Weiss properly follows; so also Plummer.

rôle of a prophet (4^{24} $13^{33,34}$). But no more in Luke than in the other Synoptists is this particularly emphasized, and in Luke, too, the prophetic character is, no doubt, conceived as part of the Messianic function,—as indeed the collocation of His prophetic calling and His redemption of Israel in the thought of the disciples going to Emmaus not obscurely suggests ($24^{19,21}$, cf. also 7^{16}).[14]

Luke also records from the mouth of the angel announcing the birth of Jesus the new designation of 'Saviour'—if we can call a designation new which is so plainly adumbrated in a passage like Mt 1^{21} (cf. also Lk 19^{10}).[15] But this is so little un-Messianic that it is not only connected with the Messianic prophecies by adjacent references (1^{47}, cf. 2^{30} 3^{6}), but is expressly defined as Messianic in the annunciation itself: "a Saviour, which is Christ the Lord" (2^{11}). Like Mt 1^{21}, this passage clearly indicates that to the circle in which Jesus moved His coming as the Messiah was connected with the great series of prophecies which promised the advent of Jehovah for the redemption of His people, as truly as with those which predicted the coming of the Davidic King. The terms, "a Saviour, which is Christ the Lord," are, indeed, an express combination of the two lines of prophecy, and import

'Saviour'

[14] Cf. Meyer on 7^{16}: "They saw in this miracle a σημεῖον of a *great prophet,* and in His appearance they saw the beginning of the Messianic deliverance (comp. 1^{68-79})." On the whole subject, cf. Stanton, *Jewish and Christian Messiah,* 126 *seq.*

[15] Cf. Plummer *in loc.:* "Here first in N. T. is σωτήρ used of Christ, and here only in Luke. Not in Matthew or Mark, and only once in John (4^{42}): twice in Acts (5^{31} 13^{23}); and frequently in Titus and 2 Peter."

that the Child who was born in the city of David was
both the promised Redeemer of Israel and the
Anointed King that was to come. Question may arise,
indeed, as to how we are to construe these collocated
designations. Some[16] would wish us to take each separately, with an indefinite article to each: " There is
born to you a Saviour, who is an Anointed One, a
Lord." Others[17] suggest that at least ' Messiah ' and
' Lord ' be kept separate: " There is born to you a
Deliverer, who is Messiah, Lord." In either of these
constructions we have three separate designations which
so far explain one another: this Child is at once a
Saviour, the promised Messiah, and Sovereign Lord
of men and angels—for it is an angel who speaks these
words. The essential meaning cannot be far from this
in any case.[18] Even if we should read " who is Messiah, the Lord, " or even " who is an anointed Lord,"[19]
we have got but little away from this general sense:
in either case what is said is that the Saviour is the
promised Messiah and therefore entitled to our obedience as our Lord. Nor is much more said if we
give the phrase the utmost definiteness possible, and
translate, " There is born to you this day in the city
of David that Deliverer who is the Messiah, the
Lord,"[20]—as, on the whole, we think we ought to read

[16] E.g. Holtzmann, Weiss.

[17] E.g. Meyer.

[18] " In any event," says Weiss, " it is meant that this Deliverer is an
Anointed Lord, and therefore destined to be the King of Israel." But
Weiss, who wishes to read only, " a Deliverer who is an Anointed
One, a Lord," takes too low a view.

[19] E.g. Paulus.

[20] So Hahn: "$\sigma\omega\tau\eta\rho$, not ' *a* Deliverer' (Paulus, Meyer, Bleek,
Ewald, Weiss, Hofmann, Keil, Nösgen, Holtzmann), but '*the* Deliv-

it, in the light of the distinction made between the two designations ' Messiah ' and ' Lord ' in such a passage as Acts 2[36], where Peter declares to the house of Israel that God has made Jesus both ' Lord ' and ' Christ.' The precise distinction intended to be signalized between ' Christ ' and ' Lord ' is, no doubt, difficult to trace: perhaps there lies in it a testimony to the wider content of the idea of Messiahship than that of mere sovereign power; perhaps a testimony to a higher connotation of the term ' Lord ' than that of mere Messianic dignity. In any event there is here a declaration that in this Child born in the city of David, the functions of Redemption, Messiahship and Supreme Lordship are united.

Almost immediately afterward we are told that it had been revealed to Simeon that " he should not see

'The Lord's Christ'

death before he had seen the Lord's Christ " (2[26])—an Old Testament expression (Ps 2[2], cf. Lk 9[20], Acts 4[26]) here applied to the infant Jesus, who is by it identified as the promised Messiah.[21] Accordingly in announcing the birth of this Child, who is thus so emphatically presented as the Messiah, the angel is represented as

erer ' (Luther, De Wette). The article is wanting not from inadvertence (De Wette), but because it is made superfluous by the succeeding relative clause. The sense is: ' the particular Deliverer, who ' . . . This Deliverer is characterized by the $X\rho\iota\sigma\tau\grave{o}\varsigma$ $\varkappa\acute{v}\rho\iota o\varsigma$ as the promised Messiah. We are not to explain: ' *a* Messiah, *a* Lord ' (Holtzmann) ; and not: ' one anointed to Lordship ' (Paulus) ; but the two expressions are two separate designations of the *expected* Messiah (cf. Acts 2[36]) : $X\rho\iota\sigma\tau\acute{o}\varsigma$, the then popularly current *name* of the Messiah; $\varkappa\acute{v}\rho\iota o\varsigma$, the designation of His Sovereign dignity."

[21] Hahn, " God's chosen and appointed Messiah "; Meyer, " God's destined and sent Messiah "; Weiss, " God's anointed and sent Messiah."

describing Him as 'the Son of the Most High God,' to whom should be given the throne of His father David, for an everlasting dominion (1^{32}); and as explaining the Divine Sonship of this Holy Child[22] as due to, or rather as evidenced by, His supernatural birth (1^{35}). The latter of these two declarations is clearly the explanation of the former. The angel had promised Mary that she should bring forth a son who should rightly bear the great name of the 'Son of the Most High God,' and he now explains that this Holy Son of hers shall be a supernatural product, and should by His supernatural advent be witnessed as rightly bearing the name of 'Son of God.' That the title 'Son of God' bears in it a Messianic implication is clear from the functions ascribed in verses 33, 34 to the child so designated, but that this Messiah was conceived as something more than human appears to be implied in the connection of His claim upon the title of 'Son of God' with the supernaturalness of His birth. Perhaps it is not reading too much into the passage to say that His preëxistence and heavenly descent are asserted,—certainly His heavenly, or supernatural, origin is asserted. This 'Son' is not merely to be attended with supernatural assistance and so to exhibit supernatural gifts: He is of supernatural origin, and therefore so far of supernatural nature. Already in the opening chapters of his Gospel, devoted to an account of the birth and infancy of Jesus, therefore, Luke makes it plain that the Jesus whose history he is to recount was first of all the Messiah of God, and as

---

[22] So (*not,* that which is begotten shall be called holy, the Son of God) Bengel, Bleek, Meyer, Weiss, Holtzmann, Godet, Hahn.

such was of supernatural origin and therefore holy, was to establish the throne of David in perpetuity, and was to be recognized as Lord of men and angels.

In accordance with these declarations, recorded in the opening of the Gospel, Luke tells us that the evil spirits knew Jesus to be 'the Christ' and greeted Him by the title 'Son of God' (4^{41}), and records Peter's great confession in the form of " Thou art the Christ of God " (9^{20}), and Jesus' ready acceptance of it, as also His acquiescence in the ascription of the title of Messiah, 'Christ,' to Him by His enemies ('the Christ,' 22^{67}, cf. 23^{39}; 'Christ a King,' 23^{2}). Such an ascription of the title 'Christ' to Him by His enemies (22^{67} $23^{2,35,39}$) is the best of all proofs that it was commonly employed of Him by His followers. But the significant fact for us is that in accepting it at their hands Jesus claims it for Himself (22^{67} 23^{2}). We are not surprised, therefore, to find Him using it of Himself when, after His resurrection, He expounded from Scripture to His followers the doctrine of the Suffering Messiah and applied it to Himself ($24^{26,46}$), even as He had at an earlier point expounded to the scribes (20^{41}) the doctrine of the Reigning Messiah with an equally clear application of it to Himself. He who was David's 'Lord' as truly as his 'Son' was to enter upon His Lordship only through suffering, a suffering which should lay the basis of a preachment in His name of repentance and remission of sins (24^{46}). Here again is the Saviour, who is the Messiah, the Lord: and the Gospel ends much on the same note on which it began.

The royal dignity of this 'Anointed King' (23^{2}) is

of course dwelt upon in Luke as in the other Synoptics.

'The King' But the precise term 'King' is not of frequent occurrence. His disciples as He entered Jerusalem on the ass's colt acclaimed Him as " the King that cometh in the name of the Lord " (19[38]), and when the Pharisees appealed to Him to rebuke them therefor—employing the simple formula of respect, 'Teacher,' in addressing Him and thereby repudiating His Messianic claim by the contrast of this address with the title of 'King'— Jesus was so far from yielding to their request that He declared that if His disciples held their peace the very stones would cry out and recognize Him as the Messianic sovereign (cf. Lk 3[8], Mt 3[9]). Similarly, when the Jews accused Him to Pilate as representing Himself to be " Christ, a King " (23[2]),[23] and that governor accordingly demanded of Him whether He was 'the King of the Jews,' our Lord was so far from denying the ascription that He expressly accepted the designation (23[3]), and thus brought it about that He was mocked on the cross by this title, and had it set over His head (23[37,38]). The equivalent title 'Son of David' also is recorded as having been given Him by an applicant for His mercy as a recognition of His authority to heal (18[38,39], cf. 1[32,69]), and by no means repudiated when (20[41 seq.]) Jesus explained that He was something much more than David's son.

[23] So Holtzmann, Weiss and others. Weiss: "'King Messiah,' or more naturally, 'Messiah, a King' (cf. on 2[11]), so that the political significance of the Messianic title expressly explained is made to tell." That is to say, Jesus has declared Himself to be 'Christ,' which is the same as to say 'King.' The term 'Christ' is employed appellatively, but so that it might easily be taken as a proper name, as it was taken (see Matthew) by Pilate. Hahn less naturally wishes to read " an anointed King." It would be more natural to take 'Christ' as a proper name—as Pilate appears to have taken it.

In the midst of the designations we have somewhat rapidly adduced, clustering around the central title 'Christ,' there is one which we should ' God's Elect ' not pass over unnoticed because it has not met us heretofore. The mocking Jews, scoffing at Jesus as He hung on the cross, are represented as flinging in His face His claim to be ' the Christ of God, *His Chosen* ' (23³⁵). The same designation occurs in the account of the transfiguration, where the voice from heaven is represented by Luke as declaring of Jesus, " This is my Son, *my Chosen* " (9³⁵). No doubt the Greek is not quite the same in each instance: ὁ ἐκλεκτός of the one is replaced by ὁ ἐκλελεγμένος in the other.[24] But doubtless the underlying Messianic title is the same in both instances. It is rooted in Isaiah 42¹, " Behold my servant whom I uphold; my chosen in whom my soul delighteth," etc. (where the parallel terms are ὁ παῖς and ὁ ἐκλεκτός), and emerges into view even in pre-Christian Jewish usage (Enoch 40⁵ 45³ 53⁶ 39⁹, etc.).[25] The conception seems to be not essentially different from a designation which has already met us in Mark (1²⁴) and which occurs also in the parallel passage of Luke (4³⁴), but elsewhere in the New Testament only at Jno 6⁶⁹—' the Holy One of God.' For it does not seem likely that ' God's this epithet, in the first instance at least, Holy One ' refers to the moral purity of the Messiah,[26] but rather probable that it designates Him as One whom God has " separated out,

[24] Cf. on these terms and on the general matter, W. C. Allen, Hastings' *D. C. G.,* I. 308.

[25] Cf. Charles, *Book of Enoch,* p. 112; Bousset, *Die Religion des Judentums,* p. 249; Schürer, *Jewish People,* etc., II. 2. p. 158.

[26] So Keil on Lk 4³⁴.

equipped and dedicated to His service,"[27] in a word as 'the Consecrated One.' In this understanding of it, it stands in close relation to the epithet, 'the Elect One,' and unites with it in emphasizing the unique loftiness of the Messianic office. At the same time it seems difficult to believe that there is no implication of moral purity, or perhaps we would better say moral exaltation, in the epithet, as used whether by Peter (Jno 6[69]) or by the demoniacs (Mk 1[24], Lk 4[34]), although this reference may be secondary. It is scarcely conceivable that the demons could recognize a mere official-standing on sight (Mk 3[11]), while the contrast between the moral perfection or exalted nature of

[27] This language is borrowed from Holtzmann, *Hand-Com.*, p. 76: "The demon recognizes in Him the Holy One of God, i.e., Him whom God has separated out, equipped and dedicated to His service (cf. Jno 6[69] 10[36]—the 'Elect One' of the Book of Enoch), whom the demoniacs (Mk 3[11]) immediately recognize and fear as such: for the Messiah's task is to judge and *destroy* the demons (the evil spirit speaks in the name of his fellows, too, '*us*'). They divine, therefore, at once Jesus' greatness and their own fate." In this view it is not the moral purity of Jesus over against their wickedness that the demons divine; but the official task of Jesus which they are aware of. Similarly Ernst Issel, *Der Begriff der Heiligkeit im N. T.*, 1887, p. 67 *seq.:* "In Mk 1[24], cf. Lk 4[34], we have the most original application of the notion [of holiness] to Jesus. The title 'the Holy One of God' is clearly a well known one, on hearing which no one could be in doubt who was meant. The same evangelist [Mk], at 3[11], opens the way to understanding it by recording that the demons cried out 'Thou art the Son of God.' That, however, is the title of the theocratic King . . . In the title of the theocratic ruler, the eye is just as little directed by the 'holy' to ethical perfection as in the expression 'Son of God.' The Messiah is 'the Holy One of God,' as He whom the Father has sanctified, Jno 10[36], that is, as He whom God has chosen and endowed for His special possession and service. There speaks for this also the designation 'the Chosen One,' Lk 23[35] 9[35]. To this election to God's possession and service limits itself also the designation in Lk 1[35] . . . and the representation of Jesus in the Temple, Lk 2[23] . . .

Jesus and their uncleanness may be presumed to have obtruded itself upon their consciousness, whenever they were brought into His presence.[23] Along with these titles we must note also that Luke, too, makes use of the title 'the Beloved,' though only at the baptism of our Lord (3^{22}), replacing it at the transfiguration by 'the Chosen One' (9^{35}), and thus exhibiting the essential synonymy of the two.[29]

It may be profitable to recall at this point that the epithet 'holy' is applied to our Lord also at the annunciation of His birth by the angel, when it was explained that it was the circumstance that His birth was not according to nature, but due to the coming down upon Mary of the Holy Ghost and the overshadowing of her by the power of the Most High, which justified the Holy Thing which was being begotten in being called 'the Son of God' (1^{35}). The epithet is not elsewhere applied to Jesus in this Gospel, except in 2^{23}, where the precept of the law is quoted in reference to Him, that "every male that openeth the womb shall be called holy to the Lord "—where it is obviously the conception of consecration which is prominent. In the present passage, however, it seems equally plain that it is not the notion of being set apart for God so much as that of being in Himself worthy of reverence and calling out veneration which is prominent. He who is thus supernaturally born is " holy " in the sense that He brings with Him something of the superhuman

Meaning of 'Holy'

[28] On the title 'Holy One of God' see J. B. Bristow, Hastings' *D. C. G.*, I. 730-31. He thinks it connects Jesus with God the Holy One; but in these passages refers particularly to Christ's dedication to a mission.

[29] Cf. J. A. Robinson, as cited, esp. *Eph.*, pp. 229 *seq.*

character belonging to His origin, and is thus not set apart among men, but is by nature distinguished from men—shall we not say, " separate from sinners " ?[30]

Nevertheless, the title ' Son of God ' as applied to our Lord in Luke is closely connected with His Messianic office: though, of course, it is not limited to that office in its implications. It occurs in this precise form but seldom. Besides the declaration of the announcing angel that He shall be called the ' Son of the Most High ' (1[32])—evidently with a Messianic connotation, as the subsequent context shows, but by no means equally evidently with none but a human connotation, as also the subsequent context assures us (1[35]),—it occurs only in the narrative of the Temptation, on the lips of Satan (4[3,9]),[31] and elsewhere on the lips of evil spirits (4[41], 8[28] ' Son of the Most High God ') who knew He was the Christ, and in the mouth of His judges when they adjured Him to tell whether He were ' the Christ,' and on His answering that they should from thenceforth see Him, ' the Son of Man,' seated at the right hand of God, demanded afresh, " Art thou, then, the Son of God? " (22[70]).[32] It seems clear, indeed, from these passages that the title ' Son of God ' was conceived as a Messianic title, and so far as the synonym of the simple ' Christ '; but it is

[30] Knowling, *The Testimony of St. Paul to Christ*, 1905, p. 314, thinks the epithet here means frankly "sinlessness" (cf. Plummer *in loc.*). Perhaps, however, while this implication of "holiness" cannot be excluded, it is going too far to find it prominent here.

[31] Cf. Plummer *in loc.:* "The reference is to the relation to God rather than to the office of the Messiah. The emphatic word is υἱός."

[32] Cf. Plummer *in loc.:* "In the allusion to Daniel 7[13] they recognize a claim to divinity, and they translate ὁ υἱὸς τοῦ ἀνθρώπου into ὁ υἱὸς τοῦ θεοῦ. But it is not clear whether by the latter they mean the Messiah or something higher."

difficult not to gather from them also that it gave expression to a higher Messianic conception than was conveyed by the simple ' Christ.' The brief conversation recorded as taking place between our Lord and His judges seems to have, in fact, the precise purport that in accepting the designation of ' the Christ ' He does so in such a manner as to pour into it a higher content than His judges were willing to accord to it —a higher content which they felt was more appropriately expressed by another title,—the ' Son of God.' Whence it seems to follow that ' Son of God,' while a current Messianic designation, was a Messianic designation charged with a higher connotation than merely that of the Messianic King—a conclusion we have already drawn from 1^{32,35}.[33]

The higher connotation of Sonship to God is, however, in Luke, as in the other Synoptists, most clearly expressed by the undefined term ' Son.'

'The Son' Luke, as well as the others, records the divine proclamation of the Sonship of Jesus from heaven, on the occasion as well of His baptism as of His transfiguration: '' Thou art my Son, the Beloved; in thee I am well pleased '' (3^{22}), '' This is my Son, the Chosen '' (9^{35}) : and gives us the parable in which Jesus, with evident reference to Himself (20^{13,14}), talks of the wicked husbandmen, to whom, after they had evil-entreated his servants, the lord of the vineyard sent in the end his ' beloved son ' who was the heir. Luke also records a number of

[33] This seems to be the truth in the view of such commentators as Godet and Hahn, as over against those who, like Weiss, insist that ' Son of God ' is " *only* another Messianic designation." It is only another Messianic designation ; but a Messianic designation charged with a higher Messianic conception as its content.

those pregnant sayings in which Jesus appeals to God
as in a unique sense His ' Father ': and he begins this
series of pregnant sayings at so early a period as to
make it clear to us that it represents a unique filial consciousness coeval with the dawn of our Lord's intelligence.   Already in His earliest youth He could speak
of being " in His Father's house " as His natural place
of abode (2^{49}),[34] even as in later life He lived in constant communion with the Father ($10^{21,21,22,27}$ $23^{34,46}$),
and equally naturally spoke of " the kingdom His
Father had appointed Him " (22^{29}), and at the end
spoke of His readiness to send forth " the promise of
His Father " (24^{49}).   The glory He expected to enter,
it is to be observed, was no less His own than His
Father's glory (22^{29}).   But above all, Luke records
for us that remarkable passage ($10^{21,22}$) in which our
Lord declares the perfect mutual knowledge which exists between the ' Father ' and ' Son,' by virtue of which
the ' Son ' is constituted the sole adequate revealer of
the ' Father '—that ' Son ' to whom all things were
declared by His ' Father ': on the basis of which He
announces that the things seen and heard in Him are
the things which prophets and kings have desired to
see and hear and have not.   The phraseology in which
Luke repeats this great saying differs slightly from that
found in Matthew.   But the two evangelists agree in
all that is essential.   In both it is unlimitedly " all
things " that are said to have been delivered by the
' Father ' to the ' Son,' so that God is affirmed to hold
back nothing, but to share all that He has with the

[34] Cf. Plummer *in loc.:* " It is notable that the first recorded words
of the Messiah are an expression of His Divine Sonship as man; and
His question implies that they knew it, or ought to know it."

' Son.'[35] In both the intimate knowledge of the ' Father '
and ' Son ' of each other is affirmed to be alike complete, exhaustive and unbrokenly continuous. In both
the ' Son ' is represented to be the sole source of knowledge of God. But in Luke it is said, not that the
' Father ' and ' Son ' know each other, but that each
knows " what the other is," that is to say, all that each
is. It would be difficult to frame a statement which
could more sharply assert the essential deity of the
' Son.'[36]

Our Lord's own favorite designation of Himself is,
however, in Luke as in the other Synoptists, ' the Son

The
' Son of Man '

of Man '; and as in the other Synoptists this designation is in Luke exclusively a self-designation of Jesus' own.
For obviously when the angel at the empty tomb is
represented as saying, " Remember how He spake unto

[35] The emphasis is on the unlimited πάντα; cf. Hahn: " Jesus gives
expression accordingly primarily to the general idea, that God has
held back nothing for Himself, but has made the Son participant in all
that is peculiar to Himself. These first words form the ground for
what follows. The emphasis in them is not on the μοί (Weiss), nor
on the ὑπὸ τοῦ πατρός (Hofmann), but on πάντα."

[36] Cf. Plummer *in loc.:* " It is impossible upon any principles of
criticism to question its genuineness, or its right to be regarded as
among the earliest materials made use of by the Evangelists. And it
contains the whole of the Christology of the Fourth Gospel. It is like
' an aërolite from the Johannine heaven ' (Hase, *Gesch, Jesu,* p. 527) ;
and for that very reason causes perplexity to those who deny the soli-
darity between the Johannine heaven and the Synoptic earth." It should
be compared with the following passages: Jno 3[35] 6[46] 8[19] 10[15,30] 14[9]
16[15] 17[6,10], and cf. further, Sanday, *Fourth Gospel,* p. 109; Keim *Jes.
of Naz.,* IV. 63 referred to by Plummer. Godet says strikingly that
Jesus' words here " become an echo of the joys of His eternal generation." He means doubtless that the continuous interchange of perfect
mutual knowledge here set forth is a reflection of the essential relation
of Father and Son to one another.

you when He was yet in Galilee, saying that the Son of Man must be delivered up into the hands of sinful men, and be crucified and the third day rise again" (24[7]),—this is not an instance of the employment of this title by another than Jesus, but only another attribution of it to Jesus. The title occurs in Luke about twenty-five times,[37] and in the same collocations and with the same import as in the other Synoptists. If we attempt, therefore, to derive from the substance of the passages in which it is employed a notion of the conception which was attached to it, we arrive at the same conclusion as in the case of the other Synoptists. In Luke, the purpose of the coming of the 'Son of Man' is declared in the form, "The Son of Man came to seek and to save that which was lost" (19[10]). Accordingly human destiny is connected absolutely with the relations of men to Him. Those are blessed whom men hate and ostracise and reproach, casting out their name as evil, if it be for the 'Son of Man's' sake (6[22]). For everyone who shall confess Him before men, him shall the 'Son of Man' confess before the angels of God (12[8]); and on the other hand every one who denies the 'Son of Man' in the presence of men shall be denied in the presence of the angels of God (12[9]), and whosoever shall be ashamed of the 'Son of Man' and of His words, of him shall the 'Son of Man' be ashamed when He comes in His own glory and that of the Father and of the holy angels (9[26]). That nevertheless blasphemy against the 'Son of Man' may be forgiven as blasphemy against the Spirit may not (12[10]), doubtless belongs to

[37] 5[24] 6[5,22] 7[34] 9[22,26,44,58] 11[30] 12[8,10,40] 17[22,24,26,30] 18[8,31] 19[10] 21[27,36] 22[22,48,69] [24[7]].

the humility of His earthly life before He has come in His glory. For in this life He comports Himself like other men, eating and drinking (7^{34}), passing a hard and suffering existence (9^{58}), and so fulfilling the Scriptures ($18^{31\ \text{seq.}}$). Meanwhile, however, He exercises even on earth the authority to regulate religious observances (6^5) and to forgive sins (5^{24}). In other words, the sufferings He endures (9^{44} 22^{48}) are not the result of fate or chance, and do not belong to Him by right, but are voluntarily undertaken as part of His mission ($18^{31,32}$ 17^{25} 24^7). They issue in death indeed (9^{22} 18^{33} 22^{22} 24^7), but after death comes resurrection (9^{22} 11^{30} 18^{33} 24^7); and after resurrection, in its own good time, a return in His appropriate glory (22^{69} 9^{26} 12^{40} $17^{22,24}$ 18^8 21^{27} 22^{69}). The humiliation over, at once the ' Son of Man ' is seated at the right hand of the power of God (22^{69}), and when He comes again He will come " in a cloud with great power and glory " (21^{27}),—a glory described as " His own glory, and the glory of His Father and of the holy angels " (9^{26}). The suddenness of this coming is adverted to (12^{40} $17^{22\text{-}24,26,30}$), and the main fact emphasized, that it is in point of significance the day of judgment, when the destinies of men shall be finally assigned them by the ' Son of Man ' (21^{36} 12^8 9^{26}) : destinies which shall be determined according to the attitude which each has occupied towards the ' Son of Man ' on earth (12^8 9^{26}). To all His enemies it is therefore a day of vengeance (18^8), and only as one prevails to stand before the ' Son of Man ' can he hope to escape the dread which His coming brings to the earth (12^{36}). The picture, it will be seen, is the picture of a Redeemer and Adjuster who comes in humiliation to save, and returns

in glory to gather up the results of His work and
finally to adjust the issues of the historical development
of the world. Whence does He come to save? There
is no plain declaration. We are left to infer it from
the obvious connection of the title with the oracle of
Daniel 7^{13}, from the more narrative portions of the
Gospel, as e. g., the opening chapters where the supernatural birth of Jesus is set forth in detail and with
all its implications, and from the very clear suggestion
that the whole career of the 'Son of Man,' in its
earthly manifestation and its subsequent glory alike,
is of a piece and is the outworking of a definite plan
of action held clearly in His own mind from the
first and carried firmly out in every detail of His
living.

The sense of His mission which is thus inherent in
the favorite Messianic designation He applied to Himself finds expression also in other forms
Jesus'
Mission
of locution which Luke reports our
Lord as employing. Thus, for ex-
ample, He is reported as speaking of Himself repeatedly as " coming " with obvious pregnancy of meaning,
possibly with some reference to the expectation of the
Messianic coming which found embodiment in the designation of the Messiah as ' the One to Come,'—a designation in Luke also reported as applied to Jesus
hypothetically by John the Baptist (7^{19,20}),—but certainly with its chief implication in a profound sense of
His mission ([3^{16}] 4^{34} 5^{32} 7^{19} [cf. 7^{33} of John the Bap-
tist], 19^{10}), and possibly with some contrast in
mind with His second coming (9^{26} [12^{36} seq.] 18^8 21^{27}).
Without essential difference of meaning this " coming "
is interchanged with " being sent "—the author of the

" mission " being thus more clearly indicated as God.
Thus Luke varies Mark's language (1^{38}) in recording
our Lord's declaration that " He had come forth " specifically to preach, by giving it rather: " for therefore was He sent " (4^{43})—plainly indicating that
" came " and " was sent " alike refer to His divine
mission.[38] Possibly in this variation there is an allusion
to the passage from Isaiah which Jesus read in the
synagogue at Nazareth (cf. Lk 4^{18}), but in any event
the term is unambiguous, and is elsewhere repeated (9^{48}
10^{16}), and from it we may at least learn that according
to the representation in Luke also Jesus prosecuted His
work on earth under a sense of performing step by
step a task which had been given Him to do and which
He had come into the world to perform.

We need call attention only in passing to the record
by Luke also ($5^{34,35}$) of Jesus' employment of the figure of the ' Bridegroom ' with refer-
The
' Bridegroom.' ence to Himself and His relations to
God's people, thus declared to be His
Bride, as they were currently represented as the Bride
of Jehovah in the Old Testament. In this remarkable
saying, preserved in all three of the Synoptics and assigned by all of them to the earlier portion of His
ministry, we have evidence not only that Jesus regarded
His ministry as a mission He had come to perform,
and already knew that it involved His death, but that
He conceived this mission as Messianic and the Messiahship as a divine function, so that His coming was

---

[38] Cf. Weiss on Lk 4^{43}: " Luke therefore already interprets the
ἐξῆλθον of Mark incorrectly of His divine Mission." But perhaps
Weiss does not know the true meaning of the expression in Mark as
well as Luke did!

the coming of Jehovah, the faithful husband of His people (Hos 2[19]).[39]

The general impression left on the mind by this series of designations is that Luke was less interested in the preëxistence of our Lord than in His divine quality and the divine nature of His mission. To him Jesus was the authoritative Teacher, the God-appointed Messiah, the heaven-sent Redeemer from sin and divine Founder of the Kingdom of righteousness, the Judge of all the earth, Lord of men and angels, and God's own Son, between whom and the Father there persists unbroken and perfect communion. If there is scarcely as full a witness to these things in his general narrative as meets us in Matthew, there is an air thrown over the whole of settled conviction which is very striking; and the reader carries away with him the impression that the engrossment of the evangelist with his narrative represses much more testimony to the divine dignity of the Messiah than actually finds expression in his pages.

---

[39] Cf. Godet *in loc.*, E. T., p. 276: "This remarkable saying was preserved with literal exactness in the tradition; accordingly we find it in identical words in the three Synoptists. It proves, first, that from the earliest period of His ministry Jesus regarded Himself as the Messiah; next, that He identified His coming with that of Jehovah, the husband of Israel and of mankind (Hos 2[19], see Gess, *Christi Zeugniss*, pp. 19, 20); lastly, that at that time He already foresaw and announced His violent death." Godet adds: "It is an error, therefore, to oppose on these three points, the fourth Gospel to the other three."

THE JESUS OF THE SYNOPTISTS

There has now passed under our observation the whole series of designations applied to Jesus in the **Variety of Titles Used** Synoptic Gospels. They are somewhat numerous, but all to much the same effect: and they unite to suggest a unitary conception of His person of the highest exaltation. Our Lord is called in these Gospels, ' Jesus,'[1] ' Jesus of Nazareth,'[1] ' the Nazarene,'[2] ' Jesus the Galilean,'[3] ' Jesus the prophet from Nazareth of Galilee,'[3] ' Jesus surnamed Christ.'[3] ' Jesus Christ,'[2] ' Jesus the Son of David,'[1] ' Jesus King of the Jews,'[1] ' Jesus, Master,'[4] ' Jesus the Son of the Most High God.'[5] He is addressed respectfully, passing up into reverently, by the titles of ' Rabbi,'[2] ' Rabboni,'[6] ' Teacher '[1] ($\delta\iota\delta\acute{a}\sigma\varkappa a\lambda\varepsilon$), ' Master '[4] ($\dot{\varepsilon}\pi\iota\sigma\tau\acute{a}\tau a$), ' Lord ' ($\varkappa\acute{v}\rho\iota\varepsilon$) :[1] and He is spoken of by Himself or others by the corresponding appellatives, ' Teacher,'[1] ' Guide ' ($\varkappa a\theta\eta\gamma\eta\tau\acute{\eta}\varsigma$),[3] ' House-Master ' ($o\dot{\iota}\varkappa o\delta\varepsilon\sigma\pi\acute{o}\tau\eta\varsigma$),[7] ' Lord.'[1] obviously with the highest implications these appellatives are capable of bearing. More specifically He is described as to His office and person by a long series of recognized Messianic titles: ' the Coming One,'[7] ' the Prophet,'[1] ' the Christ,'[1] ' the King of the Jews,'[1] ' the King of Israel,'[2] ' the King,'[7] ' the Son of David,'[1] ' the

---

[1] Matthew, Mark, Luke.
[2] Matthew, Mark.
[3] Matthew.
[4] Luke.
[5] Mark, Luke.
[6] Mark.
[7] Matthew, Luke.

Son of Abraham,'[3] 'God's Chosen One,'[4] 'the Holy One of God,'[6] 'the Servant ($\pi\alpha\tilde{\iota}\varsigma$) of God,'[3] 'the Son of God,'[1] 'the Son of the Blessed,'[6] 'the Son of the Most High,'[4] 'the Son of the Most High God,'[5] 'the Son of the Living God,'[3] 'God's Son,'[1] 'the Son,'[1] 'the Son of Man,'[1] 'the Saviour who is Christ the Lord,'[4] 'Immanuel,'[3] 'the Shepherd who is God's Fellow,'[2] 'the Bridegroom,'[1] 'the Beloved.'[1]

We have spoken of these designations as recognized Messianic titles. They emerge as such on the pages

Extent of Jewish Use

of the Gospel narrative. But it is natural that their actual use as such by the Jews contemporary with our Lord admits of illustration from the very scanty remains of their literature which has come down to us in very varying measures. Suffice it to say that those of them which are most frequently found in the Gospel narrative and which seem most significant for it, already occur in the narrow compass of the Book of Enoch, the Apocalypse of Baruch, 4 Esra, and the Psalms of Solomon: 'the Christ,' 'the Son of David,' 'the Chosen One of God,' 'the Son of God,' 'the Son of Man.'[8] The matter is of no great importance and requires to be noted chiefly that the richness of the Messianic vocabulary capable of being intelligibly employed in Jesus' day may be appreciated, and that therefore the varying designations assigned to Jesus in the Gospels may occasion no surprise.

[8] For a list of the Messianic titles in common use among the Jews see Schürer's *The Jewish People in the Time of Christ*, II. 2, 158; Bousset, *Die Religion des Judentums*, 214 *seq.*, 248-9; Drummond, *The Jewish Messiah*, II., x., pp. 283-289; and cf. Charles, *Book of Enoch*, pp. 51, 112, 301.

This rich body of designations is rooted, in all its items, not in current Messianic speculation, but in Old

Old Testament Foundation Testament prophecy; and is a witness not so much to the Messianic thought of Jesus' day as to the great variety of the modes of representation adopted in Old Testament revelation to prepare the people of God for His future intervention for their redemption. The focusing of all these lines of prediction in Jesus, and their satisfaction in His manifestation, is one of the phenomena which marked His appearance, and differentiates the movement inaugurated by Him from all other Messianic movements in Judaism—whether movements of thought merely or of action. He came forward and was recognized as the embodiment of the whole Messianic preformation of the Old Testament, moderating the current one-sided exaggeration of some elements of it and emphasizing other elements of it which had been neglected, transfiguring elements of it which had been crassly apprehended and compacting the whole into a unitary fulfillment unimagined before His appearance. What it particularly behooves us to take note of at the moment is the emphasis with which Jesus is presented, by means of this long series of designations, as the Messiah, and the exalted conception of the Messianic dignity which accompanies this emphatic attribution of it to Him. Nothing is left unsaid which could be said in simple and straightforward narratives to make it clear to the reader that Jesus is the Messiah: and nothing is lacking in what is said to make it clear that this Messiah is more than a human, even a divine, person.

It belongs to the emphasis which is placed on His Messianic character that no room is left for that de-

Jesus'   velopment of Jesus' Messianic con-
Messianic   sciousness which it has been the chief
Claims   desire of many modern students of His

career to trace. Nor, indeed, is room léft for justi-
fiable lagging of recognition of His Messiahship on
the part of His followers or of His contemporaries.
He is exhibited as already conscious of His unique relation to God as His Son, in the sole incident that is
recorded of His early youth (Lk 2^{49}). He is represented as beginning His ministry under the profound
impression necessarily made upon Him by His solemn
designation as the Messiah by John the Baptist (Mt
3^{14}), confirmed as this was by a voice from the opened
heavens proclaiming Him God's Son, His Beloved, in
whom God was well pleased (Mt 3^{17}, Mk 1^{11}, Lk 3^{22}),
and by His terrible experience of testing by Satan as
the Son of God (Mt 4^{3,6}, Lk 4^{3,9}), and His succoring
by the angels (Mk 1^{13}). Accordingly He is represented as opening His ministry by publicly applying to
Himself the prophecy of Isaiah 61^1 with its enumeration of the works of the Messiah (Lk 4$^{17,18 \text{ seq.}}$), and
as entering at once upon the performance of those
works, not merely accepting the ascriptions of Messianic dignity to Him which they elicited (Lk 5^8 4^{34,41},
Mk 1^{24,34}, Mt 8^{17}, etc.), but Himself appealing to them
as the criteria of His Messiahship (Mt 11^3, Lk 7^{19}).
He is represented as, under the impulse of His sense of
His mission (Mk 1^{38}, Lk 4^{43}), preaching throughout the land in accents of authority (Mk 1^{22}, Lk 4^{32}),
asserting His power over the religious ordinances of
the people (Mk 2^{28}, Mt 12^8, Lk 6^5), and exercising

His authority not only over unclean spirits (e. g., Mk 1^{27}) and the laws of nature (4^{41}), including even death (5^{43}), but over the moral world itself, in the divine prerogative of forgiving sins (2^{10}). Not only, however, is He represented as thus openly taking the position of Messiah and assuming the authority and functions of the Messiah (cf. Mt $7^{21,29}$) before the people: He is represented as from the first speaking of Himself as the Messiah in the use of His favorite Messianic designation, as frequently as He could be expected to do so in the circumstances in which He was placed and with the purpose which governed His entire course of life (Mt 8^{20} || Lk 9^{58}; Mt 9^6 || Mk 2^{10} Lk 5^{24}; Mt 10^{23}; Mt 11^{19}|| Lk 7^{34}; Mt 12^8 || Mk 2^{28} Lk 6^5; Mt 12^{32}; 12^{40}; Lk 6^{22}; Mt 13^{41}; before the confession of Peter at Mt 16^{16} ||).[9] When these instances of self-expression are taken in connection with those of reception of the Messianic ascription from others (e. g., Mk 1^{24} 3^{11} 5^7, Mt $4^{3,6}$ 8^{29} 14^{33}, Lk 4^{41} 8^{28} $4^{3,9}$, Mt 9^{27} 15^{22}), it will be seen that the early ministry of Jesus, as represented by the Synoptists, was marked by practically continuous assertion or confession of His Messiahship.

If, then, John the Baptist doubted in prison whether He was ' the Coming One ' (Mt 11^3), or it was only **Divergence** through a revelation from heaven that **From Current** Peter attained to confess Him with firm **Expectations** faith ' the Christ, the Son of the Living God ' (Mt $16^{16,17}$), this was not because of any lack of opportunity to learn of His Messiahship, but be-

[9] Cf. Dalman, *Words,* p. 259: "As for the Evangelists themselves, they take the view that Jesus called Himself the ' Son of Man ' at all times and before all company."

cause they were foolish and slow of heart to believe in all that the prophets had spoken and their eyes were holden that they should not know Him as He walked with them in the way (Lk 24[16,25]). So little were they left in ignorance of who it was to whom they listened as their Teacher, and obeyed as their Master and reverenced as their Lord, that it is represented that angelic messengers descended from heaven to announce Him as the promised Messiah before His birth (Lk 1[32,35] 2[11,26]), that the predicted messenger who should go before the Lord, coming to redeem His people, pointed Him out as the One who should come after Him (Mt 3[11] ||), that God Himself proclaimed Him from heaven as His Son (Mt 3[17] ||), that Satan and his subject spirits recognized Him on sight as the One who had been appointed to destroy them (Mk 1[34] 5[7] || etc.), and that His whole career and teaching alike were ordered to convey to every seeing eye the great intelligence. The difficulty, according to the representation of the evangelists, was not that there was not evidence enough that here was the Messiah of God, the King come to His Kingdom; but that the evidence was not of the nature that had been expected and therefore puzzled men's minds rather than convinced them. The gist of our Lord's message to the Baptist (Mt 11[3]) was not that John might see in His works such things as he had been looking for in the Messiah, but that he might see in them such things as he ought to be looking for. " Go and tell John that these are the kinds of things you see in me—the blind receive their sight, the lame walk, the lepers are cleansed, the deaf hear, and the dead are raised up; and the poor have the good tidings preached to them: and *blessed is he who shall find none occasion of stumbling in Me!"* It is as much as to say, " Go and tell John to revise his conception of the Messiah, and to look and see if it is not these things which, according to the Scriptures (Is 61[1]), should mark His work: go and tell John, I am indeed He who is to come, but I am not the manner of Messiah who is expected to come."[10]

Accordingly the Synoptic narrative is marked no more by the stress it lays on the Messiahship of Jesus than by the transfigured conception of this Messiahship which it in every line insists upon. This constantly vibrating note is already struck in the supernatural announcements of the birth of Jesus. It is the Son of David who is to be born (Mt 1[20], Lk 1[27,32]), the promised King (Mt 2[2], Lk 1[33]) ; but, above all else and before all else, that Saviour who is Christ the Lord (Lk 2[11]), and whose name shall be called Jesus, because it is He who in fulfillment of the ancient prophecy promising the coming of Jehovah to His people, shall save His people from their sins (Mt 1[21]). It is not merely a spiritual function which is here announced for this Messiah: it is also a divine personality. Who is that Saviour who is Christ " the *Lord,*" and whose name shall be called Jesus because He shall save from their sins *His* people—" *His* " people, let us take good note, Jesus' people, although it is clear it is Jehovah's people who are meant? No wonder that it is immediately added that in this birth there is, therefore, fulfilled the

[10] Cf. the discussion by Shailer Mathews, *The Messianic Hope in the N. T.,* 1905, pp. 95-6; although Professor Mathews' treatment is dominated by the idea that our Lord's followers saw in Jesus rather one who was after a while to do Messianic works than one who was already doing them.

prophecy of the issue from a virgin of one whose name is to be called Immanuel, which is, being interpreted, "God with us" (Mt 1²³).

The note thus struck is sustained throughout the Gospel narrative. This Messiah who Jesus is, is certainly the Son of David, the King of Israel. But the Kingdom He has come to found is the kingdom of righteousness, not merely a righteous kingdom: it is the Kingdom of Heaven, not a kingdom of the earth: the Kingdom of God, not of men. We may see its nature in Daniel's splendid dream of the heaven-founded kingdom of the saints of the Most High (Dan 7¹³,²²⁻²⁷); the method of its establishment in Isaiah's vision of the Righteous Servant of Jehovah, who bears the sins of His people and preaches the good tidings to the meek (esp. Is 53 and 61); the person of its founder in that most glorious of all prophecies of the Old Covenant: "Lo, your God will come; He will come and save you!" (Is 35⁴); "the voice of one that crieth, Prepare ye in the wilderness the way of the Lord, make straight in the desert a highway for our God; . . . the glory of the Lord shall be revealed and all flesh shall see it together, . . . Behold your God! Behold the Lord God will come . . . He shall feed His flock like a shepherd, He shall gather the lambs in His arms, and carry them in His bosom, and gently lead those that give suck" (Is 40¹ ˢᵉᑫ·).[11] To put it in one sentence, the Messianic ideal which is presented in the Synoptics as fulfilled in Jesus finds

[11] Cf. Reinhold Ziemssen, *Christus der Herr*, 1867, p. 28: "They proclaim with one voice that the Lord (Jehovah) Himself will come, that He Himself will protect His flock, that He Himself will be King in Zion, that He Himself will be found of Israel."

its Old Testament basis not merely in the prediction of a Davidic King who reigns forever over the people of God, but, interpreting that kingdom in the terms of Daniel's dream of a heaven-founded kingdom of saints, interweaves with it the portraitures of the Servant of Jehovah of Isaiah and the fundamental promise that Jehovah shall visit His people for redemption.

The special vehicles of the exalted view of the person of the Messiah embodied in this ideal are, so far as the Messianic designations are concerned, first of all that of the 'Son of Man,' then that of 'the Son of God,' or rather, in the more pregnant simple form, of 'the Son'; and outside of the Messianic titles proper, the high title of 'Lord.' The history of these designations is somewhat obscure, and, although they all have their roots set in the Old Testament, is illustrated by only scanty usage of them in Jewish literature prior to our Lord's time. 'The Son of Man' occurs only in the Similitudes of Enoch and in 4 Ezra:[12] the exact title 'Son of God' does not seem to occur at all,[13] though

Highest Designations

---

[12] Cf. Dalman, *Words*, p. 242: "From the first Christian century there are only two Jewish writings known which deal with Dan 7[13], the Similitudes of the Book of Enoch and the Second [al. Fourth] Book of Esdras. The two agree in regarding the one like to a Son of Man as an individual person. And as they combine Dan 7 with Messianic prophecies from the O. T. they clearly show that they regard this individual as the Messiah." Cf. p. 248.

[13] Cf. Stanton, *The Jewish and Christian Messiah*, p. 147, and esp. 288; and Dalman, *Words*, 269-71: also Shailer Mathews, *The Messianic Hope in the N. T.*, 1905, p. 46 and note 4. Dr. Sanday on Rom 1[4] writes as follows: "'Son of God,' like 'Son of Man,' was a recognized title of the Messiah (cf. Enoch 105[2]; 4 Ezra 7[28,29] 13[32,37,52] 14[9], in all which places the Almighty speaks of the Messiah as 'My Son,' though the exact phrase 'Son of God' does not occur). It is remarkable that in the Gospels we very rarely find it used by our

in an interpolated fragment of the Book of Enoch
(105^2) and in 4 Ezra the Messiah is represented as
spoken of by God as ' My Son.'[14] It is noteworthy that
in this rare Jewish usage both titles appear in connection with a transcendental doctrine of the Messiah,[15]
and it may be that it is the unwontedness of a transcendental doctrine of the Messiah in Judaism which accounts for the little use made in Jewish speculation of
them, because these titles were felt to be implicative
of more than human qualities. Their emergence into
more frequent use in the Gospels would in that case
be connected with the emphasis laid, according to their

Lord Himself, though in the face of Mt 27^{43}, Jno 10^{36}, cf. Mt 21^{31}
et al., it cannot be said that He did not use it. It is more often used
to describe the impression made upon others (e.g. the demonized, Mk
3^{11} 5^7 ||, the centurion, Mk 15^{39} ||), and it is implied by the words of
the tempter (Mt $4^{3,6}$ ||), and the voice from heaven (Mk 1^{11} 9^7 ||).
The crowning instance is the confession of St. Peter . . . Mt 16^{16}."

[14] Cf. Dalman, *Words,* 269-70; Charles, *Enoch,* 301.

[15] Cf. Bousset, *Die Religion des Judentums,* etc., 248 : " But here and
there there springs up, now, in the Jewish Apocalyptics a new transcendental Messiah-conception, that fits into these transcendental sur-
roundings. In the first line there comes here under consideration the
Similitudes of Enoch, springing from the pre-Herodian time. The
standing designation of this peculiar Messiah is the ' Son of Man ' . . .
Still more remarkable and unusual than, in part, the name is now the
figure of this Son of Man. He is in no respect an earthly phenomenon; he is not, like the Messiah of the stock of David, born on earth;
he is an angel-like being, whose dwelling place is in heaven under
the pinions of the Lord of spirits; He is preëxistent . . . Emphasis
must be laid on the Son of Man in the great judgment upon the kings
of the earth and the evil angels; He takes His place by the side of
God and indeed supplants Him . . . This representation of the
Messiah, singular in the sphere of Judaism, has only one, though by no
means so far-going a, parallel in the vision of the Son of Man of 4
Ezra. . . . Here too the Son of Man . . . is conceived as a
preëxistent (heavenly?) being. Here too he holds the great judgment,
and, according to the original disposition of the apocalypse, seems also

representation, upon the essential divinity of the Messiah by Jesus and His followers.

Certainly the Messianic conception represented as expressed by Jesus through His constant employment of the title 'Son of Man' of Himself, is that of a supermundane Being entering the sphere of earthly life upon a high and beneficent mission, upon the accomplishment of which He returns to the heavenly sphere, whence He shall once more come back to earth, now, however, not in humiliation, but in His appropriate majesty, to gather up the fruits of His work and consummate all things. The characteristic note of 'the Son of Man' on earth is therefore a lowliness which is not so much a humility as a humiliation, a voluntary self-abnegation for a purpose. He came under the conditions of human life (Mt 11^{19} ||) on a mission of mercy (Lk 19^{10}) which involved His self-sacrifice (Mk 10^{45}||), and therefore lives a life unbefitting His essential nature (Mt 8^{20}). For, when He tells the questioning scribe that the 'Son of Man' is worse off than the very foxes, who have holes, and the birds of the air, who have nests, since He has not where to lay His head (Mt 8^{20}), the very point of the remark is the incongruity

Meaning of 'Son of Man'

to bring in the definitive end, and not merely a preliminary closing . . ." So also p. 215: "The title Son of God, closely connected though it is with the conception of the Son of David and the Anointed, is comparatively very rare. It is found in the address in Psalm 2, which also became typical for the title 'Messiah' (verse 7, cf. Ps 89^{27}). In 4 Ezra 7^{29} the *filius* is not textually assured; in I. Enoch 105^2 the words " and My Son," as perhaps also the whole clause, is a later interpolation. Accordingly the apposition, 'My Son,' is found only in 4 Ez $1^{13,32,37,52}$,—that is to say, in the section in which along with the Similitudes, the transcendent conception of the Messiah comes forward most vitally—and also in 4 Ezra 14^9 (Dalman, 219)."

of the situation. Accordingly even on earth He exercises an authority which does not belong to His condition: though destined to be set at naught by men, to be evil-entreated and slain, yet He has power to regulate the religious observances of the people of God (Mk 2^{28}) and even to forgive sins (2^{10}). And when His lowly mission is accomplished He ascends the throne of the universe (Mk 14^{62}, Mt 19^{28}); and in due time will return in His glory and render to every man according to his works, seated as King on the universal judgment seat (Mk 8^{38}, Mt 25^{31}). The connection of the title with the dream of Daniel $7^{13,14}$ is obvious: the point of connection lying in the conception of the Kingdom of God, which Jesus came to introduce, and which He finds particularly promised in Daniel $7^{13,14}$, apparently because it is there depicted, specifically in contrast with the earthly kingdoms which it supercedes, as a Kingdom of heaven. But there is much more expressed by the title than is discernible in the dream of Daniel, and that not least with reference to the person of the founder, who is conceived, in Jesus' idea, as represented by the Synoptic record, not merely as a supermundane, perhaps angelic, figure,[16] but distinctly as superangelic, transcending all creaturely re-

---

[16] Cf. Stanton, *Jewish and Christian Messiah*, 286-7: "I may remark that the idea of the preëxistence of Christ as an angel, is irreconcilable with that of a true Incarnation. Those who have thought of Christ as essentially an angel have never in fact conceived, and could not conceive, His human life to be real. A whole and complete human nature could not be united to another finite being, whether angel or man, as it could be united to, and could become the perfect organ of, God. Wherever, then, we find a belief in the real human nature of Jesus Christ, there we may confidently say the idea formed of His superhuman preëxistence and personality is not that of an angel. . . . Hellwag fails altogether to see this when he attributes such a conception of Christ's person to St. Paul, *Theol. Jahrb.*, 1848, pp. 240 ff. . . .

lations,[17] and finding His appropriate place only by the side of God Himself, whose functions He performs[18] and whose throne He occupies as King.[19]

The conception attached in these Gospels to the designation 'Son of God' is in no respect less exalted.

Meaning of 'Son of God' The title does occasionally occur, to be sure, in circumstances in which this exalted significance seems more or less in danger of being missed. For example, it is employed by the Jewish officers at the trial of Christ as in some sense a synonym of the general Messianic title 'Christ' (Mk 14^{62}, Mt 26^{63}, Lk 22^{70}, cf. Mt $27^{40,43}$); it is also employed, according to Matthew's account, by Peter in his great confession alongside of the term 'Christ' (16^{16}); and on one occasion Jesus' disciples, having witnessed a notable miracle, cried out as they did Him reverence, " Of a truth Thou are the [or, a] Son of God " (Mt 14^{33}). Such passages, no doubt, illustrate the use of the term as a Messianic title. But it seems clear enough that they illustrate its use as a Messianic title of inherently higher connotation than, say, the simple term 'the Christ' as a general synonym of which it is employed. The very point of the Jews' approaching Jesus with this particular Messianic title appears to have been—as the form of the narrative in Luke may suggest—to obtain a confession which would enable them from their point of view to charge

Hellwag is the writer who has most insisted on the influence of a Jewish doctrine of the Messiah's preëxistence upon Christian belief." The speculative element in this remark is perhaps too dogmatically put: but there is food for thought in it.

[17] The angels are subject to Him and do His bidding: Mt 13^{41} 16^{27} 24^{31}; and also Mt 4^{11} 13^{39}, Mk 1^{13} 8^{38} 13^{27}, Lk 9^{26}.

[18] Especially forgiveness of sins (Mk 2^5) and judgment of the world (e.g. Mt 25^{31} seq.)—two inalienable divine functions.

[19] E.g. Mt 25^{31}.

Him with blasphemy. That is to say, the implications of this Messianic title in their minds seem to have been such that its use by a mere man, or by one seemingly a mere man, would involve him in claims for himself which were tantamount to blasphemy. It seems equally clear that Peter in acknowledging Jesus to be the Messiah (Mt 16[16]) intended by adjoining to the simple, " Thou art the Christ " the defining phrase " the Son of the Living God " to attach an exalted conception of the Messiahship to Him. And it is fairly obvious that the frightened disciples in the boat (Mt 14[33]),—though certainly they understood not and their heart was hardened (Mk 6[51]),—yet expressed out of their distracted minds at least the sense of a supernatural presence when they cried out, " Truly Thou art "—possibly " a," not " the "—" Son of God." Their exclamation thus may in its own degree be paralleled at least with that of the centurion at the cross (Mk 15[39], Mt 27[54]), " Truly this man was a Son of God "—which surely is the natural expression, from his own point of view, of his awe in the presence of the supernatural.

This series of exceptional instances of the employment of the term ' Son of God ' will scarcely, therefore, avail to lessen the general impression we get from the current use of the title, that it designates the Messiah from a point of view which differentiates Him as ' the Son of God ' from the children of men, and throws into emphasis a distinct implication of the supernaturalness of His person. It seems to be on this account that it is characteristically employed by voices from the unseen universe. It is by this term, for instance, that Satan addresses Jesus in the temptation, seeking to induce Him by this exploitation of His supernatural character to perform supernatural deeds (Mt 4³،⁶, Lk 4³،⁹). It is by this term (Lk 4⁴¹) that the demons greet Him when they recognize in Him the judge and destroyer of all that is evil (Mk 3¹¹ 5⁷, Mt 8²⁹, Lk 8²⁸; 4⁴¹). It is by this term that the angel of the annunciation is represented as describing the nature of her miraculous child to Mary: " He shall be great," he announced, " and shall be called the Son of the Most High God." And in doing this, it must be noted, the angel connects the title no more with His appointment to a supernatural service than with the supernatural-ness of His origin: because Mary's conception should be supernatural, therefore, that holy thing which was being begotten should bear the name of the ' Son of God ' (Lk 1³²،³⁵). It is by the term ' My Son ' above all that God Himself bore witness to Him on the two occasions when He spoke from heaven to give Him His testimony (Mk 1¹¹ 9⁷, Mt 3¹⁷ 17⁵, Lk 3²² 9³⁵)— adding to it moreover epithets which emphasized the uniqueness of the Sonship thus solemnly announced. It would seem quite clear, therefore, that the title ' Son of God ' stands in the pages of the Synoptics as the supernatural Messianic designation by way of eminence, and represents the Messiah in contradistinction from children of men as of a supernatural origin and nature.

It is, however, from our Lord's own application of the term ' the Son ' to Himself that we derive our plainest insight into the loftiness of its implications. Already in the Parable of the Wicked Husbandmen (Mk 12⁶, Mt 21³⁷, Lk 20¹³, cf. Mt 22¹), He sets Himself as God's Son and Heir over against all His servants, of whatever quality; which would seem to withdraw Him out of the category of creatures altogether. And this tremendous inference is fully supported by the remarkable utterance in which, in declaring His ignorance of the time of His future coming, He places Himself outside of the category even of angels, that is of creatures of the highest rank, and assimilates Himself as Son to the Father (Mk 13[32], Mt 24[36]). It is carried out of the region of inference into that of assertion in the two remarkable passages in which He gives didactic expression to His relation as Son to the Father (Mt 11[27], Lk 10[22], Mt 28[19]). In these, He tells us He is co-sharer in the one Name with the Father, and co-exists with the Father in a complete, perfect and unbroken interpenetration of mutual knowledge and being. The essential deity of the Son could not receive more absolute expression.

The difficulty of forming a precise estimate of the implications of the application of the term 'Lord' to Jesus in the Synoptic Gospels arises

Meaning of 'Lord'

from the confluence of two diverse streams of significance in that term. On the one hand Jesus may be and is called 'Lord' by the application to Him of a title expressive of authority and sovereignty commonly in use among men: above all others who have a right to rule He has a right to rule. On the other hand, Jesus may be and is called 'Lord' by the application to Him of a current Biblical title expressive of the divine majesty: much that was said of the 'Lord' in the Old Testament Scriptures was carried over to Him and with it the term itself.[20] When, then, we meet with an instance in

[20] Cf. Reinhold Ziemssen, *Christus der Herr*, 1867, p. 22: "But this is meant: that just as κύριος, 'Lord,' occurs in the O. T. (1) as the equivalent of Jehovah; (2) as the rendering of Adhonai; and (3) as a transference of the human honorific title to God,—so also in the

which Jesus is called ' Lord ' we are puzzled to determine whether there is merely attributed to Him supreme authority and jurisdiction, or there is given to Him the Name that is above every name.

That the designation ' the Lord ' had attached itself to Jesus during His lifetime so that He was thus familiarly spoken of among His followers is perfectly clear from the Gospel narrative. It is indeed already implied in the instruction given His disciples by Jesus to bring Him the ass's colt on which He might make His entry into Jerusalem. He could not have instructed them to say to possible objectors, " The Lord hath need of him " (Mk 11³, Mt 21³, Lk 19³¹), unless He had been accustomed to be spoken of as ' the Lord.' That He was accustomed to thinking of Himself as their ' Lord ' follows also from such a passage as Mt 24⁴² (cf. Mk 13³⁵) : " Watch, therefore, for ye know not on what day your Lord cometh "; and indeed from the didactic use of the term of Himself

N. T. the Saviour is called χύριος, 'Lord,' (1) in the sense of Adhonai-Jehovah; (2) by a heightening of the human sense or an adaptation from the relations of human sovereignty: and that the name ' Lord ' belongs to the Saviour according to the N. T. essentially and fundamentally in the sense of Adhonai or Jehovah, not as the transference or heightening of the human relation of sovereignty." The use of χύριος in the N. T. of our Lord, he says again, " has in the first instance nothing to do with glory, δόξα, and just as truly stands in the N. T. in no essential connection with χυριεύειν, ruling " (p. 10). This is not to contend that ὁ χύριος in N. T. when applied to Christ always means Jehovah. In almost all the passages in the Gospels where χύριος appears as a formula of address it is a human honorific. In certain others, as Lk 19³¹,³⁴, Lk 6⁴⁶, Mt 7²¹, something may be said for either interpretation (p. 21). But there are passages where it must be taken as the divine χύριος, viz., Lk 2⁹. Ὁ χύριος Zeimssen holds, is the name of Jesus as the Son of God, just as Jesus is His name as the Son of man, and Christ is His office-name (p. 30) ; and refers back to the prophecies of Jehovah's advent, such as Ezek 34¹¹ (p. 20).

in encouraging or warning His followers (Mt 10[24]),
and its free employment in parabolic pictures, where
He represents Himself as the ' Lord ' over against His
servants (Lk 12[36,43]). In what sense the term is used
in such allusions is not, however, immediately obvious.
The opposition of it to " slaves " in such passages as
Mt 10[24], Lk 12[36,43] leads to its instinctive interpretation
in the sense of ownership and sovereignty, and does not
appear to call for direct divine implications save as the
absoluteness of the sovereignty which is suggested may
surpass that enjoyed by men. Perhaps something to
the same effect may be said of Luke 1[43] where Elisabeth,
under the influence of the Holy Spirit, expresses her
wondering joy that " the mother of her Lord " should
come to her. Clearly she intends to express by the
designation the height of at least Messianic glory: but
it does not seem obvious that her thought went beyond
the delegated glory of the divine representative. In
a passage like Luke 5[8], however, there seems to be
an ascription to Jesus of a majesty which is distinctly
recognized as supernatural: not only is the contrast
of ' Lord ' with ' Master ' here express (cf. v. 5), but
the phrase " Depart from me; for I am a sinful man "
(v. 8) is the natural utterance of that sense of unworthi-
ness which overwhelms men in the presence of the
divine, and which is signalized in Scripture as the
mark of recognition of the divine presence. The
' Lord, Lord ' of Mt 7[21,22] also obviously involves a
recognition of Jesus as the Lord of life, and in Mt
25[37,44] ' Lord ' is the appropriate address to the King
on the judgment throne of the whole earth. In these
instances the sense of the mere supernatural gives way
to the apprehension of that absolute sovereignty over

the destinies of men which can belong to deity alone; it is this ' Lord ' in whose name all the works of life are done, by whose determination all the issues of life are fixed.

If in such instances we appear to be employing the word in its highest connotation of sovereignty, in such instances as the discussion of David's words in the 110th Psalm we seem to rise into a region of actual divine ascription. Here, with obvious reference to Himself, our Lord argues that when David in the Spirit represents the Lord as saying to his Lord, " Sit thou on My right hand," he ascribes a dignity to the Messiah very much greater than could belong to Him simply as David's son (Mk $12^{36,37}$).[21] That seems as much as to say that sovereignty of the royal order, however absolute, is too low a category under which to subsume this Lordship: and therefore appears to point to a connotation of ' Lord ' beyond illustration from human analogies. The question inevitably obtrudes itself whether our Lord does not intend to suggest that David applies the divine name itself to the Messiah. That the evangelists may very readily have so understood Him seems evident from their own application to Jesus of the term ' Lord ' in Isaiah 40^3,—representing the incommunicable name of Jehovah as it does,—in their account of the mission of the Baptist, whom they consentiently speak of as the forerunner of Jesus, fulfilling the prophecy of the coming of the voice of one crying, " Prepare ye in the wilderness the way of the Lord, make His paths straight " (Mk 1^3, Mt 3^3, Lk

[21] Cf. Bengel on Mt 22^{43}: *signum subjectionis, dominatio, cujus subditus est ipse David, coelestem et Regis majestatem et Regni indolem ostendit.*

3^4). And there remains the remarkable passage in the angelic annunciation to the shepherds of the birth in the city of David of that " Saviour " who is " Christ the Lord " (Lk 2^{11}). It seems impossible to suppose that the term ' the Lord ' here adds nothing to the term ' the Christ '—else why is it added? But what can the term ' Lord ' add as a climax to ' Christ '? In ' Christ ' itself, the Anointed King, there is already expressed the height of sovereignty and authority as the delegate of Jehovah. The appearance is very strong that the adjunction of ' Lord ' is intended to convey the intelligence that the ' Christ ' now born is a divine Christ.[22]

This appearance is greatly strengthened by the consideration that the appeal to prophecy in calling the Messiah ' the Saviour ' is an appeal to the great series of predictions of the advent of Jehovah for the redemption of His people (cf. Mt 1^{21}): and also by the general context in which this annunciation is placed, which contains a sustained attempt to make the supernaturalism of this birth impressive, and includes the declaration that the child here designated " the Saviour who is Christ the Lord " is in His person the ' Son of the Most High God ' (Lk 1^{32}) and is marked out as such by a supernatural birth (1^{35}). Nor should we permit to fall out of our sight the circumstance that this passage occurs in a context in which the term ' Lord ' appears unusually frequently, and always, with this exception and that of 1^{45}, of Jehovah. It would be very difficult for the simple reader to read of the angel of

---

[22] Cf. R. Ziemssen, *Christus der Herr,* 1867, p. 19: " In any event its significance is gained by the angelic annunciation only if we take it in this sense—Christ-Adhonai, that is, Christ-Jehovah."

'the Lord' and of the glory of 'the Lord' in Lk 2⁹, and of 'the Lord' making known in verse 15, and, in the middle of these statements, of 'Christ the Lord' in verse 11, and not institute some connection between it and its ever-repeated fellows: especially when he would soon read in verse 26, of "the Christ of the Lord." That at least a superhuman majesty is here ascribed to Jesus seems scarcely disputable: and there appears a strong likelihood that this supernaturalness is meant to rise to the divine. In any event it is clear that the term 'Lord' is sometimes applied to Jesus in the Synoptics in a height of connotation which imports His deity.[23]

It is not necessary to add further evidence, derived from less frequently employed designations of our

Synoptical Christ Divine

Lord, that a true deity is ascribed to His person in the Synoptic Gospels. On the basis of the considerations already presented it is abundantly clear that the Synoptists conceived Jesus, whom they identify with the Messiah, as a divine person; and represent Him as exercising divine prerogatives and asserting for Himself a divine personality and participation in the divine Name.

[23] The nature of the κυριότης ascribed to Jesus in the Synoptics is very interestingly expounded by Professor Erich Schaeder in two lectures on "The Christology of the Creeds and the Modern Theology," printed in Schlatter and Lütgert's *Beiträge zur Förderung christlicher Theologie,* ix. 5. (1905). That this Lord of spirits and of the world is not conceived as of the world, he makes very obvious. "It is nonsense to suggest that the world itself can produce its Lord. The world can produce only what is like it, not one who stands above it" (p. 201).

THE JESUS OF THE SYNOPTISTS THE PRIMITIVE JESUS

That we may estimate the significance of the testimony to the Divine Christ which we have seen to be
Significance of Synoptical Testimony borne by the Synoptists, we must bear in mind that it cannot be taken as merely the individual opinion of three writers. It must be recognized as reflecting the consentient conviction of the community which these three writers represent and for which they wrote. And this is equivalent to saying that we have here the conception of Jesus which prevailed in the primitive age of the Christian propaganda.[1]

This might not be so obvious if we could follow certain extremists who, largely in order to escape this
Date of the Synoptics very conclusion, have wished—formerly in much greater numbers than more recently—to assign the composition of the Synoptic Gospels to a period somewhat late in the second century. It will be allowed by most reasonable men to-day that these Gospels were all written before A. D. 80, and belong at latest to the seventh and eighth decades of the first century. Our own conviction is very clear that they were all written before A. D. 70, and therefore belong to the seventh decade at the

[1] Cf. O. Schmiedel, *Die Hauptprobleme der Leben-Jesu Forschung*, 1906, p. 35: "The early Church in whose circles the narratives of the life of Jesus originated, . . . was at one in its acknowledgment of Christ, its exalted Lord."

latest. In the seventh decade of the first century, there-fore, it was of faith in the Christian community that Jesus Christ was a divine person. And this evidence is retrospective. What was with such firmness uni-versally believed of the nature of the founder of the Christian religion in the seventh decade of the first century, had not first in that decade become the faith of the Church. But only a short generation, as we conventionally count generations—something like five and thirty years—intervened between the death of Jesus and the composition of the Synoptic Gospels. It is impossible to suppose that the conception of Jesus had radically altered in this brief interval; that a primi-tive humanitarianism for example had in the course of thirty or forty years been transformed into a universal conviction of the deity of Jesus, such as is expressed with simplicity and unstudied emphasis in our Gospels. The witness of the Synoptic Gospels is accordingly a witness to the aboriginal faith of Christians.

Nor is the force of this conclusion weakened by at-tempting to get behind our Gospels and appealing to **Earlier Documentary Basis** the yet earlier documents out of which they may be thought to have been framed. Grant that our Gospels belong to the second generation of documents; and that behind them lie still earlier documents upon which they de-pend. These earlier documents cannot be presumed to have presented a portrait of Jesus radically different from that which all three of their representatives have derived from them. We have simply pushed back ten, fifteen, or twenty years our literary testimony to the deity of Jesus: and how can we suppose that the de-terminative expression of the Church's faith in A. D.

50 or A. D. 40 differed radically from the Church's faith in A. D. 30—the year in which Jesus died? The assurance that our Gospels rest on earlier documentary sources becomes thus an additional assurance that the conception of the person of Jesus which they present in concert is the conception which held the mind and heart of the Church from the very beginning.

How fully justified this conclusion is may be illustrated by examining the conception of Jesus imbedded in the hypothetical sources which the several schools of criticism reconstruct for our Synoptics. In each and all of them is found the same portrait of the supernatural Christ. Probably the theory of the origin of the Synoptics most in vogue just now is still the so-called " two-source " theory, in some one or other of its forms. According to this theory, our three Synoptics in their main substance are compounded out of two important primitive documents, which may be conveniently called 'the original Mark' and 'the Matthean sayings.' The former of these is supposed to be substantially and, in the view of many critics, very closely indeed, represented by our present Mark; while from the latter a good portion of the material in Matthew and Luke not also contained in Mark is thought to be derived, —certainly what is common to these two Gospels apart from Mark, and doubtless also something not reproduced in both of them. According to the present most fashionable form of this theory, then, we are reading substantially a primitive evangelical document when we read our present Mark. Some suppose the primitive Mark to have been a longer document than our present Mark, some suppose it to have been a shorter

[margin note:] The Sources of the Synoptics

document, some suppose it to have differed from it not more than one textual recension may differ from another,—say a " Western " MS. of Luke from a " Neutral " one. But few would care to contend that the general portrait of Jesus drawn in it differed markedly from that which lies on the pages of our present Mark. The Jesus brought before us in our present Mark, however, is, as we have seen, distinctly and distinctively a supernatural person: and it must have been this same distinctly and distinctively supernatural Jesus, therefore, which was set forth in the primitive Mark.

Indeed, we can demonstrate this without difficulty. For it is easy to show that it is impossible to construct
Christology a primitive Mark which will not contain
of the this portrait of a supernatural Jesus.
Primitive Mark Take what is probably the most irrational hypothesis of the nature of the primitive Mark which has ever been suggested,—that which would confine its contents strictly to the matter common to all three Synoptics, as if each Gospel must be supposed to have transferred into its substance every word which stood in this common source of them all. Even in the broken sentences of the absurd " telegraphese " Gospel,[2] which on this hypothesis is supposed to represent the primitive evangelical document, the portrait of the divine Christ is ineffaceably imbedded. In it, as in the larger Mark, the stress of the presentation is laid

---

[2] Cf. E. A. Abbott and W. G. Rushbrooke, *The Common Tradition of the Synoptic Gospels,* etc., 1884, p. XI: " Is it not possible that the condensed narrative which we can pick out of the three Synoptic records represents the 'elliptical style' of the earliest Gospel notes or Memoirs, which needed to be 'expanded' before they could be used for the purpose of teaching . . . ? "

on the Messiahship of Jesus, which is copiously and
variously witnessed. Peter in his great confession declares Him the 'Christ' (8²⁹) and the declaration is
accepted by Jesus Himself; as also, when adjured by
the High Priest at His trial to say whether He is the
'Christ,' He acknowledges that He is, in the highest
sense (14⁶¹,⁶²). The implied claim to kingly estate
He also expressly makes (15²,³²); as also the involved
claim of being the promised 'Son of David' (10⁴⁷,⁴⁸),
—although His conception of the Messiahship was so
little exhausted by this claim that He takes pains to
point out that the Messiah was acknowledged by David
himself to be his 'Lord,' using the term obviously in
a high sense (12³⁵). That He was familiarly spoken
of by His disciples as 'Lord' is also made evident
(11³); and He Himself asserts that His Lordship is
high enough to give Him authority over the religious
ordinances of Israel (2²⁸). The tradition applies, indeed, the term 'Lord' to Him in citations from the
Old Testament, where it stands for Jehovah Himself
(1³). The evil spirits greet Him by the high title of
'Son of God' (5⁷), and the same title is suggested
to Him as a synonym of the Messiah in His accusation (14⁶¹), and in neither case is it repelled. He
Himself indeed in a parable represents Himself as in a
unique sense the 'Son' and 'Heir' of God, differen-
tiated as such from all "servants" whatsoever (12⁶,⁷);
and receives the testimony of heaven itself that He is
God's 'Son' and His 'beloved Son' (1¹¹ 9⁷). He
speaks of Himself, however, with more predilection as
the 'Son of Man'; and under this self-designation
He asserts for Himself power over the religious ordinances of Israel (2²⁸), and even the divine prerogative

of forgiving sins (2^{10}), although He anticipates for Himself only a career of suffering, predicting that He will be betrayed (14^{20}) into the hands of men (9^{31}) who shall mock and scourge and kill Him (10^{33}). Afterwards, however, He shall rise again (10^{34}) and ascend to the right hand of power (14^{62}), whence He shall return in clouds with great power and glory (13^{26}), the glory of the Father and the angels (8^{38}). It is clear that the designation 'Son of Man' is derived from Daniel $7^{13,14}$ (13^{20} 8^{28} 14^{62}) and the portrait presented under it is that of a being of more than human powers and attributes. In complete harmony with this portrait He is represented as calling Himself also 'the Bridegroom' ($2^{19,20}$), charged as that term was with Old Testament associations with Jehovah (cf. 'Lord' of 1^3); and in immediate connection with this high designation, too, He speaks of His death, thus instituting a close parallel between this designation and that of the 'Son of Man.' In both alike, indeed, He evidently is regarded as presenting Himself as a personage of superhuman, or rather of divine quality, who has come to earth (12^{17}) only on a mission and who suffers and dies here only to fulfill that mission.[3]

[3] There may be compared with this sketch the minimizing account which von Soden (*History of Early Christian Literature*, 1906, p. 144), gives of the christology of the primitive "Mark," which according to him was of somewhat wider compass than what we have allowed it. "Somewhat more frequently," he says, "than in the Logia of St. Matthew, stress is laid upon the Messianic character of Jesus—for instance, in the narrative of the Baptism (1^{10} seq.), in the cry of the possessed (1^{24}), in the simile of the bridegroom (2^{19}), in the question concerning the Davidic sonship of the Messiah (12^{35} seq.), perhaps in the claim to forgive sin (2^{10}); again, on the part of the disciples in their confession (8^{29}), and in the petition of the sons of the Zebedee (10^{37});

No doubt there are some striking phrases occurring in our present Mark which are lacking from this series Other Possible of broken extracts from it. But the Elements in the same figure is here outlined. And most Primitive Mark of even these striking phrases are restored if we will attend also to passages common to Mark and one of the other evangelists, of which it would be hard to deny that they may therefore have had a place in the primitive document underlying all three. Thus, for example, in the fragments peculiar to Matthew and Mark, while Jesus is not addressed as ' Lord ' except by the Syro-Phœnician woman (Mk 7^{28}, Mt 15^{27}), and is not spoken of at all by the general Messianic designation, ' the Christ,' He yet does call Himself both the ' Son of Man,' and undefinedly, ' the Son.' As ' Son of Man,' he asserts, He " came " to execute a great mission, not to be ministered unto but to minister, and to give His life a ransom for many (Mk 10^{45}, Mt 20^{28}), and therefore has a prospect of suffering before Him (Mk 9^{12}, Mt 17^{12}, Mk 14^{41},

finally on the part of our Lord, the disciples, and the people, in the story of the entry into Jerusalem (11^{1} seq.). However, the expression ' Son of God ' never occurs except in the voice at the Baptism (1^{11}), and in the utterance of 13^{32}, though elsewhere in the Gospel it forms the proper formula for profession of belief (1^{1} 3^{11} 5^{7} 9^{7} 14^{61} 15^{39}); and the word ' Christ ' only occurs in the Confession of the Twelve (8^{29}), and in the theological dispute of 12^{25}, though it likewise is often employed elsewhere by the evangelist ($1^{1,34}$ 13^{21} 14^{61} 15^{32}). The term ' Son of Man ' is found in $2^{10,28}$ $10^{33,45}$, as also in $14^{21,41,62}$, if indeed these parts of the story of the Passion belong to the group of which we are speaking; while in the sections due to the evangelist it occurs only in $9^{9,12,31}$ after the pattern of 8^{31} and 10^{33}." One cannot help admiring the skill with which the attention of the reader is kept from dwelling on the fact that all the significant, high designations of Jesus are left in the fragment of the Gospel which is allowed to be primitive; but the fact cannot even so be totally obscured.

Mt 26⁴⁵), but dies only to rise again (Mk 9⁹, Mt 17⁹). As 'Son' He represents Himself as of superangelic dignity, and therefore above all creatures, standing next to God Himself (Mk 13³², Mt 24³⁶). In the passages peculiar to Mark and Luke, we find Him testified to as the Messiah by the demons, who, although they know His earthly origin ('Jesus of Nazareth'), profess to know Him also to be the 'Holy One of God' (Mk 1²⁴, Lk 4³⁴) and the 'Son of the Most High God' (Mk 5⁷, Lk 8²⁸). Not only does He not repel these ascriptions, but He speaks of Himself as the 'Son of Man,' teaching that He is to suffer many things and be killed, but after three days to rise again (Mk 8³¹, Lk 9²²). A primitive gospel containing all this falls short in nothing of the testimony borne by our present Mark to our Lord's higher nature.

It is not neccessary for our purpose to expend effort in endeavoring to ascertain the compass most commonly attributed to the second hypothetical document supposed to underlie our Synoptics, the so-called, and let us add, very much miscalled, "Logia."[4] We may as well at once direct our eyes to its minimum contents,—the

Christology of the 'Primitive Sayings'

---

[4] The reconstruction of these so-called "Logia" by Harnack in his *Sprüche und Reden Jesu,* etc., 1907, pp. 88-102, provides one of the most convenient and accessible forms in which they may be studied, although Harnack (like Wellhausen) deprives them of the Passion story, and even eliminates the conception of the Passion from them (see to the contrary, Burkitt, *The Gospel History and its Transmission,* 1907). Their christology is minimizingly described by von Soden, *History of Early Christian Literature,* 1906, pp. 136, 137. While asserting that the claim advanced for Jesus in this document is "scarcely more than any master might make on his disciples," von Soden is yet constrained to allow that "a higher self-consciousness may be clearly traced in the background." "The word 'Christ,'" he con-

passages peculiar to Matthew and Luke,—even in the meager compass of which we shall find evidence enough that this document, whatever its extent, presented Jesus as a Divine Being. That He was the Messiah He is represented as Himself indicating by pointing to His works (Mt 11^3, Lk 7^{19}), which, He intimates, evidently on the basis of Isaiah 61^1, accredit Him as the 'One who was to Come.' It is apparently as Messiah that He is addressed as 'Lord' (Mt 8^8, Lk 7^6), and He is represented as adverting to this customary mode of addressing Him in order to declare that it is not merely verbal recognition of His authority but actual obedience to His words alone which will constitute a claim upon His mercy (Mt 7^{21}, Lk 6^{46})—where, it is to be noted, He presents Himself as 'Lord' of the destinies of men, by their relations to whom men stand or fall. He is accordingly appropriately spoken to by Satan as 'Son of God' (Mt $4^{3,6}$, Lk $4^{3,9}$); and currently calls Himself by the great Danielic title of 'Son of Man.' He explains that this 'Son of Man' has come in the fashion of men, "eating and drinking" (Mt 11^{19}, Lk 7^{34}), and living a hard life (Mt 8^{20}, Lk 9^{58})—ending in betrayal and death (Mt 26^{48}, Lk 22^{47}); but after death is to rise again (Mt 12^{40}, Lk 11^{30}). But even while on earth He asserts for Himself an unbroken communion with God, or rather a continuous intercommunion of Himself as 'Son' with

tinues, "which occurs twelve times elsewhere in St. Luke, together with the expression 'Son of God,' which elsewhere occurs nine times, does not occur in our compilation of sayings. Messianic tone and coloring, however, declare themselves in the sayings (17^{23} seq., 26 10^{22}), and in the parable (12^{35} seq.), and, besides, the expression 'Son of Man.'" How inadequate this is as a representation of the teaching of the material common to Matthew and Luke concerning our Lord's self-description, the text will show.

the ' Father ' (Mt 11²⁷, Lk 10²²) ; knowing the Father as perfectly as He is known by the Father, and therefore able to make known the Father as His sole adequate revelation to men. In this great passage we have what must be considered the culminating assertion on our Lord's part of His essential deity.

It is clear, then, that the documents which, even in the view of the most unreasonable criticism, are sup-

Resort to 'Historical Criticism' posed to underlie the structure of our present Synoptics are freighted with the same teaching which these Gospels themselves embody as to the person of our Lord. Literary criticism cannot penetrate to any stratum of belief more primitive than this. We may sink our trial shafts down through the soil of the Gospel tradition at any point we please; it is only conformable strata that we pierce. So far as the tradition goes, it gives consentient testimony to an aboriginal faith in the deity of the founder of the religion of Christianity. In these circumstances it is not strange that another mode of analysis is attempted. Literary criticism is abandoned for historical criticism : and we are invited to distinguish in our Gospels not between later and older documentary strata, but between narrative and reportorial elements. We do not wish to know, it is said, what Matthew, Mark or Luke thought, or what was thought by those represented by them or by any predecessor of theirs—the Christian community to wit, even the. primitive Christian community. What we wish to know is what Jesus Himself thought. We appeal from the representation of Jesus given by His followers to the self-testimony of Jesus. Let us have Jesus' own conception of Himself.

It is not necessary to spend much time upon this demand in its simplest form, that, namely, which would merely separate out from the Synoptic Gospels as they stand the words attributed to Jesus, and seek to ascertain from them Jesus' witness to the nature of His person and the quality of His dignity. It must have been observed as we ran over the designations applied to our Lord in the Gospels and sought to estimate their significance, that the most remarkable of them are drawn from the words of Jesus. The fact is too patent and striking to have failed to attract attention: the higher teaching of the Gospels as to our Lord's person is embodied very especially in His own words. It is on His lips, for example, that the term 'Lord' appears when employed in its loftiest connections. It is He alone who applies to Himself the significant title of 'Son of Man,' the vehicle of the most constant claim for Him of a superhuman nature. It is He alone who, speaking out of His own consciousness, proclaims Himself superior to those highest of God's creatures, the angels (Mk 13^{32}, Mt 24^{35}): represents Himself as living in continuous and perfect intercommunion with the Father, knowing Him even as He is known by Him and acting as the sole adequate mediator alike of the knowledge of God and of the grace of God to men (Mt 11^{27}, Lk 10^{22}): and in His great closing utterance places Himself, along with the Father and Holy Spirit and equally with them, even in the awful precincts of the Divine Name itself (Mt 28^{19}). To separate between the narrative and reportorial elements of the Gospels, therefore, only brings home to us with peculiar poignancy the testimony they bear to the deity

The Reportorial Element in the Gospels

of our Lord, resting this testimony, as they do, on the firm basis of our Lord's own self-testimony—a self-testimony in which He at times lays bare to us the innermost depths of His divine self-consciousness.

There can be no question of the deity of our Lord, therefore, if we can trust the report which the evangelists give of His words. It is at this point, however, Trustworthiness that the assault on the validity of their of the Evangel- representation is made. We are not ical Report asked to distinguish between what the evangelists say in their own person and what they say in the person of Jesus. We are asked to distinguish between what is really theirs in their account of the life and teaching of Jesus and what is really Jesus' own transcribed into their narratives. It is suggested that they may have, or rather that they must have, and actually have, attributed much to Jesus which He never said; that they have read back their own ideas into His teaching, and unconsciously—or more or less consciously—placed on His lips what was in point of fact the dogmatic elaborations of the later Christian community. And it is demanded that we, therefore, subject the whole body of the evangelic representation of Jesus' teaching to the most searchingly critical scrutiny with a view to sifting out from it what may really be depended upon as Jesus' own. Thus only, we are told, will it be possible to find firm footing. Faith is the foe of fact: and in the enthusiasm of their devotion to Jesus it was inevitable that His followers should clothe Him in their thought of Him with attributes which He did not possess and never dreamed of claiming: and it was equally inevitable that they should imagine that He must have claimed them and have ended by representing Him as claiming them. We shall never know the truth about Jesus, therefore, we are told, until we penetrate behind the Jesus of the evangelists to the Jesus that really was.

The situation might not have been so bad, we are told, if the evangelists had been merely transmitters

Faith the Foe of Fact

of a tradition, like, say, the rabbinical schools. But there is an essential difference between the two cases, a difference which casts us with respect to the evangelic tradition into grave doubt. This difference is due to the unfortunate fact that the evangelists themselves believed in Jesus and loved Him. " In our case," therefore, we are told,[5] " we have not merely pupils transmitting the teaching of their master, but a believing community speaking of one they honor as the exalted Lord. Even the oldest Gospel is written from the standpoint of faith; already for Mark Jesus is not only the Messiah of the Jewish people, but the miraculous eternal Son of God whose glory shone in the world."[6] " And it has been rightly emphasized that in this regard our three first Gospels are distinguished from the fourth only in degree. Must there not, then, have taken place here a complete repainting from the standpoint of faith? For there is a certain propriety in saying that faith is the enemy of history. Where we believe and honor, we no longer see objectively." Accordingly we are told that the deepest longing of men's hearts to-day is to rediscover the real Jesus.

---

[5] By Bousset, *Was wissen wir von Jesus?* 1904, pp. 54 *seq.*

[6] Cf. p. 57 : " For the belief of the community, which is shared already by the oldest evangelist, Jesus is the miraculous Son of God, on whom men believe, whom men put wholly by God's side." And cf. Wrede, *Das Messiasgeheimnis in den Evangelien,* 1901, *passim.*

" There is a great desire to know Him at first hand,"
it is said,[7] " not merely through the loving vision of
His earliest interpreters, but as He looked and spoke
and worked and thought." Which is as much as to say
that the vision the evangelists give us of Jesus is
not conformable to the reality, but has been distorted
by their love. If we wish the bald truth about Him
and His claims we must go behind them.

This point of view, it will be observed, is definite
enough. The evangelists are not to be trusted in the
Primary
Canon of
Criticism report they give of the teaching of
Jesus about Himself. But embarrassing
questions remain. Above all, these embarrassing questions: Why should we not trust the
evangelists' report of Jesus' teaching as to His own
nature? And, distrusting them, how are we to get behind their report? That the evangelists believed in
Jesus and loved Him does not seem in itself an absolutely compelling reason why we should distrust their
report of His teaching concerning His own nature.
Suppose we assume for the moment that Jesus did
assert for Himself superhuman dignity. How does it
throw doubt upon that fact that those who report it
to us were led—possibly by overwhelming evidence of
its truth—to believe that in so asserting He spoke truly?
Are we to lay it down as the primary canon of criticism
that no sympathetic report of a master's teaching is
trustworthy; that only inimical reporters are credible
reporters?

Absurd as it seems, this is the actual canon of critical
reconstruction upon which our would-be guides, in re-

[7] *Jesus the Prophet,* by Charles S. MacFarland, Ph.D., 1905; introduction by Prof. Frank K. Sanders.

covering from the obscuring hands of the evangelists the real Jesus, would have us proceed. It has found somewhat notorious enunciation in Professor Schmiedel's article " Gospels " in the *Encyclopædia Biblica*.[8] But it is so far from being peculiar to Professor Schmiedel that it is the common foundation stone upon which the whole school of criticism with which we are now concerned builds its attempt to penetrate behind the evangelical narratives and to recover from these an earlier and therefore presumably truer picture of Jesus and His claims.[9] Under its guidance we are set to searching diligently through the evangelical narratives (as if for hid treasures) for sentences or fragments of sentences in the reported words of Jesus, which appear, or may be made to appear, out of harmony with the high claims He is consentiently and constantly reported by all the evangelists to have made for Himself: and on these few broken passages, torn from their

[8] P. 1872: "When a profane historian finds before him a historical document which testifies to the worship of a hero unknown to other sources, he attaches first and foremost importance to those features which cannot be deduced merely from the fact of this worship, and he does so on the simple and sufficient ground that they would not be found in this source unless the author had met with them as the fixed data of tradition. The same fundamental principle may safely be applied in the case of the Gospels, for they also are all of them written by worshipers of Jesus."

[9] Cf. e.g. Shailer Mathews, *The Messianic Hope in the N. T.*, 1905, p. 58: "At this point we may safely use this canon: that saying is more probably genuine which treats of Messianic matters in any other way than that which characterized apostolic belief." "The trustworthiness of sayings which do not contradict, but agree with, apostolic belief must be decided on . . . more general critical grounds." It is the same canon which Prof. N. Schmidt, *The Prophet of Nazareth*, 1905, lays down in the words (p. 235): "These sayings possess evidential value just in proportion as they contradict the notions current in the circles through which they were transmitted."

context and shredded in their own contents, is erected, as on its foundation stone, a totally new portrait of Jesus, expressing a totally new self-consciousness,—which stands related to the Jesus of the evangelists and the self-consciousness which is ascribed to Him in their account, of course, as its precise contradictory,—seeing that it is precisely on the principle of contradiction that it has been concocted.

Surely we do not need to pause to point out that the procedure we are here invited to adopt is a prescription for historical investigation which must always issue in reversing the portraiture of the historical characters to the records of whose lives it is applied. The result of its universal application would be, so to speak, the writing of all history backwards and the adornment of its annals with a series of portraits which would have this only to recommend them, that they represent every historical character as the exact contrast to what each was thought to be by all who knew and esteemed him. The absurdity and wrong of invoking such a canon in the case of our Synoptic Gospels are peculiarly flagrant, inasmuch as these Gospels, as we have seen, and as these very critics are frank to allow, are themselves of very early date and rest on a documentary basis, quite at one with them in the portrait they draw of Jesus, which is naturally earlier than themselves; and therefore reflect the universal conviction of the first generation of Christians. It is really impossible to doubt that they bring to us the aboriginal testimony of the primitive Church—a Church which included in its membership a considerable number of actual eye-witnesses of Jesus and ear-witnesses of His teaching, —as to His claims and personality.

The absolute unanimity of that Church in its view of Jesus is very strikingly illustrated by the difficulty of

Futility of This Canon

discovering passages imbedded in our Gospels which can be used as a foundation for the opposing portraiture of Jesus which the critics would fain draw. Professor Schmiedel can by the utmost sharpness of inquisition find only five, which by applying more exegetical pressure he can increase only to nine. The groundlessness of this assault on the trustworthiness of the portrait of Jesus presented in our Synoptics may fairly be said, therefore, to be matched by its resultlessness. Material cannot be gathered from our Gospels out of which a naturalistic Christ can be created. The method of criticism adopted being purely subjective, moreover, the assumed results naturally vary endlessly. We feel a certain sympathy, therefore, with the position assumed by those writers who frankly admit that, the evangelical portraiture of Jesus being distrusted, the real Jesus is hopelessly lost to our sight. Strive as we may, we are told, we cannot penetrate behind the Jesus of our first informants—the writers of the New Testament, upon whose palette had already been mingled, nevertheless, colors derived from Jewish prophecy, Rabbinic teaching, Oriental gnosis and Christian philosophy. " All that can be determined with certainty from these writings," it is declared, " is that conception of Christ which was the object of faith of the early Christian communities and their teachers ": the real Jesus is hopelessly hidden under the incrustations with which faith has enveloped it.[10] Nor does there seem to be

[10] So, Pfleiderer, *The Early Christian Conception of Christ,* E. T., 1905.

lacking a certain logical force in the reasoning of bolder souls[11] who drive the inference one step further and ask what need there is of assuming a real Jesus at all. The "real Jesus" whom the critics invent certainly was not the author of the Christianity that exists. If the Christianity that actually exists in the world can get along without the Jesus which alone would account for it, why, they argue, must there be assumed behind it a Jesus which will not account for it; of whom this only may be said,—that He is a useless figure, the assumption of whom is so far from accounting for that great religious movement which we call Christianity, that it is certain that the movement did not arise in Him and did not derive its fundamental convictions from Him? Let us, then, assume, they say, that there never was any such person as Jesus at all, and the picture drawn of Him in the evangelists is pure myth.

It is interesting—almost amusing—to observe our disintegrating critics over against this more radical em-

Can We Save Any Jesus at All? ployment of their own methods, suddenly taking up the *rôle* of "apologists"[12] and writing so in the spirit and with the adoption of so many of the exact arguments of the "apologists," whom they have been wont to despise, as to lead the reader to exclaim, "Are these, too, among the prophets?" It is all, however, in vain. The fatal subjectivity which underlies their own view reasserts itself in the end and leaves them without adequate defense against extremists, simply because whether one

[11] E.g. Albert Kalthoff, *Das Christus-Problem*, and *Die Entstehung des Christentums*, 1904; and William Benjamin Smith, *New Testament Criticism, Status and Drift of*, Art. in the "Encyclopædia Americana," and, more fully, *Der vorchristliche Jesus*, etc., 1906.

[12] E.g. Bousset, *Was wissen wir von Jesus?* 1904.

stops with them or goes on with the others is not a matter of principle, but only of temperament. It is just as impossible that Christianity can have sprung from the Jesus which these critics give us, as that it should have sprung up without any Jesus behind it at all, as the radicals assert. There is just as little reason in a sound historical criticism to discover the Jesus of Bousset behind the Jesus of the evangelists, as there is for discovering with Kalthoff that there was no real Jesus at all behind the Jesus of the evangelists. The plain fact is that the evangelists give us the primitive Jesus, behind which there is none other; and the attempt to set the Jesus they give us aside in favor of an assumed more primitive Jesus can mean nothing but the confounding of all historical sequences. The real impulse for the whole assault upon the trustworthiness of the portrait of Jesus drawn in the Gospels lies not in the region of historical investigation but in that of dogmatic prejudice,—or to be more specific, of naturalistic preconception. The moving spring of the critical reconstruction is the determination to have a " natural " as over against the " supernatural " Jesus of the evangelists. There must be a more primitive Jesus than the evangelists'—this is the actual movement of thought—because their Jesus is already a supernatural Jesus,—" a miraculous Son of God, in whom men believe, whom men elevate to a place by the side of God."[13] The plain fact, however, is that this supernatural Jesus is the only Jesus historically witnessed to us; the only Jesus historically discoverable by us; the only Jesus historically tolerable. We can rid ourselves of Him only by doing violence to the whole historical testimony and to the whole historical development as

[13] Bousset, *as cited,* p. 57.

well. Not only is there no other Jesus witnessed in the documents, but no other Jesus can have formed the starting point of the great movement which, springing from Him, has conquered to itself the civilized world.

What must absorb our attention immediately, however, is the difficulty that is found even on these naturalistic presuppositions in eliminating from the portrait of Jesus drawn in the Gospels all supernatural traits and all claims on His own part to a supernatural personality. To be successful here, there is required such a policy of thoroughgoing rejection as Kalthoff's and W. B. Smith's, who sweep away the whole figure of Jesus itself as a myth, or at least as Wrede's, who would have us believe that Jesus made no claim to even Messianic dignity, so that the entire picture drawn of His career in our Gospels is false; or else such a policy of "*ignoramus*" as Pfleiderer's who declines to form any picture of the real Jesus at all. The majority of naturalistic critics recoil, however, from these extremes with an energy which seems to betray at least a semi-consciousness that there may haply be found in them the *reductio ad absurdum* of their whole method. Their position is certainly a hard one between these extremes from which they recoil and the portrait of the evangelists toward which their recoil brings them back. In endeavoring to avoid conclusions recognized by them as intolerable they are compelled to give recognition to facts as to the claims of the real Jesus which are fatal to their whole elaborately argued position.

They are forced, for example, to allow that Jesus did announce Himself as the Messiah.[14] And they are

[14] Bousset, *Jesus*, 168, argues: "We have certain knowledge that the belief existed from the very beginning among the Christian commu-

forced to admit that, in developing His Messianic conception, He was wont to call Himself 'the

Jesus Certainly Claimed to be Messiah and 'Son of Man' Son of Man.' [15]   It makes very entertaining reading to observe Bousset, for example, grudgingly conceding the fact, and then nervously endeavoring to save himself from the consequences of the damaging acknowledgment. He cannot deny that this title "represents a perfectly definite conception of the Messiah," a conception which sees in the Messiah a supernatural figure who comes down from heaven for a mission, and who is clothed with no less a function than that of the Judge of the world: and he cannot deny that Jesus represents Himself as

nity that Jesus was the Messiah, and, arguing backwards, we can assert that the rise of such a belief would be absolutely inexplicable if Jesus had not declared to His disciples in His life-time that He was Messiah." It is consequently "now definitely assured, in spite of continual discussions in which it is still frequently disputed," "that Jesus considered Himself to be the Messiah of His people" (107). Cf. Volkmar Fritzsche, *Das Berufsbewusstsein Jesu,* 13, and Schwartzkopff there quoted. For a *précis* of the literature in which it is altogether denied that Jesus claimed to be the Messiah, see Holtzmann *N. T. Theologie,* I. 280, note. Of course it is not disputable that it was a "self-evident assumption" on the part of the Synoptists that He was the Messiah (Bousset, 167): for the later community—the community which gave birth to the evangelical narratives—says Bousset (171), "the Messiahship of Jesus was the surest, most self-evident, and most precious thing about Him." Cf. Dalman, *Words,* 306.

[15] Professor N. Schmidt may be taken as the type of those extremists who find it more convenient just to deny that Jesus used this title of Himself at all: "Jesus never used this title concerning Himself either to claim Messiahship in any sense, or to hint that He was 'a mere man' or 'the true man'; but in some pregnant utterances used it in reference to man in general, his duties, rights and privileges" (*The Prophet of Nazareth,* p. vii.). Mt 8[20] according to him means that the life of man is "full of danger and uncertainty," whereas a beast is "not deprived of his home and hearth by his convictions" (p. 111)!

'the Son of Man.' But he wishes us to believe that
Jesus did this only under great pressure, as the close
of His life drew near and evil fate closed about Him,
—seizing and clinging to the Danielic prophecy to com-
fort Himself in the face of the fast-coming disaster.
And He assures us that Jesus did not adopt the title
even then in its full content "including the idea of
preëxistence and His own judgeship of the world."
"To Him," he tells us, "the idea of the Son of Man
meant only one thing,—His return in glory."[16] "He
did not thereby place Himself on a level with God.
Above all, He did not lay claim to the judgeship of
the world, although that conception was, strictly speaking, included in that of the Son of Man." "It is true,"
he adds, "in the narrative of our Gospels, the opposite
seems to be the case. But it is inconceivable   .   .   .
that Jesus   .   .   .   should have arrogated to Himself
the judgeship of the world in place of God. This is
an instance of the faith of the community working upon
the tradition.   .   .   .   As the tradition was handed
down by the community, Jesus was gradually removed
from the position of a simple witness for His followers
before God's tribunal to that of the actual judgeship
of the world."[17] That is to say, in brief, Bousset does
not like the consequences of allowing that Jesus applied
to Himself the title of 'Son of Man,' and, finding
Himself unable nevertheless to deny that He did apply

[16] *Jesus,* p. 194. Cf. among naturalistic writers who admit that Jesus
used the title 'Son of Man' in connection with promises of returning
in glory: Weisse, *Evang. Geschichte* i. 593 *seq.*: Keim, *Jesus of Naz.,*
III. 85-87; Wittichen, *Idee des Reiches Gottes,* 166-172; Vernes, *Idées
Mess.,* 229-233, and note on 243; Schenkel, *Character of Jesus,* 145;
Zeller, *Strauss und Renan,* 88-91. These are brought together by Stanton, p. 249, note 1.

[17] P. 203-5.

this title to Himself, contents himself simply with denying the consequences,—Jesus could not have meant it.
Those who prefer to determine historical facts by the
testimony of credible witnesses, rather than by the witness of Bousset's consciousness as to what were fitting,
will probably think otherwise.[18]

Similarly it cannot be even plausibly denied that
Jesus spoke the remarkable words attributed to Him
in which He acknowledges His ig-
norance of the time of His promised
second coming. The critics are indeed
in a great quandary as to this passage. It is not the
kind of a passage they can assume the evangelists
to have invented. On their fundamental canon that
statements which are, or seem to be, in conflict with the
evangelists' hero-worship of Jesus, bear the inerad-
icable stamp of genuineness, they are bound to attribute
these words of Jesus. For was not Jesus to the evangelists the omniscient Son of God? And how could they
put on His lips a confession of ignorance of so simple
a matter as the time of His return? In point of fact,
accordingly, this passage is found among the nine " absolutely credible " passages which Schmiedel declares
" the foundation pillars for a truly scientific life of
Jesus,"[19] and is pronounced by him to have been " most

Jesus Certainly Claimed to be Superangelic

---

[18] Cf. Shailer Mathews, *The Messianic Hope in the N. T.*, p. 103:
" The phrase is represented as being used by Jesus to refer to Himself
as Judge (Mk 8[38] 14[62]). To argue that these passages are Christian
comments added to the words of Jesus is certainly to base conclusions
on no clear evidence." Nor is it easy to be rid of Jesus' claim to be
judge of the world; says Dalman (*Words*, 314), justly: " The right
to judge the world was assumed by Jesus when He forgave sins,"—and
the assertion of a function of forgiveness by Jesus is pervasive.

[19] *Encyc. Biblica*, 1881; *ibid.*, 1888, cf. 1872 and Dr. E. A. Abbott,
1773. Shailer Mathews (*Messianic Hope in the N. T.*) on the other

certainly " spoken by Jesus. Yet in this passage Jesus proclaims Himself a being superior to angels, separated, that is, from the entire category of creaturely existences, and assimilated to the divine: " No one, not even the angels in heaven, nor yet the Son, but God only."

And if it must be allowed that the " real Jesus " currently called Himself ' the Son of Man,' no doubt with full consciousness of its implications, and asserted for Himself super-angelic dignity, it would seem mere hypercriticism which would deny to Him the great assertion of intercommunion with the Father made in Mt 11[27], Lk 10[22]. On the general critical canon that sayings reported by both Matthew and Luke " are to be used with confidence as representing the thought of Jesus,"[20] this passage must be accepted as an authoritative utterance of His.[21] But, in that case, the " real Jesus " must be credited with conceiving His relation to the Father less as that of a servant than as that of a fellow: as the ' Son ' He moves in the sphere of the divine life. And, this once allowed, what reason re-

And God

hand, thinks that " it must be admitted that this verse sounds much like a gloss or editorial comment "; and Dalman (*Words*), p. 194, that " the ending, ' nor the Son, but the Father only,' should be regarded as an accretion." Of course writers like Martineau (*Seat of Authority in Religion,* 590), and N. Schmidt (*The Prophet of Nazareth,* 147, 231) take fright at the language, which seems to them redolent of a later time; and thereby bear their unwilling witness to the implications of the passage. In refutation of Dalman see Sanday, Hastings' *B. D., IV.* 573, whose general remarks are quite convincing.

[20] Cf. Shailer Mathews, p. 58. This is but to say—with the whole body of critics—that passages found in both Matthew and Luke belong to what Weiss calls " the Apostolic source," which contains the oldest (and most trustworthy) record of words of Jesus.

[21] A strong defense of the genuineness of the passage is made by

mains for denying to Him the culminating expression
of His divine self-consciousness, the sublime utterance
in which He gives the Son a share in the Divine Name
itself (Mt 28[19]) ? Of course it is denied to Him by
the critics of the school we have been considering. But
the denial is in the circumstances purely arbitrary and
creates a situation which leaves an important historical
sequence unaccounted for. It is undeniable, for example, that the trinitarian mode of speech here illustrated was current in the Church from its earliest origin:
it already appears in Paul's Epistles, for example,—
especially, as a familiar and well-understood form of
speech, in 2 Cor 13[14], which was written not more than
twenty-five years after our Lord's death and antedates
all our Gospels. This current form of speech among
Christians of the first age finds its complete account if
the usage were rooted in utterances of our Lord, but
it hangs inexplicably in the air without some such supposition. The occurrence of the passage in Mt 28[19]
in the records of our Lord's teaching is thus too closely

Volkmar Fritzsche, *Das Berufsbewust. Jesu,* pp. 32 *seq.* Harnack (*Das
Wesen des Christentums,* p. 81) pronounces it authentic, and treats it
as the most important and characteristic of the words of Jesus. Even
Schmiedel does not venture to reject it: he only, by appealing to the
"Western" text, attempts to reduce its meaning. The Abbé Loisy,
however, (*l'Evangile et l'Eglise,* 45; *Autour un petit Livre,* 130), casts
it out; but on the express ground that the declaration is too high an
one for Jesus to have made; which is at least an admission that the
words involve a claim to ontological Sonship. Prof. N. Schmidt, *The
Prophet of Nazareth,* p. 152, considers "such an utterance out of harmony with the admittedly genuine sayings of Jesus," and even "to
cast an undeserved reflection upon His character." For "how can the
gentle Teacher . . . be supposed to have imagined Himself possessed of all knowledge and regarded all other men as ignorant of
God?" Certainly this is an unanswerable query if Jesus is to be conceived as thinking of Himself only as a man among other men: the

linked to a historical situation to permit its displacement on the purely subjective grounds on which alone its genuineness can be assailed.[22]

It would seem to be reasonably clear, therefore, that the attempt to penetrate behind the Synoptic tradition with a view to discovering a "real Jesus," differing from the Synoptic Jesus as the natural differs from the supernatural, has failed. The purely subjective grounds on which such an attempt must proceed in order to reach its goal, lays it open to the exaggeration which would eliminate the figure of Jesus from history altogether. From this exaggeration, it can save itself only by imposing arbitrary limitations upon the applica-

The Synoptic Jesus the Real Jesus

saying is, however, in point of fact, an express claim to be something very different from this. "The occurrence of this verse in both Matthew and Luke," says W. C. Allen, *in loc.*, "even if the two Evangelists borrow from a single source, proves that this saying reaches back to an early stage of the Gospel tradition. If, as is probable, the two writers drew from different sources, this tradition was wide-spread. If we add the fact that a similar use of the Son-the Father occurs in Mk 13[32], this usage as a traditional saying of Christ is as strongly supported as any saying in the Gospels." Cf. Plummer on Luke's report of the saying, quoted above (p. 119).

22 Schmiedel, *Encyc. Bib.*, 1876, gives a summary of the reasons relied on to exclude the passage. The history of its criticism is briefly sketched by Holtzmann, *N. T. Theologie*, ed. 1, I. 378-379, note. F. C. Conybeare alone has sought to put a documentary basis under the rejection: see esp. his articles in Preuschen's *Zeitschrift für N. T. Wissenschaft*, etc., 1901, Heft 4, pp. 175-78, and *Hibbert Journal*, I. 1. The findings of Conybeare have been taken up and repeated with extraordinary avidity by nearly the whole critical school. Only Harnack holds back: "No positive proofs can be adduced for regarding 28[19 seq.] as an interpolation" (*Expansion of Christianity*, E. T., I. 44-45, note). E. Riggenbach has sufficiently answered Conybeare—who indeed required no answer—(Schlatter and Cremer's *Beiträge zur Förderung christlicher Theologie*, 1903. VII.; also 1906, X.).; Men like Harnack, while vindicating the genuineness of the passage in Matthew, and supposing it

tion of its subjective principle, which render it nugatory for the end for which it is invoked. In any event no reasonable grounds can be assigned for discarding the portrait of Jesus drawn by the Synoptists, or for depriving Him of the great sayings by which He is represented by them as testifying to His essential deity. It is impossible to deny on any reasonable grounds that Jesus called Himself the ' Son of Man ' by predilection, and it is purely arbitrary to suppose that in doing so He did not mean what the term implies. It is equally impossible to deny that He represented Himself under the denomination of ' Son ' as of superangelic dignity, and as standing in a relation of intimate continuous intercourse with God the Father. This prepares the way for allowing farther that He represented Himself as sharer with the Father in the divine Name itself, and makes nugatory all subjective objection to it. The strictest scrutiny of the Synoptic record of Jesus' teaching, in other words, renders an appeal from their representation to Jesus' own teaching meaningless. It is not only the Synoptists who testify that Jesus is a divine person, but the Jesus they report: it is not only the Jesus as reported by them who bears this witness to Himself, but the only Jesus of history.

pre-Pauline in origin (*op. cit.* p. 111), yet deny it to Jesus. For reasons why it must be vindicated to Jesus see Hort. on 1 P 1^{1-12}; Sanday *Criticism of the Fourth Gospel*, 218, 219; Hastings' *B. D.*, II. 213-14, IV. 573, 574; P. H. Chase, *The Lord's Command to Baptize,* in the *Journal of Theological Studies,* July, 1905. Cf. also Bruce, *The Kingdom of God,* 1889, p. 258: "With reference to the trinity of the Baptismal formula, it is to be observed that it simply sums up in brief compass the teaching of Jesus"; and especially Zahn on Mt 28^{18-20} (p. 711, note 7): "The text of verses 18-20 is transmitted with certainty in all essential elements. With reference to the almost stereotyped abbreviation which recurs in Eusebius (for example *Demonstr.*

On the basis of the Synoptic record, in other words, we can be fully assured that Jesus not only was believed to have taught that He was a divine person, but actually did so teach.[23]

Evang., III. 6, 32, πορευθέντες μαθητεύσατε πάντα τὰ ἔθνη ἐν τῷ ὀνόματί μου, διδάσκοντες κτλ.), in which Conybeare, *Ztschr. für N. T. Wiss,* 1901, p. 175 *seq.* supposes that he has discovered the original text, cf. E. Riggenbach, *Der Trinit. Tanfbefehl,* 1903 (Schlatter-Cremer, *Beitr.* VII. 1), by whom the matter is set at rest (erledigt). From Eus. *Epist. ad Cæsar.* (Socr. *h. e.* I. 8) ; *c. Marc.* I. 1; *Hist. Eccl.,* III. 5, and other passages, it may be seen that Eusebius recognized the received text as that which had been transmitted to him too, and as that which alone could be employed in dogmatic discussion."

[23] Cf. Stanton, *Jewish and Christian Messiah,* p. 252: "His own express language claimed the title [of Messiah] in a sense not one whit less supernatural and glorious than that in which it was afterwards understood." So p. 390: "I have endeavored to show that Jesus must have claimed to be the Christ in a sense involving His deity." Cf. pp. 154, 155.

THE DESIGNATIONS OF OUR LORD IN JOHN AND THEIR SIGNIFICANCE

It may certainly be said that, on this showing, little is left by the Synoptists to John, in the way of ascrib-

Same Christology in Synoptics and John

ing essential deity to Jesus. This is true enough. Those who are familiar with the recent literature of the subject will not need to be told that the contradiction which used to be instituted between the Synoptists and John in this matter tends of late to be abandoned. Not only does Dr. Sanday, for example, speak of the teaching of John as only " a series of variations upon the one theme which has its classical expression " in the culminating christological passage of the Synoptists,[1] and remark that it is in Matthew rather than in John that the " only approach to a formulation of the doctrine of the Trinity " occurs in the Gospels;[2] but, as we have already seen, purely naturalistic critics like Bousset are emphatic in asserting that between the Synoptists and John, in the matter of the ascription of deity to our Lord, there exists only a difference of degree, not of kind.[3] Whatever else we must say of

---

[1] *Criticism of N. T.: St. Margaret's Lectures,* 1902, by a company of scholars, p. 17. Cf. his early work, *The Authorship and Historical Character of the Fourth Gospel,* 1872, p. 109, where he speaks of Mt 11²⁷ as containing "the essence of the Johannine theology," and as leaving "nothing in the Johannine christology" which it does not cover.

[2] *Criticism of the Fourth Gospel,* 1905, pp. 218-19.

[3] *Was wissen wir von Jesus?* 1904, p. 54: cf. Schmiedel, *Encyclopedia Biblica,* 1872.

Wilhelm Wrede's work on the Gospel of Mark, he has certainly rendered it impossible hereafter to appeal from the christology of John to that of the Synoptists.[4] Those who will not have a divine Christ must henceforth seek their human Jesus outside the entire evangelical literature. It is not merely his own individual opinion, then, which Professor Shailer Mathews is giving when he declares that " generally speaking, outside the references to the early Messianic career of Jesus, the Fourth Gospel contains nothing from Jesus that is new ": and that, after all, the differences between the Synoptists and John are " a question of degree rather than of sort of treatment."[5] He might have omitted, indeed, the qualification with respect to the references to the early Messianic career of Jesus. We have already seen that to the Synoptists also Jesus was consciously the Messiah from the very inception of His work; or rather, in their case, let us say, from the very beginning of His life. After all, it is the Synoptists, not John, who tell us of the proclamation of the Messianic character of this Child before His birth: and it is Luke, not John, who tells us that He was conscious of His unique relation to God as in a very special sense His Father from His earliest childhood.

The Synoptists and John certainly stand on the same level in their estimate of the person of Jesus, and differ **Differences in Method** in their presentation of it only in the relative emphasis they throw on this or the other aspect of it. In the Synoptists it is the Messiahship of Jesus which receives the primary emphasis, while His proper deity is introduced

[4] *Das Messiasgeheimnis*, etc.
[5] *The Messianic Hope in the N. T.,* p. 61.

incidentally in the course of making clear the greatness of His Messianic dignity. In John, on the contrary, it is the deity of our Lord which takes the first place, and His Messiahship is treated subsidiarily as the appropriate instrumentality through which this divine Being works in bringing life to the dead world. The differences in point of view between them receive a fair illustration in the introductions which the evangelists have severally prefixed to their narratives. Luke begins his Gospel with a short paragraph designed to establish confidence in the trustworthiness of his account of the life and work of the world's Redeemer. Mark opens his with a few words which connect Jesus' career with the subsequent expansion of the religion He founded. Matthew's commences with a reference to the previous development of the people of God, and presents the apparition of Jesus as the culminating act of the God of Israel in establishing His Kingdom in the world. All these take their starting-point in the phenomenal, and busy themselves with exhibiting the superhuman majesty of this man of God's appointment, the Christ of God. John, on the other hand, takes his readers back at once into the noumenal; and invites them to observe how this divine Being came into the world to save the world, and how His saving work was wrought in the capacity of the Messiah of Israel. It is in his prologue, therefore, that John sets forth the platform of his Gospel, which is written with the distinct purpose that its readers may be led to believe that Jesus is not merely the 'Christ,' but the 'Son of God' (20^{31}); for, that the term 'Son of God' here has a metaphys-

ical significance is scarcely open to question. In this
sense John's Gospel is the Gospel of the deity of
Christ; although it is clear that we can call it such in
contrast with the Synoptists only relatively, not absolutely. In a sense not so fully true of them, however,
it was written to manifest the deity of Christ.

In his prologue, then, John tells us with clear and
even crisp distinctness what in His essential Being he

**The Prologue
of John**

conceives the Jesus to be whose life and
teaching in the world he is to give an
account of in his Gospel. And what he
tells us is, in one word, that this Jesus is God. In telling this he makes use of a phraseology not only not
found in the other evangelists, but absolutely peculiar
to himself. The person of whom he is speaking he
identifies at the close of the prologue (1^{17}) by the
solemn compound name of 'Jesus Christ,' as Mark
and Matthew also at the opening of their Gospels had
made use of the same great name to identify the subject of their discourse; and, like them, John also makes
no further use of this full name in his Gospel (cf.,
however, 17^3). The particular designation he applies
to this person in order to describe His essential nature
is 'the Word' (ὁ λόγος). Of this 'Word' he declares that He was in the beginning, that is, that He
is of eternal subsistence; that He was eternally " with
God," that is, that He is in some high sense distinct
from God; and yet that He was eternally Himself
God, that is, that He is in some deep sense identical
with God ($1^{1,1,1}$); and nevertheless that in due time
He became flesh, that is, that He took upon Himself
a human nature (1^{14}), and so came under the observa-

tion of men and was pointed out by John the Baptist as the ' Coming One,' that is, the Messiah. In further elucidation of His essential nature, He is described as the ' only begotten from the Father ' (1^{14}) or even more poignantly as ' God only-begotten ' (1^{18}).

All this phraseology is unique in the New Testament. Nowhere else except Rev 19^{13} is Jesus Christ called the ' Word ' ($1^{1,1,1,14}$ only, with the possible exceptions of 1 Jno 1^1, Heb 4^{12}). Nowhere else, except Jno $3^{16,18}$, 1 Jno 4^9, is He called the ' Only Begotten.' Yet the general sense intended to be conveyed is perfectly clear. John wishes to declare Jesus Christ God; but not God in such a sense that there is no other God but He. Therefore he calls Him 'the Word,'—' the Word ' who is indeed God but also alongside of God, that is to say, God as Revealer: and he adds that He is ' God only begotten,' the idea conveyed by which is not derivation of essence, but uniqueness of relation, so that what is declared is that beside Jesus Christ there is no other,—He is the sole complete representation of God on earth.[6] In harmony with these designations he calls Him also in this prologue the ' Light ' ($1^{[4,5],7,8,9}$)—a designation more fully developed by our Lord Himself in His discourses. The effect of the whole is to emphasize in the strongest manner at the inception of the Gospel the divine nature of the ' Jesus Christ ' who is to be the subject of its

[6] Cf. Westcott on 1^{14} (p. 126): "The thought is centered in the personal Being of the Son, and not in His generation. Christ is the One only Son." Meyer on 1^{14} (p. 92): " Μονογ. designates the Logos as the *only* Son besides whom the Father has none." The same essential sense is conveyed by the ἀγαπητός employed in the Synoptists, possibly of God's witness to His Son at His baptism and transfiguration, and certainly in the parable of Mk 12^6, Lk 20^{13}.

narrative: and thus to set forth the aspect in which
His life and work are here to be depicted.

The key-note of the Gospel having been thus set,
however, John, so soon as the prologue is over and he
Jesus' Narrative takes up the narrative proper, leaves
Name in John these high designations behind him and
prosecutes his narrative, like the other
evangelists, by means of the simple designation 'Jesus.'
As truly to John as to the Synoptists, thus, the narrative name of our Lord is the simple ' Jesus,' which
occurs nearly 250 times. It is varied in the narrative only by a very occasional use of ' the Lord ' in
its stead (4^1 6^{23} 11^2 20^{20} $21^{[7],12}$). No other designation is employed by John himself outside the pro-
logue, except in the closing verse of the narrative proper
(20^{31}), where he declares that he has written to the end
that it might be believed that ' Jesus '—the ' Jesus ' of
whom he had so currently spoken—is ' the Christ, the
Son of God.' It is possible, no doubt, to take the
' Jesus Christ ' of 17^3 as a parenthetical insertion from
his hand, and to assign to him the paragraph 3^{16-21},
in which Jesus is spoken of as ' the Son,' God's ' only
begotten Son,' ' the only begotten Son of God.' But
these exceptions, even if they be all allowed, only
slightly break in upon the habitual usage by which John
speaks of our Lord simply as ' Jesus,' varied occasionally to ' the Lord.' They would merely bear witness
to the fact that the high reverence to the person of
our Lord manifested in the designations of the prologue continues to condition the thought of the writer
throughout, and occasionally manifests itself in the appearance of similarly lofty designations in the narrative.

As in the other evangelists, further, the simple

'Jesus' is reserved for the narrative name, and is placed on the lips of no one of the speakers who appear in its course. It is made clear, however, that it was by this name that our Lord was known to His contemporaries, and He is accordingly distinguished by those who speak of Him as "the man that is called Jesus" (9^{11}), "Jesus, the Son of Joseph" (6^{42}), "Jesus of Nazareth, the Son of Joseph" (1^{45}), or the simple "Jesus of Nazareth" ($18^{5,7}$ 19^{19}). In the reports of remarks about Him the simple demonstrative pronoun indeed is sometimes made to do duty as the only designation needed, occasionally, possibly, with an accent of contempt ($6^{42,42,52}$ $7^{15,35}$ $9^{16,[24]}$ 18^{30}), but ordinarily merely designatorily ($1^{2,30,33,34}$ 3^{26} $4^{29,42}$ $6^{14,46,[50,58]}$ $7^{25,26,31,40,41,46}$ 9^{33} $11^{37,37,47}$). And sometimes He is represented as spoken of merely as "this man" ($ἄνθρωπος$, $9^{16,24}$ 11^{47} $18^{17,29}$), or indeed simply as a man ($ἀνήρ$, 1^{30} only; $ἄνθρωπος$, 4^{29} 5^{12} $7^{46,[51]}$ [8^{40} $9^{11,16,16,24}$ 10^{33}] $11^{47,50}$ $18^{14,17,29}$ 19^{5}).

Jesus' Popular Designations

In the narrative of John our Lord is represented as customarily addressed by His followers, as He Himself informs us ($13^{13,14}$), as 'Teacher' ($διδάσκαλε$) and 'Lord' ($κύριε$), the correlatives of which are 'disciples' ($μαθηταί$ *passim*) and 'servants,' that is 'slaves' ($δοῦλοι$, 13^{16} $15^{15,20}$). The actual formula 'Teacher,' however, occurs very rarely (1^{38} 20^{16}, in 11^{28} it is an appellative, implying its use in address; cf. 3^{2} $13^{13,14}$), although its place is in part supplied by the comparatively frequent Aramaic form 'Rabbi' ($1^{38,49}$ 3^{2} 4^{31} 6^{25} 9^{2} 11^{8}; used of John the Baptist, 3^{26}), varied on one occasion to 'Rabboni' (20^{16}). The most common

Formulas of Address

honorific form of address is ' Lord ' ($4^{11,15,19,49}$ 5^7 $6^{34,68}$ $9^{36,38}$ $11^{3,12,21,27,32,34,39}$ $13^{6,9,25,36,37}$ $14^{5,8,22}$ [20^{15}] $21^{15,20,21}$; of Philip, 12^{21}). Of course, seeing that He was currently addressed as ' Teacher,' ' Lord,' He could not but be spoken of by these titles, used appellatively: ' the Teacher ' (11^{28}, cf. $13^{13,14}$ 3^2) rarely, and comparatively frequently ' the Lord ' ($20^{2,13,18,25}$ 21^7). The latter usage the evangelist himself adopts in his own person (4^1 6^{23} 11^2 20^{20} $21^{7,12}$). It is noteworthy that the title ' the Lord ' is in this Gospel confined to Jesus, never occuring of God the Father except in a very few citations from the Old Testament ($12^{13,38}$, cf. 1^{23}). It is an odd circumstance that the appellative use of ' Lord ' of Jesus occurs, however, only after His resurrection. We say this is an odd circumstance, because our Lord is represented as Himself telling us that it was applied to Him during His life ($13^{13,14}$), as indeed it could not fail to be from the currency of the corresponding formula of address with respect to Him. This circumstance must be set down, therefore, as merely an accident of the record.

From the substance of the passages in which it is employed, we get very little guidance to the significance of ' the Lord ' as thus applied to Jesus. It is only obvious that it is used with reverential recognition of His authority. Only in the great passage (20^{28}) where Thomas' doubt breaks down at the sight of his risen Master and he cries to Him, " My Lord and my God," do we catch an unmistakable suggestion of its highest meaning. That this exclamation was addressed to Christ is expressly stated: " Thomas *answered* and said *to Him*." The strong emotion with which it was

'Lord'

spoken is obvious. It is not so clear, however, what precise connotation is to be ascribed to the term 'my Lord' in it. There may be a climax in the progress from 'my Lord' to 'my God.' But it seems impossible to doubt that in this collocation 'Lord' can fall little short of 'God' in significance; else the conjunction of the two would be incongruous. Possibly both terms should be taken as asserting deity, the former with the emphasis upon the subjection, and the latter with the emphasis on the awe, due to deity. In any event in combination the two terms express as strongly as could be expressed the deity of Jesus; and the conjoint ascription is expressly accepted and commended by Jesus. It must rank, therefore, as an item of self-testimony on our Lord's part to His Godhead.[7]

The ascription to our Lord of prophetic character is, as in the other evangelists, cursorily noted (4^{19} 6^{14} $7^{40,[52]}$ 9^{17}), as is also our Lord's
Jesus,
the 'Christ'
own acceptance of the *rôle* (4^{44}). But in John, too, it is particularly the specifically Messianic titles which attract attention. The simple designation 'the Christ' is not, indeed, frequently applied directly to our Lord, although it is made clear that He announced Himself as 'the Christ,' and was accepted as such by His followers, and therefore

[7] Cf. Westcott, *in loc.*: "The words are beyond question addressed to Christ (*saith unto Him*), and cannot but be understood as a confession of belief as to His Person . . . expressed in the form of an impassioned address. . . . His sublime confession, won from doubt, closes historically the progress of faith which St. John traces. At first (ch. 1^1) the evangelist declared his own faith: at the end he shows that this faith was gained in the actual intercourse of the disciples with Christ. . . . The words which follow show that the Lord accepted the declaration of His Divinity as the true expression of faith."

raised continual questionings in the minds of outsiders whether He were indeed ' the Christ.' John the Baptist is represented as frankly confessing that he was not himself ' the Christ,' but His forerunner ($1^{20,25}$ 3^{28}), pointing not obscurely to Jesus as the Messiah. And accordingly John's disciples following their master's suggestion find in Jesus ' the Messiah ' (1^{41}), which the evangelist interprets to us as ' the Christ.' When the woman of Samaria confesses her knowledge that ' Messiah ' (who, adds the evangelist again, is called ' Christ ') is to come, our Lord majestically declares Himself to be Him ($4^{25,26}$). The speculation of the people over His Messianic character finds repeated mention (4^{29} $7^{26,27,31,41,41,42}$ 9^{22} 10^{24} 12^{34}). Jesus Himself is represented as calling out from Martha the full confession, in which the current Messianic titles are accumulated with unwonted richness: " Yea, Lord: I have believed that Thou art the Christ, the Son of God, He that cometh into the world " (11^{27}). And the evangelist himself, with some similar repetition of titles, explains that the purpose he had in view in writing his Gospel was that it might be believed that " Jesus is the Christ, the Son of God " (20^{31}), and announces as the full name of the subject of his narrative, at its inception and possibly at one point in its course where explicit identification seemed to him useful, ' Jesus Christ ' (1^{17}, cf. 17^{3}). We must not pass over this list of passages without noting that on two occasions the Aramaic term ' Messiah ' occurs (1^{41}, 4^{25}), the only instances of its occurrence in the New Testament.

Nor should we leave unnoticed the somewhat difficult question whether ' Jesus Christ ' in 17^{3} is intended as a word of our Lord's or is to be understood as a parenthetical explanation of the evangelist's. No doubt it is easiest to take it as an insertion of the evangelist's. The term 'Jesus Christ' occurs elsewhere in the Gospels only as a form of the evangelists' own, employed in the rarest manner as the most ceremonious and solemn of all direct designations of Jesus (Mt 1[18] [16[21]], Mk 1[1], Jno 1[17]); and there seems something incongruous in placing this full name on the lips of Jesus Himself, implying as it does that 'Christ' had already for Him acquired the quality of a proper name, and indeed that the compound 'Jesus Christ' had become, though of course not with the loss of its Messianic implications, yet very much itself a proper name. Nevertheless the structure of the sentence is not favorable to its assignment to the evangelist. Our Lord, speaking in these opening verses of His great prayer in the third person ("Thy Son," "Thy Son," "to Him," "to Him," verses 1 and 2), declares that eternal life consists in knowing the Father and Him whom the Father has sent (verse 3). To each of these persons, thus formally mentioned, then, a fuller designation is descriptively added: the words run: "That they may know Thee, 'the only true God,' and Him whom Thou didst send, 'Jesus Christ.'" The balance of the clauses seem to imply that they stand together, and that accordingly if 'Jesus Christ' is to be taken as an explanatory addition, so must also 'the only true God.' Dr. Westcott accordingly makes this supposition, and urges in its support that 'the only true God' is in John's manner (cf. 1 Jno 5[20]) and not in our Lord's: and that it is in no way derogatory to John's truthfulness as a reporter that he should thus insert brief explanations,

Jesus' own Use of 'Jesus Christ'

no doubt the compressed representation of much of
our Lord's teaching. On the other hand, it may be
urged that it is very easy to exaggerate the difficulty of
supposing our Lord to have used the phrase in question. He is certainly speaking of Himself: He has
just designated Himself the ' Son ' (verse 2) ; and
now designates Himself by the phrase, " Whom Thou
didst send." Why, continuing the use of the third
person, should He not solemnly designate Himself by
name, and, doing so, why should He not employ the
full ceremonious name of ' Jesus Christ '? This, of
course, would imply that ' Christ,' in its constant application to Him, had already become, in our Lord's
life-time, at least a quasi-proper name. We have seen
already, however, that this was very much the case
(Mk 9^{41}, Mt 24^5 $27^{17,22}$) ; and if Jesus could speak of
Himself as ' Christ,' there seems no compelling reason
why He should not speak of Himself as ' Jesus Christ.'
No doubt even this difficulty might be avoided by taking ' Christ ' here predicatively: " That they may
know Thee the only true God and Him whom Thou
didst send, Jesus, as the Christ." The structure of the
sentence again, however, is not favorable to this construction, which would break the parallelism of the
clauses. It seems more natural on the whole, therefore, to take ' Jesus Christ ' together as Jesus' own
self-designation of Himself; though if any feel a difficulty in assuming that He already used ' Christ ' in
this combination completely as a proper name, there
seems no reason why it should not be understood as
appellative: " Him whom Thou didst send, even Jesus
the Messiah." It must be recognized, indeed, that this
appellative connotation is in any event not entirely lost,

but throughout the whole use of the name 'Jesus Christ' in the Apostolic Church retains its force. In this passage we have only the earliest instance of the combination of the two names 'Jesus,' as the personal, and 'Christ,' as the official designation, into one quasi-proper name: and the solemn employment of it thus by Jesus gives us the point of departure for its Apostolic use from Pentecost on (Acts 2^{38} 3^6 4^{10} $8^{12,37}$, etc.) whenever great solemnity demanded the employment of this ceremonious name. This fixed Apostolic usage from the first days of the infant Church finds its best explanation in such a solemn employment of it by our Lord as we have here recorded for us by John.[8]

We ought not to pass finally from this passage without fairly facing the apparent contrast which is drawn

Jesus' Relation to God

in it between Jesus Christ as the Sent of God and the God who sent Him, described here as "the only true God," that is to say, Him to whom alone belongs the reality of the idea of God.[9] From this contrast it has often

---

[8] Luthardt on the passage; also Godet, Ebrard, and Stier (*Reden Jesu,* ed. 3, 1873, v. 397).

[9] Cf. Westcott, *in loc.:* "To regard the juxtaposition of *Thee, the only true God,* and *Him whom Thou didst send,* as in any way impairing the true divinity of Christ, by contrast with the Father, is totally to misunderstand the passage. It is really so framed as to meet the two cardinal errors as to religious truth which arise at all times, the one which finds expression in various forms of polytheism, and the one which treats that which is preparatory in revelation as final. On the one side men make for themselves objects of worship many and imperfect. On the other side they fail to recognize Christ when He comes." Accordingly the knowledge of God which is life is represented as twofold: "a knowledge of God in His sole, supreme Majesty, and a knowledge of the revelation which He has made in its final consummation in the mission of Christ." "The *contents* of the knowl-

been rashly inferred that Jesus Christ is here by implication affirmed not to be God; at least not in the
highest and truest sense. This, however, it is obvious,
would throw the declarations in this Gospel of the
relation of Christ to the Father into the greatest confusion. He who has explained that He and the Father
are One (10^{30}, cf. 5^{18}), and that to have seen Him is
to have seen the Father (14^9, cf. 8^{19} 10^{15} 14^7), and
who commended the confession of Him by His fol-
lower as " his Lord and his God " (20^{28}), can scarcely
be supposed here so pointedly to deny Himself incidentally to be the God He so frequently affirms Himself
to be. It is quite clear, indeed, that the relation of our
Lord to the Father is not represented by John, whether
in his own person or in the words he reports from the
lips of Jesus, as a perfectly simple one. Its complexity
is already apparent in the puzzling opening words of
the Gospel, where the evangelist is not content to declare Him merely to have been from eternity with God,
or merely to have been from eternity God, but unites
the two statements as if only by their union could the
whole truth be enunciated. We may legitimately say

edge," says Meyer with his usual point, " are stated with the precision
of a Confession—a summary of faith in opposition to the *polytheistic*
τ. μόνον ἀληθ. θεόν (cf. 5^{44}, Deut 6^4, 1 Cor 8^5, 1 Thess 1^9), and the
Jewish κόσμος, the latter of which rejected *Jesus* as Messiah, although
in Him there was given, notwithstanding, the very highest revelation
of the only true God." Our Lord, in other words, is not contrasting
God and Jesus Christ ontologically, but declaring that to have eternal
life we must know not only the only true God—for there is but one
true God; but also the only Mediator between God and man, Jesus
Christ—who, however, may Himself very well be, and in the teaching
of our Lord is, Himself the true God. How He can be the true God
and yet the sent of God raises the deeper questions of the Trinity and
the Covenant and the Two Natures which are alluded to in the text.

that this double way of speaking of Christ confuses us; and that we cannot fully understand it. We are not entitled to say that it is the index of confusion in the mind of the evangelist—or in the mind of the greater Speaker whose words the evangelist reports, —unless it is perfectly clear that there is no conception of the relation to the Father of Him whom the evangelist calls by predilection the ' Son of God,' even the ' Only begotten Son ' or indeed ' God only begotten,' on the supposition of which as lying in his mind the double mode of speaking of Him which we find confusing may be reduced to a real harmony. And it is undeniable that on the supposition of that conception which has come in the Church to be called the doctrine of the Trinity,—especially as supplemented by those other two conceptions known as the doctrines of the Two Natures of Christ and of the Eternal Covenant of Redemption,—as forming the background of the evangelist's varied modes of speaking of Christ, and of our Lord's own varied mode of speaking of Himself as reported by John, all appearance of disharmony between these declarations disappears. To say this, however, is to say that these great doctrines are taught by John and by our Lord as reported by Him: for surely there is no more effective way of teaching doctrines than always to speak on their presupposition, and in a manner which is confusing and apparently self-contradictory except they be presupposed. Whatever we may ourselves find of mystery in these doctrines, it is only fair to recognize that they express part of the fundamental basis of the religious thought of the Gospel of John and of the great Teacher whose words that Gospel so richly reports to us.[10]

[10] Cf. further below. on 2 Cor. 12^{14} and on 1 Jno 5^{20}.

It is only another way of calling Jesus the ' Christ '
to call Him the ' King of Israel.' This Nathanael does

'King'

when Jesus manifested to him His superhuman knowledge of his heart, ex-
claiming: " Rabbi, Thou art the Son of
God, Thou art the King of Israel " (1^{49})—where the
order of the titles used is perhaps due to the primary
impression being that of the possession of supernatural
powers, from which the Messianic office is inferred.
It is as ' King,' too, that Jesus was acclaimed as He
made His triumphal entrance into Jerusalem: " Ho-
sanna: Blessed is He that cometh in the name of the
Lord, even the King of Israel " (12^{13}, cf. 6^{15})—in
which acclamation the evangelist sees the fulfillment of
the prophecy of Zech 9^{9} of the coming of the King
of Zion riding on the ass (12^{15}). At His trial, again,
Pilate demanded of Him whether He was the ' King
of the Jews,' using the natural heathen phraseology
(18^{33}), and received a reply which, while accepting the
ascription, was directed to undeceive Pilate with respect
to the character of His Kingship: it is not of this world
(18^{37}). In that understanding of it (18^{37}) Jesus has
no hesitation in claiming the title (18^{37}). The subsequent ascription of this title to Him was mockery and
part of His humiliation (18^{39} $19^{3,[12],14,15,15,19,21}$), but at
the same time part of the testimony that He lived and
died as the Messianic King.

We should not pass finally away from the passages
in which Jesus is called ' Christ ' and ' King ' without

Accumulation
of Titles

noting somewhat more particularly the
accumulation of Messianic designations
in such passages as 20^{31}, where the
evangelist says he has written in order to create faith

in Jesus as "the Christ, the Son of God," and 1^{49}, where Nathanael declares Him "the Son of God, the King of Israel," and especially at 11^{27}, where Martha declares her faith in Him as "the Christ, the Son of God, Him that cometh into the world." The use of the term 'Son of God' in these passages as a general synonym of 'Christ,' but yet not necessarily a synonym of no higher suggestion, we reserve for later discussion. The designation 'He that cometh,' more fully defined here by the addition of "into the world," we have already met with in Matthew (11^3) and Luke ($7^{19,20}$). A clause in Jno 6^{14}, "This is of a truth the prophet that cometh into the world," may suggest that the epithet was associated in the popular mind with the Messianic interpretation of Deuteronomy 18^{15-18}: and we have seen that our Lord associated it with the great passage in Isa $61^{1\,seq.}$. In itself, however, it appears to conceive the Messiah fundamentally simply as the promised one (cf. 4^{25}), and to emphasize with reference to Him chiefly that He is to come into the world upon a mission. As such it is supported even more copiously in John than in the other evangelists by a pervasive self-testimony of Jesus laying stress on His 'coming' or His 'having been sent,' which keeps His work sharply before us as the performance of a task which had been committed to Him and constitutes John's Gospel above all the rest the Gospel of the Mission. In the repeated assertions made by our Lord that He "came" into the world, obviously with implications of voluntariness of action (cf.

Jesus' Mission $1^{[9],11,[15],[27],[30]}$ $3^{[19]}$ $4^{[25,25]}$ 5^{43} 6^{14} $7^{[27],[31]}$ 9^{39} 10^{10} $12^{[13],[15]}$ 15^{22} 18^{37}), some are explicit as to the point whence He came, which is defined as heaven ($3^{31,31}$), or the Person from whom He came, who is named as God ($7^{28 \text{ seq.}}$ $8^{14\text{-}16,42}$ 16^{28} 17^{8}); while others declare plainly the object of His coming, which is not to judge but to save the world ($12^{46,47}$). The correlation of the coming from the Father and being sent by the Father is express in passages like 17^{8}, and the sending is most copiously testified to, sometimes in the use of the simple verb πέμπω (4^{34} $5^{23,24,30,37}$ $6^{38,39,44}$ $7^{16,18,28,33}$ $8^{16,18,26,29}$ 9^{4} $12^{44,45,49}$ 13^{20} 14^{24} 15^{21} 16^{5} 20^{21}) and sometimes rather in the use of the more specific ἀποστέλλω, which emphasizes the specialness of the mission, and is most commonly cast in the aorist tense with a reference to the actual fact of the mission ($3^{17,34}$ 5^{38} $6^{29,57}$ 7^{29} 8^{42} 10^{36} 11^{42} $17^{3,8,18,21,23,25}$), though sometimes in the perfect tense with a reference to the abiding effect of it (5^{36} 20^{21}).[11] The effect of this whole body of passages is to throw over the whole of our Lord's self-testimony in this Gospel the most intense sense of His engagement upon a definite mission, for the performance of which He, sent by the Father in His love, has come forth from God, or, more locally expressed, from heaven, into the world. They supply a most compelling mass of evidence, therefore, taken in the large, to His preëxistence, and to His superhuman dignity to which His earthly career stands related as a humiliation to be accounted for only by its being also a mission of love ($12^{46,47}$).

The fact of this mission is also, no doubt, implicated in the designation 'the Holy One of God' (6^{69}), which is elicited on one occasion as a confession from His followers; that is to say, no doubt, the One whom the Father has set apart for a given work and consecrated

[11] See the long and careful note of Westcott, *John*, p. 298.

to its performance (6^{27} 10^{36}). It would also be the implication of the designation ' the Chosen One of God,' if that were the correct reading in 1^{34}, where the Baptist bears his witness really, however, to His divine Sonship. Another designation given to Him exclusively by the Baptist throws, however, a most illuminating light on the nature of His mission. " Behold," John is reported as crying, as he saw Jesus coming

The ' Lamb of God '

towards him after His baptism, " Behold the Lamb of God which taketh away the sin of the world " : and again on the next day, as he saw Him walking by, " Behold the Lamb of God " ($1^{29,36}$).[12] That this was in intention and effect a Messianic title is made clear from the sequel. Disciples of John, following Jesus on this suggestion, report to their friends that they have " found the Messiah (which is being interpreted, Christ)" (1^{41}). The source of the phrase is, of course, the fifty-third chapter of Isaiah, through which, however, a further reference is made to the whole sacrificial system, culminating in the Passover. By it the mission of Jesus is described as including an expiatory sacrifice of Himself for the salvation of the world : it, therefore, only gives point to and explains the *modus* of what is more generally declared by our Lord Himself in such

[12] Jesus is called ἀμνός 'Lamb,' Jno $1^{29,36}$, Acts 8^{32}, 1 P 1^{19} only in the N. T. The reference is to the suffering Messiah of Is 53. In Rev. ἀρνίον is used of Christ some 29 times : and though the term has changed, the 'Lamb' is the same—the Lamb that had been slain and in whose blood is salvation. The ἀρνίον is always thus the *slain* lamb. Neither ἀμνός nor ἀρνίον occurs in N. T. of anyone else but Christ—except that the plural of ἀρνίον occurs in Jno 21^{15} of Christ's followers. In Lk 10^3 ἀρήν is used. On the use of the diminutive ἀρνίον of Jesus in Scripture, see A. B. Grosart, *Expository Times*, III. 57.

a passage as 12^{47}: " I came . . . to save the world." The Messianic character of this saving work is thrown up in a clear light by the confession of the Samaritans who, having been invited to come and see whether Jesus were not the ' Christ ' (4^{29}), when they heard Jesus concluded for themselves that He was " indeed the Saviour of the world " (4^{42}).

Quite a series of designations, mostly figurative in character, expressive of the same general conception, are

Figurative Designations applied by our Lord to Himself. Thus He calls Himself the ' Light of the world ' (8^{12} 9^5 $12^{35,36,46}$, cf. $3^{19,20,21}$ $11^{9,10}$), which is explained as the " light of life " (8^{12}), even as the evangelist himself had with the same reference to " life " called Him ' the Light of Men ' ($1^{4,5,7,8,9}$). The ultimate source of this designation is no doubt to be found in such passages in the Old Testament as Is $9^{1,2}$, which is quoted and applied to Jesus by both Matthew (4^{16}) and Luke (2^{32}). Similarly He calls Himself ' the Door ' by entering through which alone can salvation be had ($10^{7,9}$); the ' Bread of God ' or ' of Life,' by eating which alone can life be obtained (6^{33}; $6^{35,41,49}$ 7^{41}); ' the Good Shepherd ' who gives His life for the sheep ($10^{11,14}$, cf. $10^{2,16}$); and without figure definitely ' the Resurrection and the Life,' believing in whom the dead shall live and the living never die (11^{25}). Perhaps to the same general circle of ideas belongs the title ' Paraclete ' (14^{16}) or ' Advocate,'[13] which seems to imply that our Lord conceives Himself under this designation as coming to the help of the

[13] Bousset, *Die Religion des Judentums,* p. 215, connects the Paraclete with " Menachem " employed in the later Judaism as a Messianic title. That would imply that we should take ' Paraclete ' in the sense of ' Comforter.'

needy. And we should probably think of the designation 'Bridegroom' (3^{29}) in the same light: but in this Gospel our Lord's application to Himself of this designation with a reference to His death, familiar to us from the Synoptics, is not recorded: there is only an employment of it of our Lord by the Baptist with no reference to the days to come when the 'Bridegroom' should be taken away.

In this Gospel, however, as in the Synoptists, the title 'Son of Man' comes forward as one of our Lord's favorite self-designations; and it is **'Son of Man'** charged here, too, with the implication of a mission, involving suffering and death but issuing in triumph. If we seek the guidance here, as we did in the case of the Synoptist use of the title, of the substance of the passages in which it occurs, we shall learn that the 'Son of Man' is no earthly being. He came down from heaven whither He shall ultimately return (6^{62}). His sojourn on earth is due to a task which He has undertaken, and to which He is "sealed" (6^{27}). This task is to give eternal life to men (6^{27}); and He accomplishes this by giving them His flesh to eat and His blood to drink, whence they obtain life in themselves (6^{53}, cf. 6^{27}). Of course this is symbolical language for dying for men. Accordingly our Lord declares that it is necessary that the 'Son of Man' be "lifted up," that whosoever believes in Him may have eternal life (3^{15}), and He announces it as His precise mission, received of the Father, to be thus "lifted up" (8^{28} 12^{34}). Nevertheless, it is only that He may enter His glory that He dies (12^{23} 13^{31}), and it is given to Him to exercise judgment also (5^{27}). Here there is open proclamation of His preëxistence, of His humiliation for an end, and of His passage through this humiliation to His primitive glory.

The culminating Messianic designation in John, however, is ' the Son of God,' which comes fully to its rights in this Gospel. This designation **'Son of God'** occurs not only, as in the other evangelists, in the more technical form of ' the Son of God ' (1^{34} 1^{49} 5^{25} 9^{35} 10^{36} $11^{4,27}$ 19^7 20^{31}), and the simple absolute ' the Son ' ($3^{17,35,36,36}$ $5^{19,19,20,21,22,23,23,26}$ 6^{40} 8^{36} 14^{13} 17^1),[14] but also in a form peculiar to John, ' the only begotten Son,' or simply ($3^{16,17}$) ' the only begotten ' (1^{14}, cf. 1^{18}, ' God only begotten '). That the title ' Son of God ' is a Messianic title is clear from such passages as 1^{49} 11^{27} 20^{31}, in which it is used side by side with ' the Christ,' ' the King of Israel,' ' the Coming One,' as their synonym, although not necessarily as a synonym of no higher connotation. There is no reason to doubt that here, too, as in the other evangelists, ' Son of God ' carries with it the implication of supernatural origin and thus designates the Messiah from a point of view which recognized that He was more than man. What is noteworthy is that in John ' the Son of God ' becomes very distinctly a self-designation of Jesus' own (5^{25} 9^{35} 10^{36} 11^4) : and

[14] Dr. Sanday, Hastings' *D. B.*, IV., 571 b., writes: "We should not form an adequate conception of the title ' Son of God ' if we should confine ourselves to the use of that title alone. It is true that it occurs in some central passages [of the N. T.], and true that in these passages the phrase is invested with great depth of meaning. But we should not adequately appreciate this depth, and still less should we understand the mass and volume of N. T. teaching on this head, if we did not directly connect with the explicit references to the ' Son of God ' that other long series of references to God as preëminently ' the Father ' and to Christ as preëminently ' the Son.' These two lines of usage are really convergent."

it is noteworthy that in connection with this designation He claims for Himself not only miraculous powers (9^{35} 11^4), but the divine prerogative of judgment (5^{25}, cf. ^{27}) ; and that He was understood, in employing it of Himself, to " make Himself equal with God," and therefore to blaspheme ($10^{33,36}$).

It is, however, in the use of the simple ' the Son ' ($3^{17,36,36}$ $5^{19,22}$ 6^{40} 8^{36}), often set in direct correlation with ' the Father ' (3^{35} $5^{19,20,21,23,23,26}$ 14^{13} 17^1), that the deepest suggestion of the filial relation in which our Lord felt Himself to stand to the Father comes out.   And these passages must be considered in conjunction with the very numerous passages in which He who never speaks of God as " our Father," putting Himself in the same category with others who would then share with Him the filial relation,[15] speaks of God either as ' the Father,' or appropriatingly as ' My Father.' There are over eighty passages of the former kind,[16] and nearly thirty of the latter.[17]   The uniqueness of the relation indicated is brought out by the connection of the simple ' the Son ' with the emphatically unique ' only begotten Son of God ' ($3^{16,17}$). Although, of course, the passage in which this is most pointedly done may be the evangelist's and not our Lord's, the phrase ' Only begotten Son ' or even the term ' Only begot-

'Son'

[15] But in 20^{17} He speaks to Mary Magdalene of " My Father and your Father, My God and your God."

[16] 3^{35} $4^{21,23,23}$ $5^{19,20,21,22,23,23,26,36,36,36,37,45}$ $6^{27,37,44,45,46,48,57,57,65}$ $8^{16,18,27,28,38,38}$ $10^{15,15,17,29,30,32,36,38,38}$ 11^{41} $12^{26,27,28,49,50}$ $13^{1,3}$ 14^6 $14^{9,10,10,11,12,13,16,24,26,28,31,31}$ $15^{9,10,16,26,26}$ $16^{3,10,15,17,23,25,26,27,27,28}$ $16^{28,32}$ $17^{1,5,11,21,24,25}$ 18^{11} $20^{17,21}$.

[17] 2^{16} $5^{17,18,43}$ $6^{32,40}$ $8^{[19],19,19,49,54}$ $10^{18,25,29,37}$ $14^{2,7,20,21,23,28}$ $15^{1,8,15,23,24}$ 20^{17}.

ten ' applied to Christ, occurs nowhere else, except in
John's own words ($1^{14,18}$, 1 Jno 4^9, cf. Heb 11^{17}), and
that affords a reason for assigning the paragraph 3^{16-21}
to him. Such a passage as 5^{18}, however, makes perfectly clear the high connotation which was attached to
the constant claim of Jesus to be in a peculiar sense
God's ' Son,' entitled to speak of Him in an appropriating way as His ' Father.' The Jews sought to
kill Him, remarks the evangelist, because of this mode
of speech: " He called God His own Father ($\pi\alpha\tau\acute{\epsilon}\rho\alpha$
$\H{\iota}\delta\iota o\nu$), making Himself equal ($\H{\iota}\sigma o\nu$) with God." And
indeed He leaves no prerogative to the Father which
He does not claim as ' Son ' to share. There has been
given Him authority over all flesh (17^2), and the destinies of men are determined by Him (3^{17} 6^{40}) ; He
quickens whom He will (5^{21}) and executes judgment
on whom He will (5^{22}). Whatever the Father does
He knows, and indeed all that the Father does He
does (5^{19}). He even has received of the Father to
have life in Himself (5^{26}). Though He declares indeed that the Father is greater than He (14^{28}), this
must be consistent with an essential oneness with the
Father, because He explicitly asserts that He and the
Father are one (10^{30}), that He is in the Father and
the Father in Him (10^{38}), and that to have seen Him
was to have seen the Father (14^9). It may be that
some mysterious subordination of God the Son to God
the Father is suggested in the declaration that the
Father is greater than He (14^{28}), and many certainly
have so interpreted it, constructing their doctrine of
God upon that view. But it seems more likely that our
Lord is speaking on this occasion of His earthly state
in which He is not only acting as the Delegate of the

Father and hence as His subordinate—the " sent " of
the Father; but also in His dual nature as the God-man,
is of Himself in His humanity, of a lower grade of
being than God, without derogation to His equality
with the Father in His higher, truly divine nature.   If
this be what He means, there is no contradiction between the strong affirmations of His not merely equality
(5^{18}) with God, but His oneness with Him (10^{30}), His
interpenetration with Him (10^{38}) as sharer in all His
knowledge and deeds (14^9), and His equally strong
affirmation of His inferiority to Him (14^{28}), illustrated as it is by numerous assertions of dependence on
Him and of an attitude of obedience to Him.

Thus, so clear and pervasive is the assertion of deity
through the medium of His designation of Himself as

Eternal
Sonship

' Son ' and the use of this term of Him
by the evangelist,[18] that the chief point
of interest in the term rises above this
assertion and concerns a deeper matter.   Does the Sonship asserted belong to our Lord in His earthly manifestation merely; or does it set forth a relation existing
between Him as a preëxistent person and God conceived
even in eternity as His Father?   In other words, is the
term ' Son ' a term of economical or of ontological
relation?   The question is not an easy one to determine.
But, on the whole, it seems that it should be answered
in the latter sense.   The force of a passage like 3^{16}
(cf. 3^{35} 5^{20})—" God so loved the world that He gave
His only begotten Son "—seems to turn on the intimacy

[18] Cf. Sanday, Hastings' *B. D.,* IV. 576 b.: " We may say with confidence that a sonship such as is described in the Fourth Gospel would
carry with it this conclusion.   How could any inferior being either
enter so perfectly into the mind of the Father, or reflect it so perfectly
to man?   Of what created being could it be said, ' He that hath seen

of the relation expressed by the term " only begotten
Son " having been already existent before the giving:
otherwise how is the greatness of the love expressed in
the giving to be measured? Similarly in a passage
like 3[17] there seems an implication of the Sonship as
underlying the mission: He was sent on this mission
because He was Son,—He did not become Son by being sent. In like manner the remarkable phrase " God
only begotten " in Jno 1[18] appears to be most readily
explained by supposing that it was as God that He was
the unique Son: and, if so, it seems easiest to understand " the glory of an Only Begotten of the Father,"
which men saw in the incarnate Christ (1[14]) as the
glory brought with Him from heaven. In this case,
it is obvious, John goes far toward outlining the foundations of the doctrine of the Trinity for us: and it
is a mistake not to see in his doctrine of the Logos and
of the Only Begotten God and of the Divine Son, the
elements of that doctrine.

With this high doctrine of the divine Sonship in
connection with Jesus the way is prepared for the express assertion that He is God. This,
'God'   as has already been incidentally pointed
out, is done in express words in this Gospel. The evangelist declares that that ' Word,' which,
on becoming flesh, is identified with ' Jesus Christ,'
was in the beginning with God and was ' God ' (1[1]),
and calls Him in distinction from the Father, ' God
only begotten ' (1[18]). And Thomas, his doubts of the

me hath seen the Father '? We need not stop to pick out other expressions that admit of no lower interpretations, because the evangelist has
made it clear by his Prologue what construction he himself put upon
his own narrative."

resurrection removed, greets Him with the great cry,
" My Lord and my God " (20^{28}) : and more to the
point, our Lord Himself, who had elsewhere declared
Himself one with God (10^{30}), and had asserted that
He and the Father interpenetrated one another (10^{38}),
and that to have seen Him was to have seen the Father
(14^{9}), expressly commended Thomas for this great confession and thereby bore His own testimony to His
proper deity (20^{29}).   The deity of Jesus which in the
Synoptists is in every way implied is, therefore, in John
expressly asserted, and that in the use of the most
direct terminology the Greek language afforded.   To
this extent, it is to be allowed that John's Gospel is in
advance of the Synoptists.

This advance is commonly represented as the index
of the development that had taken place between the
'God' no New   time when the Synoptics were written
Title   and the much later time when John was
written.   John, coming from a period
almost a generation later than the Synoptics, it is said,
naturally reflects a later point of view.   Of course
John's Gospel was written thirty or thirty-five years
after the Synoptics.   But it is an illusion to suppose that
it therefore sets forth a later or more developed point
of view than that embedded in the Synoptics.   The
Synoptics present a divine Christ, as we have seen, and
are written out of a point of view which is simply sat-
urated with reverence for Christ as divine.   John is
written from no higher point of view, and records nothing from the life of Jesus which more profoundly re-
veals His consciousness of oneness with the Father than
the great utterance of Mt 11^{27}, or which more clearly announces the fundamental idea of what we call the

Trinity than the great utterance of Mt 28[19]. There is no advance in conception in John over the Synoptics: there is only a difference in the phraseology employed to express the same conception. The Synoptics present Jesus Christ as God; only they do not happen to say 'God' when speaking of Him: they say 'Son of Man,' 'Son of God,' Sharer in 'the Name.' It did not, however, require thirty years for men who thoroughly believed Jesus to be divine to learn to express it by calling Him 'God.' In a word, it is in the mere accident of literary expression, not in the substance of doctrine, that the Synoptics and John differ in their assertion of the deity of Christ. Accidents of literary expression are not products of time, and differences in modes of expression do not argue intervals of time.

THE DESIGNATIONS OF OUR LORD IN
ACTS AND THEIR SIGNIFICANCE

How great an illusion it is to look upon John as reflecting a new phase of teaching, which had grown up

Value of Acts' Testimony

only in the course of years, in speaking of Jesus plainly as God, may be illustrated by attending to the designations employed of our Lord in the Book of Acts and in the letters of Paul. The Book of Acts and the Epistles of Paul both bring us testimony to how Jesus was thought and spoken of in Christian circles at the time, and indeed before the time, when the Synoptics were composed. The Book of Acts was not only written by the author of one of the Synoptic Gospels,[1] but purports to record conversations and discourses by the actors in the great drama of the founding of the Christian Church; and indeed could not have seriously misrepresented them,—seeing that it was published in their lifetime,—without having been at once corrected. We may learn from it, therefore, how Jesus was esteemed by His first followers, including those who had enjoyed

[1] This certainly cannot admit of doubt: and it is pleasant to be able to record that the evidence has been recognized as overwhelming even by Harnack: cf. his *Lukas der Arzt der Verfasser des dritten Evangeliums und der Apostelgeschichte,* 1906. That Harnack is unwilling to accord to Luke his true rank as an exact historian does not lessen the value of his admission of his authorship of the Gospel (including the infancy portion) that bears his name; and of the Acts, throughout.

His daily companionship throughout His ministry. The Epistles of Paul are none of them of later date, and many of them are of earlier date, than the Synoptic Gospels, and bring us, therefore, testimony to the estimation in which Christ was held in the Christian community at about the time when the Synoptic Gospels, or the sources on which they depend, were written. The conception of Jesus given expression alike in the Synoptics, in Acts and in Paul's Epistles, it cannot be doubted, was aboriginal in the Church.[2] But this conception is distinctly that expressed in its own way in the Gospel of John.

The narrative of Acts does not concern the acts of Jesus during the period of His earthly life, but those of the exalted Jesus through His servants the Apostles (1^1: "began"). It is natural, therefore, that the simple designation 'Jesus' should occur less frequently in its pages than in the Gospel narrative; and that even when Jesus is spoken of, which is of course comparatively infrequently, He should be spoken of by a designation more expressive of the relation existing between Him and His followers, whose acts it is proximately the business of this book to describe. Accordingly in Acts the reverential 'the Lord' becomes the ruling designation of Jesus, and the simple 'Jesus' takes a subordinate place, both as the narrative designation and in the reports

'Jesus' in Acts

[2] Harnack, in the Preface to the above-mentioned work, says: "The genuine epistles of Paul, the writings of Luke, and Eusebius' Church History are the pillars for the knowledge of the history of the earliest Christianity." This is true testimony: and it only remains to give to the testimony of these three pillar-witnesses its real validity to rise in our conception of early Christianity far above not only the average "critical" conception, but Harnack's own.

of the remarks of our Lord's followers incorporated in the narrative. Nevertheless it is employed by Luke himself with sufficient frequency to show that it suggested itself on all natural occasions. Thus, for example, Luke uses it in the first chapter where he is himself narrating what Jesus did before His ascension ($1^{1,14}$), and elsewhere currently in such phrases as "preaching Jesus" (5^{42} 8^{35} 9^{27} 17^{18}), "proving that Jesus is the Christ" (9^{20} $18^{5,28}$ 28^{23}), and the like ($4^{2,13,18}$ 5^{40} 7^{55} 9^{27} 18^{25}). And he records it as employed in a natural way by the two chief spokesmen in Acts, Peter in the earlier portion (1^{16} $2^{32,36}$ [$3^{13,20}$] 5^{30}, cf. $4^{27,30}$), and Paul in the later portion ([$9^{5,20}$] $13^{23,33}$ 17^3 $19^{4,[13]}$), as well as occasionally by other actors in the historical drama ($4^{18,27,30}$ 5^{40} $9^{17,[20]}$ 17^7 $19^{[13],15}$ 25^{19}), including the angel explaining the ascension (1^{11}) and Jesus Himself revealing Himself to Paul (9^5 26^{15}).

The fuller form, 'Jesus of Nazareth' (10^{38}), or more frequently, 'Jesus the Nazarene' (2^{22} 6^{14} 22^8 26^9) also occurs, not as a locution of Luke's own, indeed, but upon the lips of Peter (2^{22} 10^{38}), and Paul (22^8 26^9), and in one case as a description of Jesus by Himself (22^8); and also on the lips of the inimical Jews describing with some contempt the great claims made by His followers for "this Jesus the Nazarene" (6^{14}). Twice, indeed, the full name 'Jesus Christ the Nazarene' is employed, as a solemn designation throwing up for observation His entire personality in all its grandeur (3^6 4^{10}).

From these two last-named instances we may learn, what otherwise is sufficiently illustrated, that the full sacred name ' Jesus Christ' was in easy use by our

' Jesus Christ'

Lord's first followers, whenever they wished to speak of Him with special solemnity. Luke himself so employs it in his narrative (8^{12}), and he quotes it from Peter (2^{38} 9^{34} $10^{36,48}$) and Paul (16^{18})—in each instance as employed in circumstances of great ceremoniousness, in demanding faith or in working cures by this great Name. It is in similar conditions that the even more complete designation ' Jesus Christ the Nazarene ' (3^{6} 4^{10}) occurs; and that a designation which occurs very frequently in the Epistles, ' the Lord Jesus Christ ' (11^{17} 28^{31}) or ' our Lord Jesus Christ ' (15^{26} 20^{21}), appears as in use by the Apostles,—Peter (11^{17}), Paul (20^{21}), and the whole Apostolic body (15^{26}),—as well as by Luke himself (28^{31}). In all these instances it seems clear that the compound name ' Jesus Christ' is treated as a proper name, but of course not with any loss of the high significance of the element ' Christ.' Perhaps it would not be too much to say that the compound name is dealt with as the ' royal name ' of our Lord, the name which is given Him when He is to be designated with special ceremony and solemnity.

In 3^{20} 5^{42} $24^{24,3}$ on the other hand, it is questionable whether we are to read the names together so as to

' Christ Jesus '

yield the compound ' Christ Jesus,' which in that case meets us here for the first time in the New Testament, or are to take ' Christ ' as the predicate,—' Jesus as the Christ.' The commentators seem inclined to follow the

---

[3] 17^{3} $18^{5,28}$, where also the two names stand in conjunction, are different: the presence of the substantive verb renders the construction of the " Christ " as predicate necessary.

latter course.[4] But in 24^{24}, where the question is about Paul, who, we know from his Epistles (1 Thess 2^{14} 5^{18}, Rom *passim*), was accustomed, at an earlier date than this, to use the compound ' Christ Jesus ' freely, it seems difficult not to read that compound.[5] And this increases our hesitancy with reference to the two earlier passages. Paul's familiar use of ' Christ Jesus ' must have had a history back of it: and it seems, therefore, natural that its employment in the primitive community should emerge into light in such passages as we now have before us.[6]

Another compound designation of Jesus, which does not occur in the Gospels,[7] meets us with some frequency

'The Lord Jesus' —in Acts—' the Lord Jesus.' This is employed by Luke himself in the course of the narrative (4^{33} 8^{16} 11^{20} $19^{5,13,17}$), and is also attributed to speakers whose words are reported,

[4] So e.g. the Revised English Version at 3^{20} 5^{42}, and Meyer-Wendt at 3^{20}: and so also A. H. Blom, *De Leer van het Messiasrijk bij de eerste Christenen,* pp. 292 and 303. On 3^{20} Blom says: " There can be no doubt . . . but that $X\rho\iota\sigma\tau\grave{o}\nu$ $'I\eta\sigma o\hat{\upsilon}\nu$ is not to be taken as one name, but that $'I\eta\sigma o\hat{\upsilon}\nu$ is the epexegetic appositive of $X\rho\iota\sigma\tau\acute{o}\nu$, which has here its original significance of a dignity." On the other side, cf. Gloag, Barde, Rackham at 3^{20}.

[5] So e.g. R. V.

[6] Paul Feine, *Jesus Christus und Paulus,* 1902, p. 35, is among those (see note 4) who take the opposite view. He says: " This formula is a specifically Pauline one. The compound name $'I\eta\sigma o\hat{\upsilon}s$ $X\rho\iota\sigma\tau\acute{o}s$ is found also in the other N. T. writings. . . . But the reverse sequence meets us only in Paul. No doubt it may be possible to discover it if we wish to do so in Acts. But even in Acts 3^{20} 17^{3} $18^{5,28}$, the $X\rho\iota\sigma\tau\acute{o}s$, standing before $'I\eta\sigma o\hat{\upsilon}s$, is the predicate; 5^{42} means similarly, ' they preached the Messiah Jesus.' Then only 24^{24} is left $\tau\hat{\eta}s$ $\epsilon\hat{\iota}s$ $X\rho\iota\sigma\tau\grave{o}\nu$ $'I\eta\sigma o\hat{\upsilon}\nu$ $\pi\acute{\iota}\sigma\tau\epsilon\omega s.$ Even here, however, it is possible that we do not have the Pauline formula, but what is spoken of is faith in the Messiah Jesus."

[7] In Mk 16^{19}, Lk 24^{3}, it is not genuine.

—or to be more specific, to both Peter (1^{21} 15^{11}) and
Paul (16^{31} $20^{24,35}$ 21^{13}). It is even used as an address
by Stephen (7^{59}). Indeed the fuller designation, ' the '
or ' our ' ' Lord Jesus Christ,' is employed by Luke himself (28^{31}) and attributed alike to Peter (11^{17}), the
whole body of the Apostles (15^{26}), and Paul (20^{21}).
In this last formula we have combined the three most
usual designations of Christ, and it seems charged with
the deepest reverence and affection for His person.

Of course these phrases, ' the Lord Jesus,' ' the [our]
Lord Jesus Christ,' witness to the prevalence in the
Christian community of the simpler des-
' Lord ' ignation ' Lord ' of Jesus, and this prevalence is otherwise copiously illustrated
in Acts. As the narrative does not concern what Jesus
began to do and teach while in His own person on
earth, but what " after He was received up " He did
through His servants, His own person is not a figure in
the narrative, subsequent to the few opening verses
which tell of the period before the ascension. Accordingly outside of these verses (1^6) there is no occasion to record words directly addressed to Jesus, except
in visions ($9^{5,10,13}$ $22^{8,10,19}$ 26^{15}), or in prayers (1^{24}
$7^{59,60}$). On all these occasions, however, He is addressed by the supreme honorific ' Lord,' except in
7^{59}, where He is addressed more fully as ' Lord Jesus.'
It is clear that this formula is employed in all cases with
the profoundest reverence, and is meant to be the
vehicle of the highest possible ascription. Perhaps it
will be well to focus our attention upon the two or
three instances in which it is employed in direct prayer
to Jesus (1^{24} $7^{59,60}$). In these He is not merely treated
as divine—for to whom but God is prayer to be ad-

dressed?—but also directly characterized as the possessor of divine powers and the exerciser of divine functions. It is as He " that knoweth the hearts of all men " that He is appealed to at 1²⁴;[8] as the forgiver of sin at 7⁶⁰;[9] and as the receiver of the spirits of the dying saints at 7⁵⁹. All these traits are assigned to Jesus in the Gospel narratives, where Jesus claimed authority even on earth to forgive sins (Mk 2¹⁰ ||) and represents Himself as the judge before whom all were at length to stand and receive according to the deeds done in the body (Mt 25³²) : where He is represented as knowing what was in men and needing not that

[8] De Wette, Meyer, Wendt, Nösgen, Blass, *in loc.,* wish this passage to be understood as addressed to God; so also Sven Herner, *Die Anwendung des Wortes χύριος im N. T.,* 1903, p. 17: " In the sentence, ' Thou, Lord, who knowest the hearts of all men ' (1²⁴), God is probably meant. According to 15⁸ (4²⁹) and Lk 16¹⁵ God is the searcher of hearts, and the prayer of the primitive Church recorded at 4²⁴⁻³⁰ is also addressed to God. Several exegetes, however, are of the opinion that it is directed to the Lord Christ; and the ὁ χύριος Ἰησοῦς of v. 21 can be urged in support of this." Among the exegetes who consider it to be addressed to Christ are Bengel, Olshausen, Baumgarten, Lechler, Bisping, and van Oosterzee (see the solid statement of the last): as also Alexander, Hackett, Gloag, Barde, Felton, Rendall. Rackham prefers to leave the question undecided.

[9] That the prayer in 7⁶⁰ is addressed to Jesus is pretty generally allowed. Cf. e.g. Sven Herner, p. 16: " We think we can maintain that in Stephen's prayer the words, ' Lord, lay not this sin to their charge ' (7⁶⁰), are directed to Jesus, since the immediately preceding verse has the expression ' Lord Jesus, receive my spirit.' " Also A. H. Blom, p. 126: " It is probable that the same person is addressed by the χύριε as was called χύριε Ἰησοῦ in v. 59." Blom points out that it is the dominant conception of Acts that the forgiveness of sins is to be had in Christ: therefore men are baptized in His name (2³⁸ 22¹⁶), and He has been exalted to God's right hand as a Prince and a Saviour (5³¹), and all who believe in Him receive forgiveness through His name (10⁴³) ; " and therefore," he adds, " Stephen can have had *Him* in mind when he prayed for his foes, Lord, reckon not this sin to their charge (7⁶⁰)."

anyone should teach Him what were the thoughts of their hearts (Mk 2^8) : and where His promise to the thief was that he should be that day with Him in Paradise (Lk 23^{43}). It can occasion no surprise, therefore, that He should be appealed to after His return to His glory as at once the searcher of hearts, the forgiver of sins, and the receiver of the spirits of the saints. What we learn in the meanwhile is that to the infant community the ascended Jesus was their God, whom they addressed in prayer and from whom they sought in prayer the activities which specifically belong to God.

Quite naturally in these circumstances the chief narrative name for Jesus in Acts becomes the honorific 'the Lord,' which is employed about twice as frequently as the simple 'Jesus,'[10] and which is occasionally given more precision by taking the form of 'the Lord Jesus' (4^{33} 8^{16} 11^{20} $19^{5,13,17}$) and even 'the Lord Jesus Christ' (28^{31}). All of these designations are placed also on the lips of actors in the history recounted. Thus Peter speaks of Jesus as 'the Lord' in [2^{34}] 2^{36} 11^{16} 12^{11}, as 'the Lord Jesus' in 1^{21} 15^{11}, and as 'the Lord Jesus Christ' in 11^{17}; Paul as 'the Lord' in $13^{10,11,12}$ 20^{19} 26^{15}, as 'the Lord Jesus' in 16^{31} $20^{24,35}$ 21^{13}, and as 'the Lord Jesus Christ' in 20^{21}; and others speak of Him as 'the Lord' in $8^{22,24}$ 9^{17} 16^{15}, as 'the Lord Jesus' in 7^{59}, and as 'the Lord Jesus Christ' in 15^{26}. It is quite clear that 'the Lord' is a favorite designation of Jesus in this book, and was such also in the community whose usage it reflects.[11] And it is equally clear

'Lord' as Narrative Name

---

[10] [2^{47}][5^{14}] 8^{25} $9^{1,10,11,15,[17],27,29,31,35,42}$ $11^{21,21,23}$ 12^{17} $13^{2,49}$ $14^{3,23}$ $15^{35,[36],40}$ $16^{[14],[32]}$ $18^{8,9,25}$ 19^{20} 23^{11}.

[11] Cf. Sven Herner, *Die Anwendung des Wortes* χύριος *im N. T.*, p. 20: "The frequent employment of the word χύριος in Acts is

that in the use of this term what is primarily expressed is the profoundest reverence on the part of the community and the highest conceivable exaltation and authority on the part of Jesus Himself. It belongs to the situation that it is often extremely difficult to determine whether by ' Lord ' Jesus or God is meant.[12] That is to say, so clearly is Jesus ' God ' to this writer and

shown not merely in the cases where it refers to God, but even more where it is Christ that is spoken of. Acts loves to call Christ 'Lord.' According to 2^{36} God has made Jesus Lord and Christ; He is 'the Lord over all' (10^{36}), and, therefore, He is often spoken of by the designation of 'Lord' ($2^{20,21,34}$ $9^{1,[5,6]10,11,15,17,27}$ 11^{16} [16^{10} 18^{25}] 20^{28} [$22^{10,16}$] 23^{11} [26^{15}]). To these must be added the passages in which Christ is addressed with the term 'Lord' (1^6 $7^{59,60}$ $9^{5,[6],10,13}$ $22^{8,10,19}$ 26^{10}), and a series of citations in which He is called 'Lord,' but in connection with a 'Jesus' or 'Jesus Christ' (1^{21} 4^{33} 8^{16} [9^{28} 10^{48}] $11^{17,20}$ [14^{10}] $15^{11,26}$ 16^{31} $19^{5,13,17}$ $20^{21,24,35}$ 21^{13} 28^{31}). Acts speaks therefore extremely often of Christ by the designation 'Lord,' even if we neglect the passages adduced at an earlier point, where decision is uncertain whether God or Christ is meant."

[12] Cf. Sven Herner, *op. cit.,* p. 16: "Whereas the Gospels depict the life of Jesus on earth, the narrative in Acts revolves around the Jesus exalted to the right hand of God, whom God has made Lord and Christ (2^{36}). It is He who leads to eternal life; He is the Lord of life (3^{15}). He is the Saviour, and there is salvation in no other (4^{12}). He deals out His blessings (3^{16}) and pours out the Holy Spirit on believers (2^{33}). His power is not bounded by the limits of space (26^{17}), and His flesh shall not see corruption (2^{31}). He is not only the Lord and Master according to the ordinary representation of the Gospels (cf. e.g. Mt 21^3, Mk 11^3, Lk 19^{31} with Mt 26^{18}, Mk 14^{14}, Lk 22^{11} and John 13^{13}), but He is the Lord over all (10^{36}). Accordingly Acts can leave it undetermined whether certain assertions are to be made of God or Christ; a designation is employed which is common to both, and it can often not be decided whether God or Christ is meant,—indeed sometimes it seems almost as if Acts had chosen a common designation just because it was unnecessary more precisely to express whether what was spoken of was to be ascribed to God or Christ. It is thus characteristic of Acts that a large number of passages occur where we cannot be

those whose speech he reports that the common term 'Lord' vibrates between the two and leaves the reader often uncertain which is intended.[13] The assimilation of Jesus to God thus witnessed is illustrated also in other ways. Thus, for example, in Peter's Pentecostal sermon Jesus is conceived as sitting at the right hand of God (2^{34}) and as having been constituted "both Lord and Christ," where the conjunction is significant (2^{36}) : and more explicitly still He is designated in a later discourse of the same Peter, "Lord of all" (10^{36}), that is to say, universal sovereign, a phrase which recalls the great declaration of Rom 9^5 to the effect that He is "God over all," as indeed He who sits on the throne of God must be.[14]

sure whether κύριος means God or Christ (1^{24} 2^{47} 5^{14} $8^{25,39}$ $9^{31,35,42}$ $11^{21,21,23,24}$ $13^{2,10,11,12,[44],47,48,49}$ $14^{3,23}$ $15^{35,36}$ $16^{14,15,32}$ $18^{8,9,25}$ $19^{10,20}$ 20^{19} 21^{14})."

[13] Therefore commentators have been tempted sometimes to seek out an easy and mechanical rule of discrimination. In his *Neueste Theol. Journal*, IV., pp. 11-24 (cf. III. p. 501), Gabler, e.g., maintained that anarthrous κύριος always is God in the N. T., while articled κύριος is always Jesus. Winer in the first and second editions of his Grammar blindly repeated this. But on investigating the matter he was soon convinced of the error, and showed in his monograph, *Disputatio de sensu vocum κύριος et ὁ κύριος im Actis et Epistolis Apostolorum* (Erlang., 1828), pp. 26, that the assumed rule did not hold good. Moses Stuart had meanwhile taken up the whole subject and printed the results of his researches in a somewhat rambling but useful paper in the first volume of the *Biblical Repository* (1831, Oct.), to the same effect. Dr. A. Plummer in his commentary on Luke repeats as regards that book the artificial statement of Gabler. In truth the distribution of the usage between Christ and God cannot in any book of the N. T. be determined on such grounds: and the difficulty in determining the reference is rooted ultimately in the assimilation of the two persons in the minds of the writers. Cf. Harnack, *History of Dogma*, I. p. 183.

[14] Cf. Meyer on 2^{36} and 10^{36}.

That in this rich development of the conception of the Lordship of Jesus, His Messianic dignity is not

'Son of Man'

out of mind is already apparent from the phraseology of 2^{36}.[15] The emphasis of Peter's preaching turns, indeed, precisely on the fact that God has made the Jesus whom the Jews crucified " both Lord and Christ." It is thus with Acts as truly as with the Gospels the Messianic office of Jesus on which the greatest stress is laid. Naturally as Jesus is not a speaker in the narrative of Acts, His own favorite self-designation of 'Son of Man' is here conspicuous by its absence. It occurs only a single time, when the dying Stephen declared that he saw the heavens opened and the 'Son of Man' standing at the right hand of God (7^{56}). This is the only instance in the whole New Testament where this designation is employed by anyone except our Lord Himself: Stephen's use of it seems a reflection of our Lord's declaration, " Henceforth ye shall see the Son of Man sitting at the right hand of power " (Mt 26^{64} ||), and is at once Stephen's testimony to the greatness of his Lord in His divine Majesty, and a witness to the genuineness of the whole series of declarations attributed to our Lord in which He saw Himself in the Danielic vision and developed on that basis His conception of His Messiahship in its earthy humiliation and subsequent elevation to participation in the divine glory.

The great companion designation 'Son of God' is

[15] Cf. e.g. A. H. Blom, *De Leer van het Messiasrijk*, etc., pp. 58-9: " Christians were thoroughly convinced that the Messiah had appeared in Jesus the Nazarene. This was the main content of the preaching of the Apostles, whether they turned to the Jews (Acts 2^{22-36} $3^{13,26}$ 4^{8-12} 5^{29-32} 7^{52} 9^{20}, etc.), or to the Samaritans (8^{5}), or to the heathen (10^{34-42} 13^{16-41})."

almost as rare in Acts as the ' Son of Man.' This precise designation, indeed, occurs but once,
where we are told that Paul immediately
after his conversion began to proclaim
in the synagogues of Damascus Jesus as the ' Son of
God' (9^{20}), which is explained as meaning that he
proved Jesus to be ' the Christ ' (9^{22}). In his speech
in the synagogue of Pisidian Antioch, Paul indeed declared that by raising up Jesus God fulfilled the announcement of the second Psalm, " Thou art my Son,
this day have I begotten Thee " (13^{33}) ; and the risen
Jesus is quoted as twice speaking of God as " the
Father " ($1^{4,7}$), and Peter is cited as repeating one of
these declarations in his Pentecostal sermon (2^{33}). Occasion has been taken from the circumstance that in
all these three cases of allusion to the ' Father ' the
term employed is ' the Father ' to suggest that it is
not specifically Jesus' Father but the general Father of
spirits that is intended. To this is added the suggestion that in Paul's allusion to the second Psalm it is
of the incarnation or even perhaps of the resurrection
that he is thinking as the point when the Son was begotten. The conclusion is then drawn that in Acts
there is no allusion to a metaphysical Sonship of
Christ.[16] It must be frankly admitted that had we these

'Son of God'

[16] Cf. e.g. A. H. Blom, *De Leer van het Messiasrijk*, etc., pp. 58-9,
70, 71 : " We think we may conclude that the Christians as little as the
Jews connected with the ' Son of God ' the conception of a divine nature ; and that the ethical element in the idea of the Messiah lay more
in the $\pi\alpha\hat{\iota}\varsigma$ than in the $\upsilon\iota\acute{o}\varsigma$ of God " . . . " It attracts our attention that Jesus here and there speaks of God as ' the Father '
(Acts $1^{4,7}$), and that Peter too on one occasion made use of this designation (2^{33}). Seeing how that elsewhere in the N.T. the most intimate communion of God with men, His life for and in men, is expressed by this term, it is all the more remarkable that Jesus by speak-

passages alone to consider, we might hesitate to ascribe to Acts the doctrine of a divine Messiah. But this is by no means the case, and we need only note in passing that the title of 'Son of God' is very little in evidence in Acts either in its precise form or in its cognate modes of expression. Nevertheless, the locution 'the Father' does not appear in the usage of it here to be without suggestion of its correlative 'the Son'; and Paul's citation of the second Psalm does not seem to be without implication of a Sonship for Jesus lying deeper than either His resurrection or His incarnation.

The prevailing Messianic designation in Acts is the simple 'Christ,' and Luke tells us that the staple of the Apostolic teaching was that Jesus

Prevalence of 'Christ'

is 'the Christ' (5^{42} 8^5 9^{22} $18^{5,28}$), and illustrates this fact by instances recorded both from Peter ($2^{31,36}$ $3^{18,20}$) and from Paul (17^3 26^{23}). The general employment of the compound names, 'Jesus Christ,' 'the Lord Jesus Christ' (or 'our Lord Jesus Christ') and even 'Christ Jesus,' testifies to the fixedness of the conviction that Jesus was 'the Christ' and the close attachment of the title to His person as at least a quasi-proper name. Luke does not himself make use of any other Messianic title, except in the one instance when he tells us that Paul

ing not of *His* but of *the* Father, does not lay claim by it for Himself alone to such a relation to God. And Peter follows Him in this, since he employs the term to the Jews, who did not yet believe in Christ, from which it may be inferred that this fatherlike love of God for men was not conceived as dependent on their belief in Christ, but as grounded in His nature. . . . And if we were not arbitrary in suggesting that for the early Christians the title 'Servant of Jehovah' was of much more ethical significance than that of 'Son of God,' it would seem to follow that we should not seek a rich ethical sense in the name of Father."

on his conversion began at once " to proclaim Jesus that He is the Son of God " (9^{20}). But he quotes quite a rich variety of such titles as employed by others. To Peter there is ascribed, for example, a considerable series, which, moreover, he is represented as weaving together in a most striking way, as all alike designations of the same Jesus, which bring out the several aspects of the unitary conception fulfilled in Him. Prominent among them are those which apply to Jesus the prophecies concerning ' the Righteous Servant of Jehovah ' ($3^{13,14,26}$, cf. $4^{27,30}$) and ' the Prophet like unto Moses ' ($3^{22,28}$), which are inextricably combined with those which speak of Him as ' the Anointed King.'[17]

[17] With respect to this intermingling of designations, cf. A. H. Blom, *De Leer van het Messiasrijk bei de eerste Christenen,* 1863, p. 48: " It scarcely needs to be said that only the religious-minded were in a position rightly to understand Jesus, and that undoubtedly the most of those who became His followers in the first years belonged to this class. The question thus becomes, What was the conception which they had formed of the Messiah, when they came to know Jesus? And the Book of Acts answers us, that the Messiah, in their view, was to be the offspring and successor of David, a Prophet like to Moses, the Servant of Jehovah, the Son of God and the Son of Man. The three first of these characterizations describe His dignity, while the two last raise the question for us what nature was ascribed to Him." Again, pp. 55-56: " Diverse as were the ideas expressed in these three views of a King like David, a Prophet like Moses, and the Servant of Jehovah, and little as the particulars in which they were developed permitted themselves to be united into a unitary, consistent, concrete conception, yet since the Messiah was seen in all three, they were looked upon as identical. Accordingly what was said of one of them was considered unhesitatingly to be applicable to the others. A striking example of this is afforded by the words applied to Jesus in Mt 17^5—' This is my Son, the Beloved, in whom I am well pleased: hear ye Him.' Here the predicate, ' my Son,' belongs to the idea of the King of Ps 2; the ' in whom I am well pleased ' is a trait only of the portrait of the Servant of Jehovah (Is 42^1); and the ' hear Him ' points to what is due to the prophet (Deut 18^{15}). We meet with a like phenomenon in

In Peter's early discourses 'the Servant ($\pi\alpha\tilde{\iota}\varsigma$) of God' is one of the most notable of the designations of

Accumulation of Titles

Jesus ($3^{23,26}$, cf. $4^{27,30}$); and along with it occurs 'the Holy and Righteous One' (3^{14})[18] which belongs to the same series of designations; and in the same context appeal is made likewise to Moses' prophecy of a Prophet like unto himself ($3^{22,23}$);[19] while to these is added further

Acts. It is declared that what stands written in Ps 2^2 of the King—'The Kings of the earth set themselves and the princes take counsel together, against the Lord and against His Anointed'—is fulfilled in God's holy Servant (Acts 4^{25-27}, cf. verse 30). Similarly the idea of the prophet is brought into connection with that of the Servant of Jehovah when Peter, after adducing the words, 'A *prophet* shall the Lord your God raise up,' announces that God has actually sent him to them, 'having raised up to you His *servant* Jesus' (Acts 3^{24-26}). And if the splendid successor of David received the glory, which the Holy One of God expected (Acts $2^{27,30}$), so also the sufferings of the Servant of Jehovah were unhesitatingly assigned to the King (3^{18}), as Peter declares that God through all His prophets has proclaimed that 'His Christ should suffer.' "

[18] Cf. Blom, *op. cit.*, p. 33: "Whatever weight can be attached here to the appeal to this anointing of Jesus with the Holy Spirit of prophecy and with power, as a proof that He must be the Messiah, there was yet another side to the manifestation of Jesus which strongly impressed the Christians and by which they were led to recognize His religious greatness. He was the $\ddot{o}\sigma\iota o\varsigma$ (Acts 2^{27} 13^{35}), the $\delta\acute{\iota}\varkappa\alpha\iota o\varsigma$ (7^{52} 22^{14}, the $\ddot{\alpha}\gamma\iota o\varsigma$ $\varkappa\alpha\grave{\iota}$ $\delta\acute{\iota}\varkappa\alpha\iota o\varsigma$ (3^{14}), the $\ddot{\alpha}\gamma\iota o\varsigma$ $\pi\alpha\tilde{\iota}\varsigma$ $\tauo\tilde{\upsilon}$ $\theta\varepsilon o\tilde{\upsilon}$ ($4^{27,30}$). And this He was not only after His exaltation, but already on earth, for the guilt of the Jews was so great just because they had rejected and killed Him, the $\ddot{\alpha}\gamma\iota o\varsigma$ $\varkappa\alpha\grave{\iota}$ $\delta\acute{\iota}\varkappa\alpha\iota o\varsigma$, instead of a murderer. These general predicates, however, are not enough to give us a just notion of the perfection which they saw in Jesus. It is undoubtedly wrong for men to see nothing more in them than that He was guiltless in the matters of which He was accused by the Jews. This is already plain from the emphasis with which He is named $\acute{o}$ $\ddot{\alpha}\gamma\iota o\varsigma$, $\acute{o}$ $\delta\acute{\iota}\varkappa\alpha\iota o\varsigma$. . . . And so the predicate $\acute{o}$ $\ddot{\alpha}\gamma\iota o\varsigma$ must include in itself a religious and ethical sense . . ."

[19] Cf. Blom, *op. cit.*, pp. 50-57: "Although they [the Jews] applied these words to a particular person, they do not seem to have all thought

the striking title of the ' Prince ' or ' Author ' ' of life '
(3^{15}).   In other discourses Peter calls Jesus a ' Prince
and Saviour ' (5^{31}) and indeed even ' Judge of the
quick and the dead ' (10^{42}).   The composite portrait
which he presents of Jesus the Messiah as he passes
freely from one of these designations to another is a
complex and very lofty one: what is most apparent is
that he conceives Him as the focus upon which all the
rays of Old Testament prophecy converge, and as exalted above all earthly limitations.   A somewhat similar list of designations is placed on the lips of Paul.
To him the ' Lord Jesus ' (16^{31} $20^{21,24,35}$ 21^{13}) is ' the
Christ ' (17^{3} 26^{23}), ' the Holy One ' (13^{35})[20] ' the
Righteous One ' (22^{14}, cf. 7^{52}, Stephen)[21] who has come
as a ' Saviour ' (13^{23}) to Israel, and who though a

of the same one; and while some held ' him of whom Moses wrote   in
the law ' (Jno 1^{45}) or ' the prophet who should come into the world '
(6^{14}, cf. [15]) for the Messiah, others must have distinguished Him from
the Messiah ($1^{21, \text{cf. } 20}$, $7^{40, \text{cf. } 41}$).   According to these last, he was,
in harmony with the prophecy of Malachi (3^{1} 4^{5-6}), the returning
Elijah, who was to prepare the way before the Messiah (Mt 17^{10}).   The
Christians did not share this view.   While they also had expected an
Elijah and had found him in John the Baptist (Acts 13^{24}), they conceived that the promise of Moses had found its fulfilment only in the
Messiah; and Peter, therefore, in his preaching, appealed directly to
these words (Acts 3^{22}), and Stephen also seems to have meant the same
thing (7^{37}).   Accordingly on their basis the gift of prophecy was a
main element of the idea of the Messiah, and that, such a gift as placed
Him by the side of Moses and elevated Him above all other prophets.
There was certainly connected with this also an inner communion
with God; and God was understood to speak with Him face to face,
and to reveal to Him His counsel more clearly as in the case of Moses
(Ex 33^{11}, Numb 12^{6-8})."

[20] Cf. 2^{27}.   In both cases it is derived from Ps 16^{10}, and the term
employed is ὅσιος, not ἅγιος, as in 3^{14}, cf. Mk 1^{24}, Lk 4^{34}, Jno 6^{69},
1 Jno 2^{20}, Rev 3^{7}.   See on the titles of this sort Hastings' *D. C. G.,* I.
pp. 730-31.

[21] Cf. Stanton, *op. cit.,* p. 170.

' Man ' ($\dot{a}\nu\dot{\eta}\rho$, 17^{31}) is ' God's own Son ' (13^{33}), nay, in some high sense ' God ' Himself (20^{28}),—for it was by nothing else than " the blood of God " that the Church was purchased.[22]

A rapid enumeration of the mere titles applied to Christ, such as we have made, fails utterly to reproduce the impression which they make on the reader as he meets them in the course of the narrative. That impression is to the effect that although the true humanity of our Lord is thoroughly appreciated ($\dot{a}\nu\theta\rho\omega\pi\sigma\varsigma$, 5^{28}, cf. 7^{56}: $\dot{a}\nu\dot{\eta}\rho$, 2^{22} 17^{31}, cf. Lk 24^{19}), yet it is the majesty of this man which really fills the minds of these first Christians, as they perceive in Him not merely a man of God's appointment, representing God on earth, in whom all that they can conceive to be the source of dignity in Old Testament prophecy meets and finds its fulfillment ($10^{42,43}$), but also something far above humanity, which can be expressed only in terms of precise deity (20^{28}).

A side-light is thrown upon the high estimate which was placed among these early Christians on Jesus' person by the usurpation by it of the Old Testament pregnant use of the term " Name." As in the Old Testament we read continually of " the Name of Jehovah " as the designation of His manifested majesty, and even of simply " the Name " used absolutely with the same high connotation, so in Acts we read of the Name of

'The Name'

[22] The variant reading, " the blood of the Lord," means the same thing.   But Dr. Hort justly says, "$\tau\sigma\tilde{v}$ $\theta\varepsilon\sigma\tilde{v}$ is assuredly genuine." See for a discussion of the reading, Westcott and Hort, *The New Testament in the Original Greek*, II. pp. 98-99.

Jesus Christ, to the exclusion of the old phrase,[23] and again of simply " the Name " (5^{41}, cf. 3 Jno 7) used absolutely of Jesus. Those who were persecuted for His sake we are told rejoiced " that they were counted worthy to suffer dishonor for the Name " (5^{41}, cf. 3 Jno 7).[24] In the Old Testament this would have meant the Name of Jehovah: here it means the Name of Jesus.[25] " The Name," as it has been truly remarked, " had become a watchword of the faith, and is consequently used alone to express the name of Jesus, as it stood in former days for the Name of Jehovah (Lev 24^{11})." [26] Nothing could more convincingly bear in upon us the position to which Jesus had been exalted in men's thoughts than this constant tendency to substitute Him in their religious outlook for Jehovah.

[23] Only in citations from the O. T. (2^{21} $15^{14,17}$) does "the Name of God" appear in Acts. On the other hand the phrase "the Name of Jesus Christ" is quite frequent: 2^{38} $3^{6,(16)}$ $4^{10,18,30}$ 5^{40} $8^{12,16}$ $9^{14,16}$ $9^{16,27}$ $10^{43,48}$ 15^{26} 16^{18} $19^{5,13,17}$ 21^{13} 22^{16} 26^{9}. Instances like $4^{7,12,17}$ 5^{28} 9^{21}, where "the Name" or "this Name" is used more absolutely, are quite instructive from the point of view of the significance of the term. Only at 5^{41} is the completely absolute use of it found.

[24] Cf. Meyer on 5^{41}: "The absolute τὸ ὄνομα denotes the *name* κατ᾽, ἐξοχήν,—namely 'Jesus Messiah' (3^{6} 4^{10})—the confession and announcement of which was always the highest and holiest concern of the apostles. Analogous is the use of the absolute הַשֵּׁם (Lev $24^{11,16}$), in which the Hebrew understood the name of his Jehovah as implied of itself. Cf. 3 Jno 7." Cf. on the general question Giesebrecht, *Die alttest. Schätzung des Gottesnamens*, p. 1901; G. B. Gray, *B. D.*, III. p. 480, and also Conybeare, *J. Q. R.*, IX. p. 66, and Chase, *J. T. S.*, January, 1907.

[25] That the Name was simply "Jesus" is thought by **Hackett** and Barde: that it was "Christ," by De Wette and Gloag: that it was "the Lord Jesus Christ" is Blass' view; and that it was "the Messiah Jesus" is Wendt's, as it was Meyer's.

[26] Rashdall, *in loc.*

THE CORROBORATION OF THE EPISTLES OF PAUL

In passing from the book of Acts to Paul's Epistles, we are not advancing to a new period, in order that we Relative Early may observe how Jesus had come to be Date of Paul's thought of at a somewhat later date, in Letters the developing thought of Christians.[1] In point of fact, none of Paul's letters are of a later date than the Acts, and the earlier of them come from a time which antedates the composition of that book by ten or fifteen years. What we are passing to is merely a new form of literature,—didactic literature as distinguished from narrative. And what we are to observe is not a later development of the Christian conception of Jesus, but only more directly and precisely how the Christians of the first age thought of Jesus.

The book of Acts does indeed tell us not only how Paul and his companions thought and spoke of Jesus

[1] On the witness of Paul, see in general R. J. Knowling, *The Witness of the Epistles,* 1892; *The Testimony of St. Paul to Christ,* 1905. It used to be the fashion to attribute to Paul a very " primitive " christology supposed to find expression in Romans, 1 and 2 Corinthians and Galatians; largely on the ground of this these Epistles were allowed to be his. It is now the fashion, recognizing that the christology of these Epistles too is high, to represent Paul as the author of the deifying christology which, so it is said, has spread from him through the N. T. " Paul is everywhere the starting point," says Wernle (*Beginnings of Christianity,* II., p. 294): " it is his Gospel which now speaks to us from the words of Jesus and the original Apostles." The Gospels, from

as they presented Him to the faith of men; but also how Peter and his fellow-evangelists of the first days of the Gospel proclamation thought and spoke of Him: and to this extent the information derived from it reflects an earlier usage. But neither in Acts nor in Paul's Epistles is there any hint that Peter and Paul stand re-

The Value of their Testimony

lated to one another in their thought of Christ as representatives of a less and a more developed conception.[2] On the contrary in Acts the conception of the two, though clothed in different forms of speech, is notably the same: and in Paul's Epistles, though differences are noted between the other Apostles and himself in other matters, there is none signalized on this central point. And it

Mark (Wernle, 251 *seq.*, cf. Wrede, *Paulus*, 89) to John (Wernle, 274, Wrede, p. 96), reflect Paul's christological speculations: and the rest of the N. T. bears equally his mark. The origin of this high Pauline christology is left somewhat obscure. Wrede and Weinel are, on the whole, inclined to say that Paul had as a Jew believed in a transcendent Messiah, such as is pictured in the Similitudes of Enoch, say, and had only, on conversion, to accept Jesus as Messiah to have an exalted christology ready at hand. But if this doctrine of a transcendent Messiah was "in the air," why was it left to Paul to invent a transcendent christology for the church? And if it was "in the air" why need it be supposed to be derived from the later Apocalypses? Why might not the Apocalypses and Paul alike draw from, say, Daniel $7^{13,14}$? And why may it not have been shared by Jesus Himself? It scarcely seems logical to refer all traces of a transcendent christology in the N. T. to Paul; and then to refer Paul's doctrine to a generally active cause. The single solid result of the movement is, thus, the general recognition that the christology of the N. T. at large is "transcendent."

[2] Cf. Knowling, *The Testimony of St. Paul to Christ*, pp. 44, 45: "The Twelve and St. Paul differed, no doubt, in many ways; but there is no trace that the former opposed the Gentile Apostle in the estimate which he formed of the person of Christ and of His relationship to the Father." "If the deification of Christ was due to St. Paul, how is it that we do not hear of any such opposition, of any such violation of Jewish feeling and belief?"

is distinctly to be borne in mind that these Epistles were written not merely in the lifetime of the original apostles of Christ, but also in full view of their teaching, and with an express claim to harmony with it. Their testimony is accordingly not to Paul's distinctive doctrine with regard to the person of Jesus, but to the common doctrine of the Churches of the first age, when the Churches included in their membership the original followers of Jesus.[3] They, therefore, do not present us a different usage from that reflected in Acts and the Synoptic Gospels, but the same usage from a different point of sight. As didactic writings addressed by a Christian leader to Christian readers they enable us to observe, as the historical books do not, how Christians of the sixth and seventh decades of the first century were accustomed to speak of the Lord to one another; and accordingly what their thought of Jesus was as they sought to quicken in themselves Christian faith and hope and to bring their lives into conformity with their professions. Not merely in point of date, therefore, but also in point of intimacy of revelation, the Epistles of Paul present to us the most direct and determining evidence of the conception of Jesus prevalent in the primitive Church.

It belongs to their character as didactic rather than narrative writings, for example, that in Paul's Epistles the designation of our Lord by the simple 'Jesus' falls strikingly into the background,[4] while the designation of Him

Constant Use of 'Lord'

---

[3] Cf. Stanton, *The Jewish and Christian Messiah*, p. 156-7.

[4] Cf. Robinson on Eph 1[3] (p. 23): "To St. Paul, Jesus was preëminently 'the Christ.' Very rarely does he use the name 'Jesus' without linking it with the name or the title 'Christ.'" Cf. p. 107.

as ' Lord ' comes strikingly forward.[5] This phenomenon we already observed in Acts: it is much more
marked in Paul. The simple ' Jesus ' occurs in all these
Epistles only some seventeen times, while the simple
' Lord ' occurs some 144 or 146 times, to which may
be added 95 to 97 more instances of the use of ' Lord '
in conjunction with the proper name.[6] And this constant application of the term ' Lord ' to Jesus must not
be imagined merely a formal mark of respect.[7] It is
the definite ascription to Him of universal absolute
dominion not only over men, but over the whole universe of created beings (Phil 2^{11}, Rom 10^{12}).[8]

It is, of course, true that Paul has the exalted Jesus
in mind in thus speaking of Him. It was only on His

**Ground
of Jesus'
Lordship**
exaltation that Jesus entered upon His
dominion. But it by no means follows
that he conceived Jesus to have acquired
His ' Lordship,' in the sense of His inherent right to
reign, by His exaltation. On the contrary, to Paul it
was the ' Lord of Glory ' who was crucified (1 Cor 2^8).

[5] On the relation of ' Christ ' and ' Lord ' in Paul's usage cf. Robinson, *Com. on Ephesians*, pp. 72-90.

[6] The statistics of Paul's employment of the various designations of
our Lord are carefully given by Paul Feine, *Jesus Christus und Paulus*,
1902, pp. 21 *seq*. The text he uses is Nestle's ed. 3, 1901.

[7] Cf. Knowling *op. cit.*, pp. 39, 65, etc.: " No criticism has sufficed
to do away with the peculiar significance of this title." . . . We
must " frankly admit that St. Paul had very far overstepped the limits
of Christ's humanity when he finds in Him the Lord of the O. T."

[8] It was a notion of Baur's (*Der Lehre von der Dreieinigkeit*, I. p. 85,
N. T. Theologie, p. 193) that ' Lord ' in Paul always means ' Lord of the
Church,' through whom salvation has been brought to men. Not only
the passages cited, but many others, such as 1 Cor 8^6, negative this.
Dr. Sanday (on Rom 1^4, p. 10) supposes that this was the primary
meaning of the term: " On the lips of Christians, χύριος denotes the
idea of ' sovereignty,' primarily over themselves as the society of be-

That is to say, even in the days of His flesh, Jesus was to him intrinsically " the Lord to whom glory belongs as His native right."[9] That Paul usually has the exalted Christ in mind when speaking of Him as Lord is only thus a portion of the broader fact that, writing when he wrote, and as he wrote, he necessarily had the exalted Christ in mind in the generality of his speech of Him. He was not engaged in writing a historical retrospect of the life of the man Jesus on earth, but in proclaiming Jesus as the all-sufficient Saviour of men. That he recognized that this Jesus had entered upon the actual exercise of His universal dominion only on His resurrection and ascension, and in this sense had received it as a reward for His work on earth (Phil 2[9], Rom 14[9]) merely means that, no less than to our Lord Himself, the earthly manifestation

lievers (Col 1[18 seq.]), but also over all creation (Phil 2[10,11], Col 1[16,17])." " The title," he adds, " was given to our Lord even in His lifetime (Jno 13[13]), but without a full consciousness of its significance: it was only after the Resurrection that the Apostles took it to express their central belief (Phil 2[9 seq.])." These remarks, however, require revision. Though the term " does not in itself necessarily involve divinity " and " Jews may have applied it to their Messiah (Mk 12[36,37], Pss Sol 17[46]) without meaning that He was God "—and indeed His followers may have applied it to Jesus in its lower connotation during His lifetime and afterwards,—yet its association with the ' Lord ' of the LXX. gave it also its divine implication from the beginning, and in point of fact it is so employed from the first.

[9] Cf. T. C. Edwards on 1 Cor 2[8]; who rightly takes the genitive as genitive of characteristic quality, and explains: " The Lord to whom glory belongs as His native right. . . . Glory is the peculiar attribute of Jehovah among all the gods (Ps 29[1]). The expression is theologically important because it implies that Jesus was Lord of Glory, that is Jehovah, and that the Lord of Glory died (cf. Acts 3[15])." Passages like 1 Cor 11[26], " the Lord's death," 11[27], " the body and blood of the Lord," are quite similar in import, owing to the exalted sense of the term ' Lord.' Hence Heinrici speaks of " the paradox " in such expressions. Cf. Heinrici-Meyer, ed. 1896, pp. 353 and 363.

of Jesus was to Paul an estate of humiliation upon which the glory followed.[10] But the glory which thus followed the humiliation was to Paul, too, a glory which belonged of right to Jesus, to whom His lowly life on earth, not His subsequent exaltation, was a strange experience. It was one who was rich, he tells us, who in Jesus became poor that we might through His poverty become rich (2 Cor 8[9]); it was one who was in the form of God who abjured clinging to His essential equality with God and made Himself of no reputation by taking the form of a servant, and stooping even to the death of the cross (Phil 2[6 seq.]). When Paul speaks of Jesus, therefore, as 'Lord' it is not especially of His exaltation that he is thinking, but rather "the whole majesty of Christ lies in this predicate"[11] for him, and the recognition that Jesus is 'Lord' expresses for him accordingly the essence of Christianity

[10] Cf. on this Meyer on 2 Cor 4[4] (E. T. pp. 229-30): "For Christ in the state of His exaltation is again, as He was before His incarnation (comp. Jno 17[5]), fully $\dot{\varepsilon}\nu$ $\mu o\rho\varphi\tilde{\eta}$ $\theta\varepsilon o\tilde{v}$ and $\dot{\iota}\sigma a$ $\theta\varepsilon\tilde{\omega}$ (Phil 2[6]), hence in His glorified corporeality (Phil 3[21]) the visible image of the invisible God. . . . It is true that in the state of His humiliation He had likewise the divine $\delta o\xi a$, which he possessed $\varkappa a\tau\dot{a}$ $\pi\nu\varepsilon\tilde{v}\mu a$ $\dot{a}\gamma\iota\omega\sigma\dot{v}\nu\eta\varsigma$ (Rom 1[4]), which also, as bearer of the divine grace and truth (Jno 1[14]), and through His miracles (Jno 2[11]), He made known (Jno 14[9]); but its working and revelation were limited by His humiliation to man's estate, and He had divested Himself of the divine appearance (Phil 2[7 seq.]) till in the end, furnished through His resurrection with the mighty attestation of His divine Sonship (Rom 1[4]), He entered, through His elevation to the right hand of God, into the full communion of the glory of the Father, in which He is now the Godman, the very image and reflection of God, and will one day come to execute judgment and establish the Kingdom." "The whole acknowledgment of the heavenly $\varkappa\nu\rho\iota\dot{o}\tau\eta\varsigma$ of Jesus as the $\sigma\dot{v}\nu\theta\rho o\nu o\varsigma$ of God," says Meyer justly on Rom 10[9], "is conditioned by the acknowledgment of His previous descent from heaven, the incarnation of the Son of God, 8[3], Gal 4[4], Phil 2[6], *et al.*"

[11] The phrase is Meyer's, on 2 Cor 4[5].

(Rom 10⁹, 2 Cor 4⁵, 1 Cor 12³, Phil 2¹¹). The proc-lamation of the Gospel is summed up for him therefore in this formula (2 Cor 4⁵); the confession of Jesus as Lord is salvation (Rom 10⁹), and it is the mark of a Christian that he serves the Lord Christ (Col 3²⁴); for no one can say that Jesus is Lord except in the Holy Spirit (1 Cor 12³).

Obviously the significance of the title 'Lord' as applied to Jesus by Paul is not uninfluenced by its con-'Lord' a stant employment of God in the Greek
Proper Name Old Testament, and especially in those
of Jesus Old Testament passages which Paul ap-plies to Jesus, in which 'Lord' is the divine name (e. g., 2 Thess 1⁹, 1 Cor 1³¹ 10⁹,²⁶, 2 Cor 3¹⁶ 10¹⁷, Rom 10¹³, Eph 6⁴, 2 Tim 2¹⁹ 4¹⁴: Isaiah 45²³ is cited with reference to God in Rom 14¹¹, and with reference to Jesus in Phil 2¹⁰).**12** Under the influence of these passages the title 'Lord' becomes in Paul's hands almost a proper name, the specific designation for Jesus con-ceived as a divine person in distinction from God the Father. It is therefore employed of Jesus not merely constantly but almost exclusively. It is doubtful whether it is ever once employed of God the Father, outside of a few citations from the Old Testament: and in any case such employment of it is very excep-

¹² Cf. Paul Feine, *Jesus Christus und Paulus,* p. 38: "ὁ κύριος became to him ever more the heavenly Jesus, to whom he belonged with all his thoughts and activities. Jesus was to the Apostle the em-bodiment of God. This follows from the peculiarity which meets us also in Acts 2²⁰(?) 2²⁵, 1 P 3¹⁵, that with Paul κύριος in O. T. citations is often applied to Jesus: 2 Thess 1⁹, 1 Cor 1³¹, 2 Cor 10¹⁷, 1 Cor 10⁹, 2 Cor 3¹⁶, Rom 10¹³, Eph 6⁴, 2 Tim 2¹⁹ 4¹⁴. In Rom 14¹¹, Is 45²³ is applied to God: in Phil 2¹⁰ ˢᵉ𐞥· to Christ."

tional. It is accordingly in point of fact the determinate title for Jesus as distinguished from God the Father.[13] As such 'the Lord Jesus Christ' is coupled with 'God our Father' (or 'the Father') as the co-source of that grace and peace which Paul is accustomed to invoke on his readers in the addresses to his Epistles (1 Thess 1[1], 2 Thess 1[1,2], 1 Cor 1[3], 2 Cor 1[2], Gal 1[3], Rom 1[7], Eph 1[2], Phil 1[2], 1 Tim 1[2], 2 Tim 1[2], Titus 1[4], cf. Eph 6[23], 1 Thess 3[11], 2 Thess 1[12]). And throughout the Epistles Jesus as 'the Lord' and the Father as 'God' are set over against each other as distinct and yet conjoined objects of the reverence of Christians, and distinct and yet conjoined sources of the blessings of which Christians are the recipients.

[13] Cf. David Somerville, *St. Paul's Conception of Christ*, 1897, pp. 124 *seq.*: "The term 'Lord' occurs hundreds of times in the Epistles, and expresses the conviction of the supremacy of Christ which the Apostle shared with the entire primitive Church. In the nomenclature of the Apostle the Father is ὁ θεός, Christ is κύριος. The term 'Lord,' except when he quotes from the O. T. (in which case κύριος is used of God, being the LXX. translation), uniformly describes Christ in Paul's Epistles. That he regards it as Christ's proper designation we see from 1 Cor 8[5,6], also from Eph 4[5], 1 Cor 12[3]. Wherever 'Lord' occurs we are to understand him as referring to Christ. 1 Cor 4[19] 3[5] 7[17], Rom 14[4], which Weiss adduces as exceptions, are so only in appearance." Cf. also Sven Herner, *Die Anwendung des Wortes κύριος im N. T.*, p. 22, speaking of the Ep. to the Romans, he says: "If we direct our attention here to the verses where κύριος represents God, we find that they are all citations from the O. T.: 11[3] 12[19] 14[11] form no exception to this rule. Outside the O. T. citations, on the other hand, κύριος in Romans means our Lord Jesus Christ, and no certain exception to this rule occurs. . . . These citations are not always, however, able to alter the usage of Paul. We not only have an instance in which in Romans—as in the Gospels and Acts—a passage is applied to the Lord Christ in which in the O. T. the Lord Jehovah is spoken of (10[12]); but also two passages (11[1,2]) in which an O. T. 'Lord God' is altered to (11[8]) 'God.'"

No doubt by this elevation of Jesus as ' Lord ' to the side of God[14] certain peculiarities of expression are pro-
Jesus Embraced duced which are on a surface view suffi-
in the One ciently puzzling. Thus, for example,
Godhead in declaring the nonentity of the objects of heathen worship, Paul asserts roundly that " none is God except One," and proceeds to explicate this assertion by remarking that, although there may exist so-called gods whether in heaven or earth, as there are—obviously among the heathen—many gods and many lords, " yet to us there is one God, namely, the Father, from whom are all things and we unto Him " (1 Cor 8[4-6]). But he does not stop there, but adds at once, " And one Lord Jesus Christ, through whom are all things and we through Him " (1 Cor 8[6]). This addition might seem to a superficial reading to stultify his whole monotheistic argument: " There is no God but one; . . . for to us there is one God . . . and one Lord." There is but one possible solution. Obviously the one God whom Christians worship is conceived as, in some way not fully explained, without prejudice to His unity subsistent in both the ' one God,' viz., the Father and the ' one Lord,' viz., Jesus Christ. Otherwise there would be a flat contradiction

[14] Cf. David Somerville, *St. Paul's Conception of Christ*, p. 295 *seq.*, where the use of the term κύριος in the LXX. is examined, and it is added that it was as " accustomed to this usage that Paul confines the term κύριος to Christ and reserves θεός for the Father, God "— and " this plainly points to the belief that He whom he called Lord was in some sense God as well as He who was termed θεός" (p. 296). Cf. p. 143: " But the fact that he habitually applies to Christ the term ' Lord ' (κύριος) a term that in the LXX. is practically equivalent to God (θεός) and is the rendering of the most solemn name of Jehovah in the O. T., shows that in his regard He was entitled to the worship and obedience that are due to God."

between the emphatic assertion that " none is God but one " and the proof of this assertion offered in the explanation that to Christians there is but " one God, viz., the Father " and " one Lord, viz., Jesus Christ." And it is clear that Paul can count upon his readers understanding that the " one Lord, Jesus Christ " bears such a relation to the " one God, the Father " that these two may together be subsumed under the category of the one God who alone exists. We shall not say that there are the beginnings of the doctrine of the Trinity here. It seems truer to say that there is the clear pre-supposition of some such doctrine as that of the Trinity here.[15]

There is lacking, indeed, only the conjunction of " the Spirit" with " God the Father " and " Jesus the

Trinitarian Background

Lord " to compel us to perceive that underlying Paul's mode of speech concerning God there is a clearly conceived and firmly held conviction that these three together constitute the one God of Christian worship. And other passages enough supply this lack. For example, later on in this same Epistle the Apostle, speaking of those gifts of the Spirit with which the Apostolic Church was blessed, remarks in the most natural way in the world: " Now there are diversities of gifts but the same Spirit.

[15] Dr. Sanday, in his otherwise excellent note on Rom 1[7], neglects to consider the point here made, and speaks as if we were observing in these passages the formation of a christology and of a doctrine of the Trinity instead of the presupposition of these doctrines. He says: "The assignment of the respective titles of 'Father' and 'Lord' represents the first beginnings of christological speculation. It is stated in precise terms and with a corresponding assignment of appropriate prepositions in 1 Cor 8[6]. Not only does the juxtaposition of 'Father' and 'Lord' mark a stage in the doctrine of the Person of Christ; it also marks an important stage in the history of the doctrine of the

And there are diversities of ministrations, and the same Lord.   And there are diversities of workings, but the same God " (1 Cor 12$^{4-6}$).   " Now I beseech you, brethren," he says again towards the end of the Epistle to the Romans, " by our Lord Jesus Christ, and by the love of the Spirit, that ye strive together with me in your prayers to God for me " (Rom 15^{30}).   " There is one body and one Spirit, even as also ye were called in one hope of your calling," says he again, in a later Epistle (Eph 4$^{4\ \text{seq.}}$), " one Lord, one faith, one baptism, one God and Father of all, who is over all, and through all, and in all."   Or, perhaps, most explicitly of all, in those closing words of the Second Epistle to the Corinthians which have become the established form of benediction in the Churches: " The grace of the Lord Jesus Christ, and the love of God, and the communion of the Holy Spirit, be with you all " (2 Cor 13^{14}). From passages like these it is perfectly clear that the Christian doctrine of God as apprehended by Paul, and as currently implied in his natural modes of speech concerning Him, as he wrote in simplicity of heart and with no misgivings as to the understanding of his language by the Christian readers whom he addressed, embraced, in conjunction with the utmost stress upon the unity

Trinity.   It is already found some six years before the composition of Ep. to Romans at the time when St. Paul wrote his earliest extant Epistle (1 Thess 1^1, cf. 2 Thess 1^2).   This shows that even at that date (A. D. 52) the definition of the doctrine had begun.   It is well also to remember that although in this particular verse of Ep. to Romans the form in which it appears is incomplete, the triple formula concludes an Epistle written a few months earlier (2 Cor 13^{14}).   There is nothing more wonderful in the history of human thought than the silent and imperceptible way in which this doctrine, to us so difficult, took its place without struggle and without controversy among accepted Christian truths."   Dr. Sanday neglects to note that the triple formula is found in Romans as well as 2 Cor., viz., 15^{30}.

of God, the recognition at the same time of distinctions in the Divine Being by virtue of which the Lord Jesus Christ and the Holy Spirit were esteemed God along with the Father.

But what we require to note particularly at this point is that to Paul, the divine name—perhaps we may even be permitted to say, " the Trinitarian name "—of Jesus is apparently ' the Lord.' God, the Lord, the Spirit, —this is his triad, and when he speaks of Jesus as ' Lord ' it must be supposed that this triad is in his mind. In other words, ' Lord ' to him is not a general term of respect which he naturally applies to Jesus because he recognized Jesus as supreme, and was glad to acknowledge Him as his Master (Eph 6^9, Col 4^1), or even in the great words of Col 2^{19} as the ' Head ' of the body which is His Church (cf. Eph 4^{15}). It is to him the specific title of divinity by which he indicates to himself the relation in which Jesus stands to Deity. Jesus is not ' Lord ' to him because He has been given dominion over all creation; He has been given this universal dominion because he is ' Lord,' who with the Father and the Spirit is to be served and worshipped, and from whom all that the Christian longs for is to be expected. In His own nature the ' Lord of glory ' (1 Cor 2^8), He has died and lived again that He might enter upon His dominion as ' Lord ' of both the dead and the living (Rom 14^9), and being thus ' Lord of all ' (Rom 10^{12}) might be rich unto all that call upon Him and so fulfill the saying that whosoever " shall call upon the name of the Lord " shall be saved (Rom 10^{13}). He does not become ' Lord,' but only comes to His rights as ' Lord,' by and through

(marginal note: ' Lord ' the Trinitarian Name of Jesus)

His resurrection and ascension, which are the culminating and completing acts of His saving work. He is 'Lord' because He is in His own person the Jehovah who was to visit His people and save them from their sins.[16]

No doubt a different representation is sometimes given. We are even told that there is in these very

Appearance of Subordination

passages a distinction drawn between 'God' and 'the Lord,' by which the status of 'the Lord' is made definitely inferior to that of 'God,' to whom He is subject and whose will He executes. It is God the Father who is the source and end of all things; the 'Lord Jesus Christ' is the mediator through whom He works (1 Cor 8⁶, cf. 1 Tim 2⁵ and such passages—διά with the genitive—as the following, Rom 2¹⁶ 3²² 5¹,¹¹,¹⁷,²¹, Eph 1⁵,

---

[16] Cf. Paul Feine, *Jesus Christus und Paulus*, 1902, pp. 165 *seq.*: "If Jesus undertook to perform the redemptive acts which were in the O. T. hoped for from God's action, so in Paul, in correspondence with the advance of the redemptive work which lay in Christ's death and resurrection, there emerges even more strongly the idea of the divine activity of Christ. Paul applies to Christ words which in the O. T. refer to God,—2 Thess 1⁸,⁹ ˢᵉᑫ·, ¹² 1 Cor 1³¹ 2¹⁶ 10²², 2 Cor 3¹⁶ 8²¹ 10¹⁷, Rom 10¹⁶, Phil 2¹⁰ ˢᵉᑫ·, Eph 4⁸. 1 Thess 4⁶ is doubtful. One of the most commonly employed designations of Christ on the part of the Apostle is ὁ κύριος, the name in which the LXX. prevailingly represents the unpronounced יהוה. It is not merely in the letters to the Thessalonians uncertain in many passages whether God or Christ is intended by κύριος: even in 1 Cor we still meet with a multiform vacillation in the reference of κύριος to Christ and to God. Divine honors are given to Christ in 2 Thess 1⁹ ˢᵉᑫ·, Rom 10¹³, Phil 2¹⁰. In 2 Tim 4¹⁸ a doxology such as elsewhere is given to God is given to Him. One of the designations of Christians is 'those who call upon the name of our Lord Jesus Christ' (1 Cor 1²; similarly Rom 10¹² ˢᵉᑫ·, 2 Tim 2²²). Christ, after He has ascended above all the heavens (Eph 4¹⁰), sits at the right hand of God as sharer in the divine disposition of grace to believers (Rom 8³⁴ ˢᵉᑫ·), and has the

1 Th 5^9, Tit 3^6). The term 'Lord' as applied to Jesus, therefore, although ascribing a certain divinity to Him, appears to fall short of attributing deity to Him in its full sense. It is the appropriate designation of a sort of secondary divinity, a middle being standing in some sense between man and God. Accordingly we read that while "the head of every man is Christ," "the head of Christ is God" (1 Cor 11^3), and that "if we are Christ's," so "Christ is God's" (1 Cor 3^{23}). The whole redemptive work of Christ is represented as the working of God through Christ, as terminating ultimately on God, and as redounding specifically to His glory (Rom 3^{25} 5^{10} 8^3, 2 Cor 5^{18}, Eph $1^{6,12,14,19}$ 3^{19}, Col 1^{19}, etc.). When, then, the redemptive work is completed the 'Lordship' which has been conferred upon Christ ceases also, so that His very sovereignty appears as a derived sovereignty delegated for a purpose (1 Cor $15^{27,28}$). God is appropriately spoken of therefore distinctly as the "God of our Lord Jesus Christ" (Eph 1^{17}, cf. Rom 15^6, 2 Cor 1^3 11^{31}, Eph

power to subject all things to Himself (Phil 3^{21}). Every knee shall bow to Him in the realms of the heavenly and the earthly and the underearthly (Phil 2^{10}). He is Lord over every lordship and power and might and dominion and every name that is named (Eph $1^{20\ \text{seq.}}$, Col 2^{10}). The O. T. day of the Lord, the day of Judgment, has become *His* day (1 Thess 5^2, 2 Thess 1^{10} 2^2, 1 Cor $1^{8\ \text{seq.}}$). Christ is to carry out the world-judgment when He appears accompanied by His holy angels (1 Thess 3^{13}, 2 Thess $1^{7,10}$). All must appear before His throne (2 Cor 5^{10}). . . . The Apostle passes back and forth with references to God and Christ. Is 45^{23}, which in accord with its original meaning is referred to God in Rom 14^{11}, is applied to Christ in Phil 2^{10}. In Rom 14^{6-12} the Apostle begins with the words 'Who eats, eats to the *Lord,* for he gives thanks to *God,*' etc. (cf. 1 Cor 10^{31}). Then comes the beautiful declaration that we belong to the *Lord* in life and death; on which, however, he grounds the warning to judges that we must all stand before the judgment seat of *God.*"

1³), a locution which, while intimating that the relation subsisting between Him and Jesus is peculiarly close, yet equally clearly intimates that it is not a relation of equality but of the nature of divine master and subject servant.[17]

That a problem is raised by the passages of this class is obvious enough. But it is equally obvious that this problem cannot be solved by the attribu-

Its Impossibility with Paul

tion of a certain secondary divinity to Christ, and much less by supposing that He has merely a sort of divinity communicated to Him *quoad nos,* while in His essential nature only a creature. The strict and strongly asseverated monotheism of Paul forbids the former assumption: his definite ascription to Jesus of an eternal divine form of existence antecedent to His earthly career excludes the latter. Nothing could exceed the clearness and emphasis of Paul's

[17] Cf. for statement of this point of view Beyschlag *Die Christologie des N. T.,* 1866, pp. 203 *seq.:* "Whatever there may be great and unique lying in the εἷς κύριος, it is undeniable that Paul purposely does not apply the name θεός to Christ, but rather most distinctly distinguishes the εἷς κύριος from the εἷς θεός besides whom there is no other. The same conception and manner of expression runs exceptionlessly and in numerous instances throughout the Pauline Epistles: everywhere ' God '=the Father, our Father, the Father of our Lord Jesus Christ, and everywhere the ' Father ' and the Father only=God, our God, the ' God of Jesus Christ ' (Eph 1¹⁷) : everywhere in a word the conception of ' God ' and ' Father ' stand together, while the ' Son ' or the ' Lord ' is equally constantly distinguished from the ' Father.' " How overstated this is may be observed by comparing it with the text. Cf. the long argument to the same effect in Richard Schmidt's *Die paulinische Christologie,* etc., 1870, pp. 148 *seq.;* and the brief but pointed statement of Paul Feine, *Jesus Christus und Paulus,* 1902, pp. 168, 169; also David Somerville, *St. Paul's Conception of Christ,* etc., 1897, pp. 140, 141.

monotheism. " None is God," says he, " but one "[18]
(1 Cor 8⁴) ; and he says it, as we have seen, in immediate connection with his recognition of ' one God,
the Father " and " one Lord, Jesus Christ " (cf. Rom
3³⁰ 16²⁷, Gal 3²⁰, Eph 4⁶, 1 Tim 2⁵). How, then,
could he mean to set by the side of this " one God the
Father " the " one Lord Jesus Christ " as a second,
although somewhat inferior, God?[19] And nothing
could exceed the clearness and emphasis with which
Paul represents Jesus' divine majesty not as an attain-
ment but as an aboriginal possession. He does not
say that Jesus Christ became rich that by His riches
we might be enriched, as he must have said if he had
conceived of Jesus as a man to whom divine powers
and dignity were communicated that He might save
us. What he says is that our Lord Jesus Christ was
rich, and became poor only for our sakes, that
" through His poverty we might become rich " (2 Cor
8⁹). That is to say, that, as he expresses it in another
place, it was to make no account of Himself for Him
to take the " form of a servant " (Phil 2⁷). Nor does
he leave us in doubt as to the quality of the riches He
left when He thus made Himself of no reputation by
taking " the form of a servant." No heavenly hu-

---

[18] " No [Being] is God except One [Being]," Evans *in loc.;* cf.
Edwards *in loc.:* " There is but one God and the Christians' God is
that One."

[19] The fallacy of writers like Beyschlag, *Christologie d. N. T.,* 1866,
consists in treating the phrase " to us there is one God the Father "
as taking up and repeating the " There is no God but One," and the
phrase " and one Lord Jesus Christ " as a kind of afterthought added
to it (pp. 203-4). In truth it is the double clause: " There is one God
the Father . . . and one Lord Jesus Christ for us," which takes
up and develops the phrase, " None is God but One."

manity suffices here: not even angelic grandeur:[20] it
was "in the form of God" that He was by nature
($ὑπάρχων$) : it was "equality with God" which He did
not graspingly cling to. And to be "in the form of
God" means nothing less than to have and hold in
possession all those characterizing attributes which
make God God: having which He could not but be
equal with God, because He was just God. No wonder
then that Paul tells us that though He was crucified
by man yet was He 'the Lord of glory' (1 Cor 2[8]),
that in Him dwelt "all the fulness of the Godhead
bodily" (Col 2[9]), that Israelite as He was " according
to the flesh" He was something much more than
what He was according to the flesh—nothing less indeed than "God over all, blessed forever" (Rom 9[5]).

He certainly does not mean then to contrast Jesus
as 'Lord' with God the Father as an inferior God
or as possessing a merely delegated
divinity. Nor, indeed, does the term
'Lord' lend itself readily to such a
contrast. On the pages of Paul's Bible—the Greek
version of the Hebrew Scriptures—it stood side by side
with 'God' as the most personal and intimate name

*Implication of
Term 'Lord'*

[20] Richard Schmidt, *Die paulinische Christologie,* 1870, pp. 148
seq., represents it as difficult to fix on a formula by which to express
Paul's conception of what the preëxistent Christ was. We may at first
sight think that to suppose he conceived the antemundane Christ as
man will best meet his references: but that will soon appear inadequate. Nor can we satisfy ourselves that he thought of Him as an
angel. Nor indeed that he conceived Him after the fashion of later
Trinitarianism as of purely intro-divine relations. It is unimportant
whether he calls Christ ' God ' as, e.g. in Rom 9[5], or not: for even if
he applies the name to Him the question would still remain open
whether he means by it what we should naturally express by it. This
seems, however, in the face of Paul's repeated attribution to Jesus of
full deity in a great variety of modes of expression, very hypercritical.

of Deity: and thence he took it as we have seen and applied it to Jesus. And if it thus could not have been lower in its connotation to him than ' Jehovah ' itself, it was charged likewise to the apprehension of his Gentile readers with suggestions in no way inferior to those of ' God ' itself.[21] For him to say ' Lord ' of Jesus as His most appropriate title was therefore to say and to be understood as saying all that he could say by the designation of ' God ' itself. And if nevertheless there was to him and to his readers but one God, then there is nothing for it but that we should recognize that for Paul and his readers two might be God and yet there be but one God; and that is as much as to say that their thinking of God was already ruled by a Trinitarian consciousness.

As for the expressions in which, despite his clear intimation of the proper deity of Jesus, he yet speaks of Him as in some sense inferior or,

Subordination is Humiliation

to be more precise, subordinate, to God the Father, it is quite clear that they must find their explanation in Paul's intimation of the humiliation to which this divine Person subjected Himself for the purposes of redemption. When He who was rich became poor; when He who was and ever remains " in the form of God " made Himself of no reputation " by taking the form of a servant ": then and thus He became so far inferior to and subject to that God the Father on an equality with whom He might have remained in His riches had He so chosen. In and for the purposes of this redemptive work He

[21] Cf. Harnack, *Hist. of Dogma*, I. p. 119, note 1: " *Dominus* in certain circumstances means more than *Deus;* see Tertull *Apol.* . . . It signifies more than *Soter;* see Irenaeus I. i. 3: . . . ' They say Saviour since they do not wish to call Him Lord ' . . ."

is the Mediator of God the Father, whose He is, and who is His Head and His God; whose will He performs and whose purposes of grace He executes; and to whom, when the redemptive work is fully accomplished and its fruits garnered, He shall restore the Kingdom, that God may be all in all. In a word, there underlies Paul's statements not merely the conceptions which have found expression in the doctrine of the Trinity and the Incarnation, but those also which have found expression in the doctrine of the Covenant of Redemption in accordance with which the Persons of the Godhead carry on each His own part of the work of redemption: and he who will not recognize these conceptions in the Pauline statements must ever find those statements a confused puzzle of contradictions, which can be reduced to apparent harmony only by doing manifest violence to one or another series of them. Only on the presupposition of these conceptions can it be understood how the Apostle can speak of our Lord now as " in the form of God," " on an equality with God," nay, as " God over all," and now as subject to God as His Head and His God with reference to whom He performs all His work: and how He can speak of " God the Father " and " Jesus Christ our Lord " as each " God over all," and yet declare that there is but one Being who is God.

With this high meaning of ' Lord ' as attributed to Jesus in our mind it is interesting to observe the various forms of designation into which this epithet enters. These run through nearly all the possible combinations with the names of Jesus. ' The (or our) Lord Jesus,' which, were the title ' Lord ' a mere honorific, would

Designations Compounded with ' Lord '

be the simplest of them all, but which, since that title is an express declaration of deity, is now the most paradoxical,[22] occurs some twenty-four to twenty-six times, chiefly in the earlier Epistles; and its duplicate, 'Jesus our Lord,' twice more. 'The (or our) Lord Christ' is less frequent, occurring only twice (Rom 16[18], Col 3[24]). But the full formula, 'the (or our) Lord Jesus Christ,' is the most common of all, occurring some forty-nine times, pretty evenly scattered through all the Epistles. 'The (or our) Lord Christ Jesus' does not occur: but in the reverse order of the titles, 'Christ Jesus, the (or our, or my) Lord,' this combination occurs ten times and by its side, "Jesus Christ, our Lord" four times. In all these combinations the names, whether the simple 'Jesus,' the simple 'Christ,' or the combinations 'Jesus Christ' or 'Christ Jesus,' appear to be used as proper names, though, no doubt, the appellative 'Christ' does not in any of them become a mere proper name. Certainly in the phrase, "Ye serve the Lord Christ," the term 'Christ' is a title of dignity which is still further enhanced by the adjunction of the term 'Lord': and something of the same intention to enhance an already lofty ascription appears traceable in the instances where the fuller phrase 'Christ Jesus, our Lord' occurs (1 Cor 15[31], [2 Cor 4[5]], Rom 6[23] 8[39], [Col 2[6]], Eph 3[11], [Phil 3[8]]). But this obvious use of 'Christ' as a name of dignity

[22] Cf. Heinrici-Meyer, 1896, on 1 Cor 12[3], p. 363: "The paradoxical synthesis of the historical personal name with the divine name of dignity (cf. p. 353" [where the paradox of speaking of 'the Lord's death' in 11[26] is adverted to]) "is the crispest and most impressive form of the Christian confession. The Apostle accordingly looks upon κύριος Ἰησοῦς as the fixed watch-word of the believing heart, and the key-note of spiritual speech."

by no means implies that it is not employed practically
as a proper name. Its implications of Messiahship
remain present and suggestive, but it has become the
peculiar property of Jesus who is thought of as so
indisputably the Messiah that the title ' Messiah ' has
become His proper name.[23]

It is worthy of remark moreover that not only is

[23] As is natural, opinions differ on this matter. Says Feine, *op. cit.*
29: "It is still a much controverted question. Bornemann (Meyer's
Com. on 1 *Thess.* 1[10]) maintains that $X\rho\iota\sigma\tau\delta\varsigma$ is never a proper name
in the N. T.: on the other hand, von Soden (*Theolog. Abhandlungen
Weizsäcker gewidmet*, 1902, p. 118), considers $X\rho\iota\sigma\tau\delta\varsigma$ already to
have won the character of a proper name so fully that it has the article
only about sixty times.' Westcott-Hort also print $X\rho\iota\sigma\tau\delta\varsigma$ when it
stands without the article, as a proper name with a capital initial: on
which Schmiedel (Winer, *Grammatik*, § 54) remarks that δ $X\rho\iota\sigma\tau\delta\varsigma$
just as truly is a proper name in a series of passages.' " " Hausleiter
also (p. 9) points out that ' Christ ' has for the Apostle frequently the
significance of a proper name for designating the person of Jesus."
Feine thinks the term is appellative in such passages as Rom 9[5] 10[6,7],
2 Cor 5[16], Gal 2[17], and that the Messianic suggestion is generally
present. Dr. Sanday in his *Inspiration*, 289, speaks cautiously (but
scarcely cautiously enough): " We know how in the Epistles ' Christ '
has become almost a proper name. It may perhaps retain rather more
of its true meaning than we are apt to realize; but if not exactly a
proper name it is rapidly becoming such." So far, so good. But more
doubt attaches to the assertions that follow: " In the Gospels, on the
other hand, it nearly always means, as in the mouth of our Lord and
His strict contemporaries it must have meant, ' the Messiah ' . . .
The compound phrase ' Jesus Christ ' occurs a few times (Mt 1[1] 1[18]
(v. l.) 16[21] (v. l.), Mk 1[1], Jno 1[17] 17[3] 20[31]), but always, with one exception (Jno 17[3]), as it should do, in words of the evangelist and not
of our Lord Himself. The true phrase, the natural phrase in our
Lord's life-time, is of course that which we find three times in St. Matthew, ' Jesus *who is called Christ* ' (Mt 1[16] 27[17,22])." Dr. Sanday mis-
conceives the significance of the phrase ' Jesus who is called Christ,'
not perceiving that it presupposes that ' Christ ' had already become a
quasi-proper name, having in this respect the same implications as the
compound ' Jesus Christ.'

'Christ' a proper name of our Lord with Paul, but
it is his favorite designation for Him.[24]
For, full and rich as Paul's employment of the term 'Lord' is, it is not
nearly so frequently employed by him as 'Christ.' This
designation (more commonly with than without the
article)[25] occurs in his Epistles no fewer than 210 or
211 times in its simplicity, and many more times in
combination with other designations. It is most dom-
inantly Paul's favorite name for our Lord in the great
central Epistles—Romans, Corinthians and Galatians,
—in which it occurs some 138 to 140 times; but it is
also very frequent in the Epistles of the first imprison-

[marginal notes: 'Christ' Paul's Favorite Designation]

---

[24] Harnack, *Hist. Dog.*, E. T., I. p. 184, note 2, says: "Only in the
second half of the second century, if I am not mistaken, did the designation 'Jesus Christ' or 'Christ' become the current one, more and
more crowding out the simple Jesus." This appears to be founded on
the relative usage of the terms in the writings of the early post-Apos-
tolic age. On taking a broader outlook the appearance of things is
altered. Already in Paul the simple 'Jesus' has retired into the background and the simple 'Christ' together with compounds of 'Christ'
has taken its place. There is in fact no question here of change or
development of usage: but only of character of literature. In the
N. T. 'Jesus' is only the narrative name of our Lord: 'Christ' and its
compounds, together with 'Lord,' the didactic name. So far as appears from the evidence, Christians were from the beginning accustomed to speak of Jesus as 'Christ,' 'Lord,' whenever they were not
merely recounting His deeds in the flesh. The use of 'Lord' and its
high implications are recognized by Harnack as an early phenomenon
persisting through the succeeding eras (p. 183).

[25] Anarthrous $X\rho\iota\sigma\tau\acute{o}\varsigma$ in Paul: Rom $5^{6,8}$ $6^{4,8,9}$ $8^{9,10,17}$ 9^1 $10^{4,6,7,17}$
12^5 $14^{9,15}$ $15^{8,18,20,29}$ $16^{5,7,9,10}$, I Cor $1^{12,17,23,24}$ 2^{16} $3^{1,23,23}$ $4^{1,10,10,15}$
5^7 6^{15} 7^{22} $8^{11,12}$ 9^{21} 11^1 12^{27} $15^{3,12,13,14,16,17,18,19,20,23}$, 2 Cor 1^{21} 2^{10},
$2^{15,17}$ $3^{3,14}$ $5^{16,17,18,19,20,20}$ 6^{15} $10^{7,7}$ $11^{3,10,13,23}$ $12^{2,10,19}$ Gal
$1^{6,10,22}$ $2^{16,17,17,20,20,21}$ $3^{13,16,24,27,29}$ 4^{19} $5^{1,2,4}$, Eph 1^3 2^{12} $4^{15,32}$
$5^{21,32}$, Phil $1^{10,13,17,18,20,21,23,29}$ $2^{1,16,30}$ $3^{8,9}$, Col $1^{2,27,28}$ $2^{2,5,8,20}$ 3^{11},
Philem 6,8,20, I Thess 2^6 4^{16}; and not at all in the Pastorals; **127 in all.**

ment (67 times in Eph., Col., Phil., Philemon), and is unusual only in the Thessalonian letters (4 times only) and in the Pastorals (once only). It surprises us somewhat to observe that next to the simple 'Christ' (and 'Lord'), Paul's favorite designation for our

'Christ Jesus'

Lord is the compound 'Christ Jesus.' This form, as we have seen, seems to occur occasionally in Acts, not only as a Pauline (24^{24}) but also as a primitive Christian (3^{20}) and a Lucan formula (5^{42}).[26] But in Paul's Epistles it occurs not less than 82 (84) times, regularly anarthrously (except Eph 3^1, cf. 3^{11}, Col 2^6), and pretty evenly distributed, though with a tendency to increased frequency in the progress of time (Thess. only 2; Gal., Cor., Rom. 29; first imprisonment, 29; Pastorals 24). It is possible that the prepositing of the 'Christ' may throw greater emphasis upon the Messianic dignity of Jesus than was currently felt in the opposite compound 'Jesus Christ,'[27] which is much less frequent in Paul (only 23 times; and not at all in Thess., Col., Philemon). But in any case, both

[26] Cf. also Mt 1^{18}, v. r.

[27] So e.g. Paul Feine, *op. cit.*, p. 36: "The ground of this combination is a feeling of need on Paul's part to throw the Messianic aspect of Jesus into the foreground. This form, Χριστὸς Ἰησοῦς, accordingly has much the same significance as that in which the Apostle uses the simple 'Christ.'" In his comment on Rom 1^1, Dr. Sanday discusses the forms of the names of Jesus used by Paul in the addresses to his Epistles. He supposes that in the addresses of the earlier Epistles Paul used Ἰησοῦς Χριστός, but in those of the later Χριστὸς Ἰησοῦς. "The interest of this," he adds, "would be in the fact that in Χριστὸς Ἰησοῦς the first word would seem to be rather more distinctly a proper name than in Ἰησοῦς Χριστός. No doubt the latter phrase is rapidly passing into a proper name, but Χριστός would seem to have a little of its sense as a title still clinging to it: the

formulas are employed as practically proper names of our Lord, and it is difficult to trace any difference in the implications of their use. Along with these simple compounds Paul also employs the more elaborate formulas, 'the (or our) Lord Jesus Christ,' 'Jesus Christ our Lord,' 'Christ Jesus, the (or our, or my) Lord.' The first of these meets us most frequently, occurring indeed no fewer than 49 times, pretty evenly distributed through the Epistles. The second occurs only four times (Romans 3 and 1 Cor 1): and the last only ten times (two central groups of Epistles only). In these sonorous formulas the Apostle expresses his deep sense of reverence to the person of Jesus, and he tends to fall into one or the other of them whenever he is speaking of his Master with solemnity and exalted feeling.[28] It is noticeable that

phrase would be in fact transitional between Χριστός or ὁ Χριστός of the Gospels and the later Χριστὸς Ἰησοῦς or Χριστός simply as a proper name." He refers us to his own *Bampton Lectures*, p. 289 *seq.*, and to an article by the Rev. F. Herbert Stead in *The Expositor*, 1888, i. pp. 386 *seq.* According to Feine, then Χριστὸς Ἰησοῦς is more of a proper name; according to Sanday it is less of a proper name, than Ἰησοῦς Χριστός. The truth seems to be that both are practically proper names: and neither has lost the whole implication of office. For the rest is it not rash to speak of one as an "earlier" or a "later" form than the other? "Jesus Christ" is, indeed, placed once on our Lord's lips (Jno 17³), and is used by the evangelists (Mt 1¹,¹⁸ 16²¹, Mk 1¹, Jno 1¹⁷ [17³]), but "Christ Jesus" already appears on the lips of the earliest followers of Jesus (Acts 3²⁰), and in Paul's earliest epistle (1 Thess 2¹⁴ 5¹⁸). "Jesus Christ" appears not only in 1 Thess (1¹ 3¹ 5⁹,²³,²⁸), but also in James (1¹ 2¹).

[28] Cf. Feine, *op. cit.*, pp. 41 *seq.*: "'Ἰησοῦς Χριστός and ὁ κύριος Ἰησοῦς are already solemn names of Jesus: and this is in still higher degree the case with ὁ κύριος (ἡμῶν) Ἰησοῦς Χριστός. It gives expression formally and ceremoniously to the majesty of Jesus over against the believers, and has something in it of the nature of a

they are apt to be employed in the formal solemn opening and closing sections of his Epistles, and whenever Jesus is named in direct connection with God.

In the Pastoral Epistles the compound names ' Jesus Christ ' and ' Christ Jesus ' occur also in composition with the epithet ' Saviour ': ' Christ Jesus our Saviour ' (Titus 1⁴), ' Jesus Christ our Saviour ' (Titus 3⁶), ' our Saviour Christ Jesus ' (2 Tim 1¹⁰), ' our Saviour Jesus Christ ' (Titus 2¹³).   In the earlier Epistles, Jesus is indeed not only treated as our ' Saviour,' but the epithet is given Him as a title of honor, it being a mark of Christians that they look for a ' Saviour ' from heaven, even ' the Lord Jesus Christ ' (Phil 3²⁰, cf. Eph 5²⁰).   But the precise forms of expression occurring in the Pastorals are not found in these.   The significance of the epithet ' Saviour ' thus applied to Jesus may perhaps be suggested by the circumstance that it is in the same Epistles a standing epithet of God.   Paul describes himself as an apostle of Jesus Christ " according to the command of God our Saviour and Christ Jesus our hope " (1 Tim 1¹, cf. Titus 1³), and wishes Timothy to live so as to be acceptable " in the sight of God our Saviour " (2³, cf. Titus 2¹⁰) whose glory it is to be ' the Saviour ' of man (4¹⁰), in accordance with His love to men as our ' Saviour ' (Titus 3⁴).[29]   The ascription of this epithet thus in-

Jesus the ' Saviour '

confession. . . .   In Paul this formula occurs for the most part in the opening and closing greetings. . . .   And it occurs frequently when Jesus is named in connection with God."   " Both of the formulas [Χριστὸς Ἰησοῦς ὁ κύριος (ἡμῶν, μοῦ) and Ἰησοῦς Χριστὸς ὁ κύριος ἡμῶν] have something very solemn about them."

[29] Cf. Swete on Rev 7¹⁰: " The cry Ἡ σωτηρία τῷ θεῷ καὶ τῷ ἀρνίῳ is equivalent to attributing to Both the title of Σωτήρ, so freely

terchangeably to God and to Jesus assimilates Jesus to God and leaves us in less doubt how we are to take the passage in Titus 2¹³ which in contrast

'The Great God'

with Christ's first coming in grace speaks of the impending "appearing of the glory of "—shall we say "the great God and our Saviour Jesus Christ "?—or shall we not rather say "our great God and Saviour Jesus Christ "? If the latter construction is followed, as it seems it should be,[30] it provides us with one of the most solemn ascriptions of proper deity to Jesus Christ discoverable in the whole compass of the New Testament.

Perhaps something similar is implied in the designation of Him in Eph 1⁶ as the 'Beloved,' the epithet appearing in its simple majesty without

'The Beloved'

qualification: "His grace which He "—that is God—" freely bestowed on us in the Beloved." We have already had occasion to point out the significance of this phrase on its appear-

given by loyal or pliant cities of Asia to the Emperors, but belonging in Christian eyes only to God and to His Christ. The Pastoral Epistles supply examples of both applications, (1) 1 Tim 1¹ 2³, Tit 1³ 3⁴, (2) Tit 1⁴ 2¹³ 3⁶." Also p. clxiii.: "The phrase is perhaps suggested by the free use of σωτήρ on coins and in inscriptions in reference to certain of the heathen deities (e.g. Zeus, Asklepios), and to the Emperors. John recalls the word from these unworthy uses, and claims it for the Ultimate Source of health and life. But in this attribution he includes Jesus Christ."

[30] Cf. Weiss (Meyer) *in loc.,* correcting Huther. Cf. Schmiedel-Winer, *Grammatik,* p. 158: "In Tit 2¹³, 2 P 1¹, 2 Thess 1¹², Jude 4, Eph 5⁵, and Acts 20²⁸, according to the badly attested reading τὴν ἐκκλ. τοῦ κυρίου καὶ θεοῦ, grammar strictly requires, as well as in 2 P 1¹¹ 2²⁰ 3²,¹⁸, that there should be in every case a single person intended, and therefore Christ be called θεός or μόνος δεσπότης. Nevertheless it is possible for κύριος in 2 Thess and Jude, and θεός in Eph (and Acts) to stand as a designation of a new person (§ 19, 13 d). That σωτήρ too in Titus and 2 P can also be so construed,

ing in the Gospels as a designation of Jesus (Mt 3[17]
12[18] 17[5], Mk 1[11] 9[7], Lk 3[22]). Here the same epithet
meets us without the defining accompaniments: Jesus
Christ is in full simplicity set forth as by way of
eminence 'the Beloved,' in and through whom God
has communicated His grace to men. This designation
of Christ "makes us feel," we are told, "the greatness of the divine grace."[31] But it does this only by
making us feel the greatness of the Mediator of this
grace. It is only at the cost of the blood of the
'Beloved' that God has redeemed us. The epithet
of 'Saviour' is a designation of our Lord from the
point of view of men: this epithet of 'Beloved' tells
us what He is from the point of view of God—He
is God's own unique One, the object of His supreme
choice, who stands related to Him in the intimacy of
appropriating love. In the parallel passage in the
sister Epistle (Col 1[13]), Paul calls our Lord "the
Son of God's love." This seems a combination of
the two titles, the 'Son of God,' and the 'Beloved';
and bears witness to their close affinity,—which indeed
is inherent in their significance. We will recall that
in the evangelical use of 'the Beloved' it stands in
the closest relation with 'Son': "This is my Son, the
Beloved, in whom I am well pleased." It is only in

since it has $\dot{\eta}\mu\tilde{\omega}\nu$ with it, is acc. to § 19, 5, to be left open. In any
case no one will ground here on Grammar, but must hold a careless
construction possible, and therefore in deciding the question leave
room for material considerations." Winer (Thayer, p. 130) had on
Biblico-theological grounds decided in these passages for two persons—
that is, he had decided on the strength of his conception of what these
authors would be likely to say; but he allows that grammatically they
are flexible to the other opinion.

[31] Meyer *in loc.*

connection with the idea of ' Son,' thus, that ' Beloved ' comes to its rights.[32]

On the other side, the compound names, ' Jesus Christ ' and ' Christ Jesus,' appear in Paul's Epistles also in combination with designations which emphasize rather the human aspect of our Lord's person. We read of " the man Jesus Christ " (Rom 5^{15}), of " the man Christ Jesus " (1 Tim 2^5), and somewhat more frequently we are, apart from such a combination with His personal name, directed to contemplate our Lord as a " Man " ($\mathring{\alpha}\nu\theta\rho\omega\pi\sigma\varsigma$). In very few of these instances, it is true, is the emphasis primarily upon the fact of humanity. Most commonly it is thrown upon some point of likeness or contrast between Jesus and that other man, Adam (Rom $5^{15,[19]}$, 1 Cor $15^{21,47,[48,49]}$, cf. 15^{45}, " last Adam "), and it is the singleness or the superiority of this ' Man ' which is in question. But in a passage like 1 Tim 2^5, " There is one God, one mediator also between God and man, Himself man, Christ Jesus," it is clear that the humanity of Christ itself is insisted upon: and there is a necessary if somewhat unemphasized suggestion of humanity underlying all these passages. The lesson we must first of all draw from this series of passages seems, then, to be that neither ' Jesus Christ ' nor ' Christ Jesus ' is a designation of such supreme dignity that it could not suggest itself as an appropriate name for Jesus when

Jesus the ' Man '

[32] On this designation see the full note of· J. Armitage Robinson in his commentary on *St. Paul's Epistle to the Ephesians*, 1903, pp. 229-233; and cf. Hastings' *Dictionary of the Bible*, II. p. 501. Cf. also Charles, *The Ascension of Isaiah*, 1900, pp. 3 *seq.*, and E. Daplyn, in Hastings' *D. C. G.*, *sub voc.* (I. pp. 188, 189).

the mind of the writer was intent on precisely His humanity, as indeed no designation could be in the case of a being who was not purely divine, not even 'the Lord of Glory' (1 Cor 2⁸) or 'God' itself (Acts 20²⁸). Beyond that, we learn, therefore, that clear and strong as was Paul's conception of the proper deity of Christ, it in no wise precluded him from also recognizing with equal clarity and expounding with equal force His essential humanity. When He who was in the form of God took the form of a servant

But not Merely Man He was made in the likeness of men and was formed in fashion as a man (Phil 2⁷‧⁸); and Paul found no difficulty in so understanding, even though he also understood that the " *taking* the form of a servant " was not a supercession of " the form of God " but an addition to it: and that therefore though now made in the likeness of men and formed in fashion as a man, Jesus remained nevertheless unbrokenly " in the form of God " (ὑπάρχων, verse 6, observe the tense) and able at will to lay hold again of His essential equality with God. Accordingly, therefore, the Apostle, if he represented Jesus as of the seed of David, represented Him as this only on one side of His being,—that side which he calls " according to the flesh " (Rom 1³‧⁴): if he saw in Him, to the glory of the covenant people, an Israelite, he saw this also in Him only " according to the flesh " (Rom 9⁵). It cannot be denied that there underlies this whole mode of conception the idea of " the two natures " of Christ, on the basis of which alone can this duplex method of speaking of Him be defended or even comprehended.

In the opening verses of the greatest of his Epistles

the Apostle brings the two sides of our Lord's being
The Two Sides sharply to our apprehension. Reduced
of Christ's to its lowest terms, what he tells us
Being here is that on one side of His being
our Lord was the ' Son of David ' and on the other
side the ' Son of God.' These two sides of being he
speaks of respectively as " according to the flesh " and
" according to the Spirit of holiness," which may be
briefly paraphrased respectively as the human and the
divine sides. But he does not leave us to infer that
these two sides of our Lord's being were equally original to Him. On the contrary, he tells us that the
human side had a historical beginning, while the divine
side knew only an historical establishment: our Lord
was made—came to be ($\gamma \varepsilon \nu \acute{o} \mu \varepsilon \nu o \varsigma$)—of the seed of
David according to the flesh; He was ' designated '
—marked out as ($\acute{o} \rho \iota \sigma \theta \acute{\varepsilon} \nu \tau o \varsigma$)—the ' Son of God ' by the
resurrection of the dead. Becoming man, He brought
life and immortality to light, and thus showed Himself
more than man,—nothing less than ' the Son of God.'
The highest human exaltation is the Messiahship: but
His Messiahship was the lower side of His majesty.
That He might be the Messiah He stooped from His
prior estate of divine glory.[33] Thus clearly the Apostle
presents our Lord as essentially the ' Son of God,' and
this Sonship to God as essentially consubstantiality with
God.[34] After precisely the same fashion, at a later

[33] Cf. Lightfoot on Rom 1⁴: " The word $\gamma \varepsilon \nu \acute{o} \mu \varepsilon \nu o \varsigma$ implies a prior
existence of the Son before the Incarnation. . . . His Messiahship
was after all only the lower aspect of His Person ($\varkappa \alpha \tau \grave{\alpha} \ \sigma \acute{\alpha} \rho \varkappa \alpha$).
His personality as the Divine Word . . . was His higher aspect."
[34] Cf. Sanday on Rom 1⁴: " It is certain that St. Paul did not hold
that the Son of God *became* such by the Resurrection. The undoubted

point of the same Epistle, having occasion to mention
Christ as sprung from the seed of Israel, he at once
pauses as if to guard himself from the imputation of
insufficient reverence, to add the limitation, " according to the flesh." He was not wishing to speak of
Christ even incidentally as merely man. And so greatly
did his reverence for His person swell in his heart,
that, in adjoining a designation of His higher nature, he is content with nothing lower than the
highest conceivable. " From whom is Christ, as according to the flesh,"—that Christ " who is in His
essential being (ὁ ὢν) none other than God over all
blessed for ever " (9⁵). On the side in which He
was not " according to the flesh," He was the Supreme
God ruling over all things.

It is, however, significant rather than copious use
which the Apostle makes of the category of the ' Son

Epistles are clear on this point (esp. 2 Cor 4⁴ 8⁹, cf. Col 1¹⁵⁻¹⁹). At
the same time he *did* regard the Resurrection as making a difference—
if not in the transcendental relations of the Father to the Son (which
lie beyond our cognizance), yet in the visible manifestation of Sonship
as addressed to the understanding of men (cf. esp. Phil 2⁹ . . .). This
is sufficiently expressed by our word ' designated,' which might perhaps
with advantage also be used in the two places in the Acts (10⁴² 17³¹).
It is true that Christ *becomes* Judge in a sense in which He does not
become Son; but He is Judge too not wholly by an external creation,
but by an internal right. The Divine declaration, as it were, endorses
and proclaims that right. . . . It is as certain that when St. Paul
speaks of Him as ὁ ἴδιος υἱός (Rom 8³²), ὁ ἑαυτοῦ υἱός (8³),
he intends to cover the period of preëxistence as that St. John identifies the μονογενής with the preëxistent Logos." Cf. also Robinson on
Eph. 4¹³ (p. 100): When Paul is treating of the relation of our Lord
to the Church he speaks of Him as ' the Christ'; but when he would
describe Him as the object of saving faith, he speaks of Him as the
' Son of God '—" thereby suggesting, it would seem, the thought of His
eternal existence in relation to the Divine Father."

of God' in his presentation of the personality of
'Son of God' Jesus to his readers.[35] It is doubtless
at least in part due to his predilection
for the term 'Lord' as the Trinitarian name of
Jesus that Paul speaks of Him only some seventeen
times as 'the Son.'[36] In a number of these instances[37]
there is naturally little indication of the particular implication of deity which it nevertheless always carries
with it in Paul's usage.[38] In others, however, the whole
point of the employment of the term hangs on the
uniqueness of the relation to God which it intimates.
This is the case, for instance, when this uniqueness of
relation is emphasized by the added term " own ":
God, we are told for example (Rom 8³), sent " His
own Son " (τὸν ἑαυτοῦ υἱόν) " in the likeness of sinful
flesh " " to condemn sin in the flesh ": and again God
spared not " His own Son " (τοῦ ἰδίου υἱοῦ) but " delivered Him up for us all " (Rom 8³²). Obviously
we are expected to estimate the greatness of the gift

[35] It is a usage which he was so far from inventing that he seems to
have brought it with him when he entered on his career as a preacher
of the Gospel. " It is most significant," remarks Knowling (*The Testimony of St. Paul to Christ*, p. 43), " that the first and earliest intimation which we have in Acts of St. Paul's Christian teaching is this, that
' in the synagogues,' not to Greeks and Romans, but to Jews and prose-
lytes, ' he proclaimed Jesus that He is the Son of God' (Acts 9²⁰)."
It is already an old form of speech with him when he wrote his first
Epistle (cf. 1 Thess 1¹⁰ and see Knowling, pp. 229 *seq.*).

[36] Rom 1³,⁴,⁹ 5¹⁰ 8³,²⁹,³², 1 Cor 1⁹ 15²⁸, 2 Cor 1¹⁹, Gal 1¹⁶ 2²⁰ 4⁴,⁶,
Eph 4¹³, Col 1¹³, 1 Thess 1¹⁰.

[37] E.g. 1 Thess 1¹⁰, Gal 1¹⁶ 2²⁰, Col 1¹³, Eph 4¹³.

[38] Cf. Meyer on Rom 1³,⁴ (E. T., pp. 43, 44): " The Apostle *never*
designates Christ as the υἱὸς θεοῦ otherwise (cf. Gess. *v. d. Pers.
Christi*, p. 89 *seq.*; Weiss, *Bibl. Theol.*, p. 309) than from the standpoint of the knowledge of God given him by revelation (Gal 1¹⁶) of
the metaphysical Sonship (8³,³², Gal 4⁴, Col 1¹³, Phil 2⁶, *al*)."

by the closeness of the relation indicated: it is because it was His own Son whom He gave that the love of God to us was so splendidly manifested in the gift of Jesus, who, we are further told, was for this gift "sent forth from" Himself (Gal 4[4], ἐξαπέστειλεν). This closeness of relation, amounting really to identity, is somewhat oddly suggested by the argument in Rom 5[8-10]. Here we are told that scarcely for a righteous man would one die: but God commends His love to us —or as it is strengtheningly put, His *own* love to us— by dying for us while we were yet sinners? No,— by *Christ's* dying for us while we were sinners! But how does God commend His *own* love for us—by someone else's dying for us? Obviously the relation between Christ and God is thought of as so intimate that Christ's dying is equivalent to God Himself dying. And so, we read further that this Christ is God's Son (v. 10) and His dying for us is to such an extent the pledge of God's love that it carries with it the promise and potency of all good things (vv. 10, 11).

With this emphasis on the Sonship of Christ and its high significance it is a little strange that the correlative Fatherhood of God is brought so little into immediate connection with it.

God
'the Father'

The explanation is doubtless again that Paul prefers the title 'Lord' to express our Lord's Trinitarian relations. The Fatherhood of God is in any event not very frequently adverted to by Paul, and is very seldom brought into immediate relation with Jesus. Indeed God is expressly called the Father of Jesus Christ only in those few passages in which He is spoken of as "the God and Father of our Lord Jesus Christ" (Rom 15[6], 2 Cor 1[3] 11[31], Eph 1[3], [Col

1³]). In a number of other passages in which God is called 'the Father' the Trinitarian relation seems in mind (Rom 6⁴, 1 Cor 8⁶ 15²⁴, Gal 1³, Eph 2¹⁸ 6²³, 1 Thess 1¹, 2 Thess 1², 1 Tim 1², 2 Tim 1², Titus 1⁴). In the other instances of the application of the name of Father to God the reference is rather to His relation to us (Rom 1⁷ [8¹⁵], 1 Cor 1³, Gal 1⁴ [4⁶], Eph 1² 4⁶, Phil 1² 2¹¹ 4²⁰, Col 1², 1 Thess 1³ 3¹¹,¹³, 2 Thess 1¹ [2 var. lec.] 2¹⁶, Philem 3, cf. 2 Cor 1³, Eph 1¹⁷ 3¹⁴ 5²⁰, Col 1¹² 3¹⁷). In only three passages are the correlatives 'Son' and 'Father' brought together (1 Cor 15²⁸, Gal 4⁴⁻⁶, Col 1¹³), and in no one of these instances is it clear that the term 'Father' is employed in sole reference to Jesus, the unique 'Son.' In one of them we are told that the Father has delivered us out of the power of darkness and translated us into the Kingdom of 'the Son of His love' (Col 1¹³), where there seems certainly a reference to God's Fatherly relation not only to Jesus 'the Son of His love' but also to us who are by His grace introduced into a similar relation to God with Christ's own. So, in another, we are told that because we are sons God has sent forth the Spirit of His Son into our hearts, crying, Abba, Father (Gal 4⁶)—where it is quite clear that 'Father' has relation to us, too, as the brethren of Christ. Even in the remaining instance, where we are told that at the end Christ shall deliver up the Kingdom to God even the Father, and even 'the Son' Himself shall be subjected to Him, that God may be all in all (1 Cor 15²⁸), it is by no means obvious that the term Father may not again embrace with Christ all those who have been brought by Christ into the Kingdom. We may see in all three instances that the peculiar relation of the 'Father' and 'Son' lies at the basis of the thought: but this peculiar relation does not in any of them absorb the whole thought. It seems to be treated by Paul as a matter too well understood to require particular insistence upon. He could count on his readers, when he spoke of Jesus as 'the Son of God,' understanding without further elucidation that he was thereby attributing to Him a unique relation, including proper deity along with the Father, while our co-sonship was to be realized only in and through Him.

Another method employed by Paul to indicate the relation of Jesus to God is the presentation of Him

Christ All that God Is

as the 'image of God' (2 Cor 4⁴, Col 1¹⁵). He is the image of God, we are told, and the light of the knowledge of the glory of God shines in His face (2 Cor 4⁴). And, again, He is the image of the invisible God, the firstborn of all creation (Col 1¹⁵). The meaning is that we may see in Christ what God is: all God's glory is reflected in Him; and when we see Him we see the Father also. Perhaps the mere term falls short of expressly asserting proper deity, though it would certainly gain force and significance if proper deity were understood to be asserted. In that case it would suggest that Jesus Christ is just the invisible God made visible. And that this is its actual significance with Paul can scarcely be doubted when we recall that he does not hesitate to ascribe proper deity to Jesus, not only by means of the designations 'Lord' and 'Son of God,' but by the direct application to Him of the name 'God' itself and that in its most enhanced form —'God over all' (Rom 9⁵), the 'Great God' (Titus

2^{13}). That Jesus Christ is intended in both instances by these great designations, seems, despite sustained efforts to deny them to Him, beyond legitimate question.[39] The natural interpretation of the passages themselves compels it: and no surprise can be felt that Paul, who everywhere thinks and speaks of Christ as very God, should occasionally call Him by the appropriate designation. These passages in effect supply only the to-be-expected expression in plain language of Paul's most intimate thought of Jesus. He is always and everywhere to his thought just 'our Great God and Saviour,' 'God over all, blessed for ever.'

It was thus, then, that Jesus was thought of, and familiarly spoken of, in the Christian communities throughout the epoch in which the Synoptic Gospels were composed or, if we choose to use such misleading language, were compounded. The testimony of Paul's letters comes from the sixth and seventh decades of the century; and assures us that at that time Jesus was to His followers a man indeed and the chosen Messiah who had come to redeem God's people, but in His essential Being just the great God Himself. In the light of this testimony it is impossible to believe there

Paul's Jesus the Primitive Jesus

[39] On Rom 9^5 see Dwight, *Journal of Exegetical Society,* 1881, p. 22; and Sanday *in loc.* with the literature there mentioned. Dr. R. B. Drummond significantly writes (*The Academy,* March 30, 1895, p. 273): "I must confess that I feel very strongly the grammatical difficulty of the Unitarian interpretation; but on the other hand the improbability of Paul attributing not only deity, but supreme deity (ἐπὶ πάντων θεός) to Christ, seems to me so great as to outweigh all other considerations." On Titus 2^{13} see Weiss' note (in Meyer's *Com.*). The case against the application of these titles to Christ may be read, as well as elsewhere, in Ezra Abbott, *Journal of Exegetical Society,* 1881, reprinted in his *Critical Essays.*

ever was a different conception of Jesus prevalent in
the Church: the mark of Christians from the beginning was obviously that they looked to Jesus as their
'Lord' and 'called on His name' in their worship.

The general significance of the testimony of Paul, we
may say, is universally recognized. Bousset, for example, when engaged in repelling the crudities of
Kalthoff points it out with great distinctness. In Paul,
he tells us, we have "a witness of indubitable value
from the bosom of the Christian community for the
existence and the significance of the Person of Jesus."
"His conversion, according to the tradition, goes back
very nearly to the death of Jesus. His chief activity
falls in any case in the forties and fifties. From his
letters the historical existence of Jesus stands out before us in all clearness. And not merely does Paul
presuppose this, as we perceive from these letters: he
had intercourse with the first generation of Christians,
who had themselves seen the Lord Jesus." "Whoever
would question the existence of Jesus must erase also
the existence of Paul, as he meets us in his letters."
"With the person of Paul the person of Jesus, too,
stands established." Nor is it merely the existence of
a Jesus which Paul thus substantiates for us: he rati-
fies also the fact that the person of Jesus had for the
faith of the first Christian community "no indeter-
minate but a perfectly determinate significance."[40]
In the presence of Paul's letters, therefore, it is impossible to deny that there underlies the whole Chris-

[40] *Was wissen wir von Jesus?* 1904, pp. 17-26. This much, says
Bousset, is certain from the general testimony of Paul: "First, the fact
of a historical Jesus is assured. . . . Secondly, however, it is assured
that the Person of Jesus had for the faith of His first community no
indefinite but a perfectly determinate significance."

tian movement the great personality of Jesus, or that
the primitive Christian community looked to Him as
its founder and Lord. Is it not equally impossible to
deny in the presence of these letters that the primitive
Christian community looked upon this Jesus as their
divine founder and divine Lord?

Strange to say, Bousset draws back at this point.
Paul's testimony to the existence of the historical
Jesus and to His significance to the primitive Church
is decisive. But Paul's testimony to the estimate
placed upon the personality of this historical Jesus
is not trustworthy. It is, indeed, impossible to
doubt in the light of his testimony, that " the
earthly Jesus worked in the souls of His disciples
with inexpressible power " (p. 26) : and that they
had come to believe that He had risen from the
dead. But it does not follow that they who had com-
panied with Him in His life shared Paul's idea that
He was " essentially a heavenly being " (p. 26). The
inconsequence here is flagrant. Paul is not writing a
generation or two later, when the faith of the first disciples was a matter only of memory, perhaps of fading
memory; and when it was possible for him to represent
it as other than it was. He is writing out of the very
bosom of this primitive community and under its very
eye. His witness to the kind of Jesus this community
believed in is just as valid and just as compelling,
therefore, as his testimony that it believed in Jesus at
all. In and through him the voice of the primitive
community itself speaks, proclaiming its assured faith
in its divine Lord. This would be true quite apart
from the consentient witness of the Acts and the Gospels. In the presence of this consentient witness it

is impossible to contend that Paul has misrepresented or misconceived the faith of Christians. The same divine Jesus which Paul presents as the universal and aboriginal object of Christian faith, Luke sets before us in Acts from the mouth of the primitive disciples —Peter and John and James and the rest—as from the beginning believed on in the Church; and the same Luke with his companion evangelists represents as Himself asserting His divine dignity. The testimony of Paul merely adds to this witness a new and thoroughly trustworthy voice; and renders it so much the more impossible to doubt that from the very beginning the entire Christian community was firmly convinced of the deity of its Lord.

Nor can the force of this testimony be broken or even weakened by suggesting doubts as to the genu-

Inaccessibility   ineness of more or fewer of Paul's let-
to Critical   ters, or raising question of a development
Doubts   of the doctrine of the person of our
Lord through their course. We have treated them all as genuine products of Paul's mind and pen and as all of a piece: because, shortly, the facts warrant such a treatment of them. But the conclusion to be drawn from them in the matter in hand does not depend on so taking them. The conception of Jesus embedded in these letters is the same in them all: if they are not all Paul's they are all Pauline. You may discard any number of them you choose, therefore, as not Paul's personal product: the conception of Jesus in those that remain is not altered thereby. Take the extremest hypothesis which has ever even temporarily commanded the assent of any considerable number of scholars,— the old Tübingen theory which allowed to Paul only the

four great Epistles, Romans, 1 and 2 Corinthians and Galatians.[41] In these Epistles may be found Paul's entire witness to the deity of Christ. It is from them that we learn that Jesus Christ, while on the side of His flesh of the seed of David, had another side to His being, on which He was the Son of God (Rom 1[3,4]); that as God's own Son He was rich before He became poor by becoming of the seed of David (2 Cor 8[9]); and that in His real nature He is not merely God's Son but Himself God over all, blessed for ever (Rom 9[5]). When we add to these four great Epistles one after another of the others—such as Philippians, and 1 Thessalonians and Colossians, as practically all living critics do[42]—and even Ephesians and Second Timothy, as many are willing to do—we merely add to the mass of the testimony, and in no respect alter its character or effect. These letters one and all only repeat, and in repeating more or less clarify, the teaching of the four chief Epistles as to the dignity of our Lord's person.

[41] The extreme radicalism of the so-called Dutch school, the best representative of which is probably van Manen (or in Germany, Steck), may safely be neglected.

[42] Bousset, *Was wissen wir,* etc., pp. 19, 20, says: " It is not, however, at all the case that the critical theology denies to Paul all others of the letters ascribed to him with the exception of the four chief Epistles (and possibly also the Epistle to the Philippians). If the critical theology once did that, it has since corrected itself here. Thus with ever increasing confidence it has again accredited to Paul, together with the Epistle to the Philippians, 1 Thessalonians also, and Colossians, with the exception of perhaps a few verses. Lately a theologian like Jülicher, whom no one can accuse of anti-critical prepossessions, has again defended the genuineness of Ephesians on striking grounds. With ever greater clearness and definiteness doubts are confining themselves to particular Epistles—2 Thess., 1 Tim. and Titus." Weinel bases his picture of *St. Paul the Man and His Work* (E. T., 1906), on Romans,

For this same reason nothing is gained for our present purpose by treating the Epistles not all together,

No Substantial Development

but in small chronologically arranged groups. Slight differences may be observed, it is true, from group to group in modes of expression and relatively favorite forms of statement. But no differences can be traced in the conceptions which are brought to expression in these varying forms of statements. For example, the ruling designation of Christ in the Thessalonians is ' the Lord ' (22), with ' the Lord Jesus Christ ' (14) a somewhat close second, and ' the Lord Jesus ' (10) third, while the simple ' Christ ' occurs only four times. In Romans, Corinthians, Galatians, on the other hand, it is the simple ' Christ ' which becomes the favorite designation, with ' Lord ' a good second: and the same is true of the Epistles of the first imprisonment. In the Pastorals, on the other hand, while ' Lord ' is still common, ' Christ,' as in Thessalonians, falls into the background, and ' Christ Jesus ' becomes the favorite designation. Variations like these, it is obvious, are rather interesting to those who are engaged in studying the literary form of the Epistles than important in estimating their witness to the deity of our Lord. Through all such variations, the product of circumstance, the essential teaching of all these Epistles upon

1 and 2 Cor, Gal, Phil, and 1 Thess only: but he is willing to admit that " the vast majority of critics consider the Epistle to the Colossians and the short note to Philemon to be genuine," and that some not unworthy of the name of critics add Eph. and 2 Thess. (p. ix.)   Wrede (*Paulus,* 1905) uses Romans, 1 and 2 Cor., Gal., Philip., 1 Thess., Col., Philem.; while Wernle makes use of all except the Pastorals (*Beginnings of Christianity,* 1903).

the person of Christ remains the same. In them all alike He is the divine ' Lord,' whose right it is to rule: the ' Son of God,' consubstantial with the Father: the ' great God and Saviour ' of sinners: ' God over all, blessed forever.' And in their consentient testimony to the deity of Christ they make it clear to us that upon this point, at least, the whole primitive Church was of one unvarying mind.

THE WITNESS OF THE CATHOLIC
EPISTLES

There yet remains a certain amount of corroborative evidence for the conclusions which we have reached, Catholic borne by a series of letters which have Epistles been preserved to us, purporting to be Corroborative the compositions of primitive followers of our Lord. We use the term " purporting " not because we have any doubt that they are all that they profess to be, but because their descriptions of themselves have not been accepted as valid in all critical circles, and because we do not consider it necessary to pause to vindicate their authenticity here. If their testimony were substantially different from that of the more extended documents which we have already passed in review, it might be required of us to validate their claim to give testimony to the primitive conception of Christ, before admitting their witness. As, however, they yield only corroborative testimony, we may be content to present it for what it seems to each individual to be worth. In any event it helps to make clear to us the absolute harmony of early Christianity taken in a wide sense in its lofty conception of its Lord's person, and thus adds weight to what we have learned, from the more important documents, of the conception current in the first age. And just in proportion as we recognize these letters, too, as a legacy of the first age, reflecting the belief of the first generation of

Christians, their corroborative evidence will become more and more significant to us. If, as in our own judgment they ought to be, they are accepted at their face value, their testimony becomes of primary importance, and would suffice of itself to assure us of the attitude of mind our Lord's followers cherished towards Him from the beginning. We shall present their testimony then frankly from this our own point of view, without stopping to argue our right to do so. It will thus at least be made apparent that the whole body of writings gathered into what we call the New Testament unite in commending to us one lofty view of Christ's person. For in all these letters, too, as in those which have already claimed our attention, Jesus appears fundamentally as the divine object of the reverential service of Christians.

Among these letters a special interest attaches to the Epistles of James and Jude, because of their authorship by kinsmen of our Lord according to the flesh, who moreover did not believe in Him during His earthly manifestation (Jno 7[5]) : to which is added in the case of the Epistle of James, its exceedingly early date (A. D. 45),—a date antecedent to that of any other of the canonical books. Not only does not the simple ' Jesus ' occur in either of these Epistles or even the simple ' Christ,' but our Lord is uniformly spoken of by designations expressive of marked reverence. Both writers describe themselves simply as " servants "—that is, " bond-servants," " slaves,"[1]—James " of God and of

James' and Jude's Christology High

---

[1] We must not press, however, the ignoble connotations of " slaves " to our modern minds: entire subjection is all that is imputed. Cf. Mayor on Jude 1.

the Lord Jesus Christ " (1^1), and Jude with striking directness simply " of Jesus Christ " (1). The acknowledgment of Jesus as their ' Lord ' implied in this self-designation is emphasized in both Epistles by the constant employment of this title in speaking of Jesus.

James speaks of our Lord by name only twice, and on both occasions he gives Him the full title of reverence: ' the (or our) Lord Jesus Christ ' (1^1 2^1)— coupling Him in the one case on equal terms with God, and in the other adding further epithets of divine dignity. Elsewhere he speaks of Him simply as ' the Lord ' ($5^{7,8 [14],15}$)[2] in contexts which greatly enhance the significance of the term. The pregnant use of ' the Name,' absolutely, which we found current among the early Christians as reported in the Acts, recurs here; and James advises in the case of sick people that they be prayed over, while they are anointed with oil " in the Name " (5^{14}). The " Name " intended is clearly that of Jesus, which is thus in Christian usage substituted for that of Jehovah. A unique epithet, equally implying the deity of the Lord, is applied to Him in the exhortation, " My brethren, hold not the

Christ
'the Glory'
faith of our Lord Jesus Christ, the Glory, with respect of persons " (2^1). ' The Glory ' seems to stand here in apposition to the name, " our Lord Jesus Christ," further

---

[2] Sven Herner, *op. cit.,* thinks that ' Lord ' is used of Jesus only at $5^{7,8}$. Mayor on 1^7 thinks it probable that it is used of Jesus also at $5^{[14],15}$. Herner remarks (p. 42) : " The Epistle of James knows the expression ' The Lord Jesus Christ ' (1^1 2^1) and, therefore, uses χύριος of Christ. Since this is the case, we do not venture definitely to deny that Christ is meant in the expression ' the coming of the Lord ' (5^7 seq.),

defining Him in His majesty.³ There is here some‑
thing more than merely the association of our Lord
with glory, as when we are told that He had glory with
God before the world was (Jno 17⁵), and after His
humiliation on earth (though even on earth He mani‑
fested His glory to seeing eyes, Jno 1¹⁴ 2¹¹ 17²²) entered
again into His glory (Lk 24²⁶, Jno 17²⁴, 1 Tim 3¹⁶, Heb
2⁹, cf. Mt 19²⁸ 25³¹, [Mk 10³⁷]), and is to come again
in this glory (Mt 16²⁷ 24³⁰ 25³¹, Mk 8³⁸ 13²⁶, Lk 9²⁶
21²⁷, Titus 2¹³, 1 P 4¹³). We come nearer to what is
implied when we read of Jesus being ' the Lord of
Glory ' (1 Cor 2⁸), that is He to whom glory belongs
as His characterizing quality; or when He is described
to us as " the effulgence of the glory of God " (Heb
1³). The thought of the writer seems to be fixed on
those Old Testament passages in which Jehovah is de‑
scribed as the " Glory ": e. g., " For I, saith Jehovah,
will be unto her a wall of fire round about, and I will
be the Glory in the midst of her " (Zech 2⁵). In the
Lord Jesus Christ, James sees the fulfillment of these
promises: He is Jehovah come to be with His people;
and, as He has tabernacled among them, they have
seen His glory. He is, in a word, the Glory of God,
the Shekinah: God manifest to men. It is thus that
James thought and spoke of his own brother who died
a violent and shameful death while still in His first
youth! Surely there is a phenomenon here which may
well waken inquiry.

The attitude of Jude is precisely the same. He does

although Peter's remark on the advent of the day of God (2 P 3¹²)
makes such an ascription unlikely, and it is to be noted that in the
preceding and following verses (5¹⁰,¹¹) κύριος is used of God."

³ Bengel, Bassett, Mayor.

indeed speak of Christ in the address of his Epistle
by the simpler formal title of 'Jesus
Christ,' but in accordance with his description of himself at that point as
the " slave " of this ' Jesus Christ,' he tends to multiply
reverential titles in speaking of Him elsewhere. To
Him our Lord is always ' our Lord Jesus Christ '
(17, 21), ' Jesus Christ our Lord ' (25), ' our only
Master (δεσπότης) and Lord, Jesus Christ ' (4)—a
phrase, this last one, so strong that many commentators
balk at it and wish to render it ' the only Master, viz.,
God, and our Lord Jesus Christ.'[4]   But we cannot feel
surprised that one who pointedly calls himself in the
first verse of his Epistle " slave " of Jesus Christ,
should apply the correlative of that term, " Despotic
Master and Lord " to Jesus Christ, three verses later.
No doubt " no Jew could use " such a phrase " without
thinking of the one Master in heaven ";[5] but that is
only evidence that this Jew thought of Jesus who was
his ' Lord ' and whose " slave " he recognized himself
as being, as, in this eminent sense, his " Master in
heaven " (cf. 2 P 2[1]).   Obviously it is the testimony
of these two Epistles that Jesus was conceived by His
first disciples as their divine Lord and Master.

*Christ
'the Despot'*

The designations of our Lord in 1 Peter are notably
simple, but none the less significant.   Peter's favorite
designation for Him (as it is Paul's)
is the simple ' Christ,' used, ordinarily
at least, as a proper name, though of

*Christology
of 1 Peter*

---

[4] See on the passage, Bigg and Mayor *in loc.*

[5] The phrase is Mayor's (*in loc.*)*:* who notes also the use of the word
δεσπόσυνοι by Julius Africanus (Eus. *H. E.,* i. 7) to denote the kins-
folk of Jesus, and justly remarks that this implies a current earlier
employment of δεσπότης of our Lord.

course not without its appellative significance still clinging to it and in one or two instances ($1^{11,11}$) becoming
prominent ($1^{11,11,19}$ 2^{21} $3^{15,16,18}$ $4^{1,13,14}$ $5^{1,10,14}$). Next to
the simple ' Christ ' Peter uses by predilection the sim-
plest of the solemn compound names, ' Jesus Christ '
($1^{1,2,3,7,13}$ 2^5 3^{21} 4^{11}). In the address to the Epistle he
sets this designation in its place in the trine formula
of Father, Spirit and Jesus Christ, with the effect of
suggesting the Threefold Name, that is to say, with
underlying implication of the Trinity.[6] Similarly in
1^{11} where " the Spirit of Christ," that is, most naturally,
the Spirit which proceeds from and represents Christ,
is spoken of as having resided in the ancient prophets,
the preëxistence of Christ is assumed.[7] Besides these
proper names, Peter speaks of our Lord by the desig-
nation ' Lord ' ($2^{3,13}$ 3^{15}, cf. 2^{25} and Bigg *in loc.* and p.
109) and in doing so applies an Old Testament text
to Him in which ' Lord ' stands for ' Jehovah,' and

[6] Cf. Hort *in loc.* (pp. 17, 18): "The three clauses of this verse beyond all reasonable question set forth the operation of the Father, the
Holy Spirit and the Son, respectively. Here, therefore, as in several
Epistles of Paul (1 Cor 12^{4-6}, 2 Cor 13^{14}, Eph 4^{4-6}), there is an implicit
reference to the Threefold Name. In no passage is there any indica-
tion that the writer was independently working out a doctrinal scheme:
a recognized belief or idea seems to be everywhere presupposed. How
such an idea could arise in the mind of St. Paul or any other Apostle
without sanction from a word of the Lord it is difficult to imagine: and
this consideration is a sufficient answer to the doubts which have, by no
means unnaturally, been raised whether Mt 28^{19} may not have been
added or recast in a later generation. St. Peter, like St. Paul, associ-
ates with the subject of each clause, if one may so speak, a distinctive
function as towards mankind: on their relations to the Divine Unity
he is silent."

[7] Cf. Bigg *in loc.* (p. 108), "*The words* τὸ ἐν αὐτοῖς πνεῦμα
Χριστοῦ must be accepted quite frankly. Christ was in the prophets,
and from Him came their inspiration."

thus assimilates Him to the divine Being. By a combination of this great title and the solemn Messianic name of ' Jesus Christ,' he calls Jesus ' our Lord Jesus Christ ' (1^3) ;[8] and it is noticeable that it is by this significant title that he designates Jesus when he is speaking of God as not only His Father but His God —having reference doubtless to "the days of His flesh " (Heb 5^7), that is to say, to His humiliation.[9] No other titles are applied to our Lord in this Epistle, except that in 2^{25} He is spoken of as ' the Shepherd and Bishop of our souls,' and at $5^{3,4}$ as ' Chief Sheph rd,' modes of description in which the soteriological rather than the ontological element is prominent.

In comparison with 1 Peter, 2 Peter makes use of more elaborate designations in speaking of Christ.

2 Peter and the Deity of Our Lord Not only does the simple ' Jesus ' not occur in this Epistle, but not even the simple ' Christ ': and the less complex compound ' Jesus Christ ' occurs in its simplicity only once—in the formality of the address. The simple ' Lord,' on the other hand, seems to be used of Christ in a few cases ($3^{8,9,10,15}$),[10] and a number of more or

[8] Cf. Hort *in loc.*, p. 30, who has a long, analytical discussion of it.
[9] Cf. Bigg *in loc.*

[10] Bigg on 3^9: "The Lord is certainly Christ "; on 3^{15}: " 'Our Lord ' must undoubtedly signify Christ, to whom alone the doxology in verse 18 is addressed." Less decidedly, Sven Herner, *op. cit.*, pp. 44, 45: " 2 Peter has some passages about which, in our opinion, no clear decision can be come to. According to 3^3 seq. scornful mockers shall come and say, ' Where is the promise of His coming?' It is almost the universal judgment that the reference here is to the coming of Christ. Against the scorn of the mockers the Apostle suggests that a day with our Lord is as a thousand years (v. 8), and therefore there can be no talk of slackness. The Lord is not slack with His promise, but is long-suffering to us-ward and not willing that any should perish (v. 9).

less sonorous combinations of it occur: 'Jesus our Lord' (1²), 'our Lord Jesus Christ' (1⁸,¹⁴,¹⁶), 'the Lord and Saviour' (3²), 'our Lord and Saviour Jesus Christ' (1¹¹ 2²⁰ 3¹⁸), with the last of which may be connected the great phrase 'our God and Saviour, Jesus Christ' (1¹). Two things that are notable in this list of designations are the repeated use of 'Saviour' of our Lord, and the clear note of deity which is struck in their ascriptions. 'Saviour' itself is a divine appellation transferred to Christ:[11] to whom it is applied fifteen times out of the twenty-three in which it occurs in the New Testament. In 2 Peter

The day of the Lord, however, will come as a thief (v. 10). In verse 15 the course of thought in verse 9 is repeated, and the reader is exhorted to account the long-suffering of the Lord salvation. This interpretation has in its favor that the expression 'our Lord' (v. 15) can be referred to Christ. Apart from Rev 4¹¹ 11¹⁵ (2 Tim 1⁸) it is the constant rule in the N. T. and in this Epistle (1²,⁸,¹¹,¹⁴,¹⁶ 2²⁰ 3¹⁸) that the pronoun ἡμῶν is adjoined to κύριος only when κύριος refers to Christ; and already on this ground κύριος in v. 15 can scarcely designate God. The declaration in v. 8 that a day with the Lord is as a thousand years, causes no great difficulty, since it is no unwonted occurrence in the N. T. that a statement made of Lord Jehovah is referred to Lord Christ, wholly apart from the circumstance that the statement in question is scarcely an Old Test. citation. On the other hand, our explanation is rendered uncertain by the expression in v. 12, 'the coming of the day of God.' Since v. 12 speaks of 'the day of God,' 'the day of the Lord' is commonly explained in connection with it; and as ultimate result there emerges that nothing assured can be attained concerning the meaning of 3⁸,⁹,¹⁰,¹⁵."

[11] Cf. Isaiah 43¹¹, "I, even I, am the Lord and beside me there is no Saviour"; Is 43³, "The Holy One of Israel, thy Saviour," cf. 45¹⁵,²¹ 49²⁶ 60¹⁶ 63⁸, Jer 14⁸, "O thou hope of Israel, the Saviour thereof in time of trouble; Hos 13⁴, "Beside me there is no Saviour" (cf. 1 Sam 10¹⁹ 14³⁹, 2 Sam 22³, Ps 7¹⁰ 17⁷ 106²¹). But cf. Is 19²⁰ where the Lord promises to send "a Saviour and a mighty one": and such passages as Judges 3⁹,¹⁵, where the Saviour sent is a man raised up by God for the purpose (cf. Judges 6³⁶, 2 Kings 13⁵, Neh 9²). The O. T. term for Saviour is the Hiphal participle of ישע, viz., מושיע

it occurs five times, always of Christ, and never alone, but always coupled under a single article with another designation, and so forming a solemn formula. In this respect the two phrases, ' our Lord and Saviour Jesus Christ ' (1^{11} 2^{20} 3^{18}) and ' our God and Saviour Jesus Christ ' (1^1) are perfectly similar and must stand or fall together. Not only, however, is the deity of our Lord openly asserted in the direct naming of Him here ' our God and Saviour.'[12] It is almost equally clearly asserted in the parallel phrase, ' our Lord and Saviour Jesus Christ.' And it is implied in the conjunction of ' God ' and ' Jesus our Lord ' in 1^2 as co-objects of saving knowledge (cf. 1^8 2^{20} 3^{18}), and in the ascription to ' our Lord and Saviour Jesus Christ ' of an eternal Kingdom (1^{11}).[13] Besides these designations, our Lord is called by Peter, as by Jude (4), our ' Master ' ($\delta\varepsilon\sigma\pi\acute{o}\tau\eta\varsigma$) with the same high implications (2^1) ;[14] and the declaration of God the Father at the transfiguration that He is ' God's Son,' ' God's Beloved,' is cited (1^{17}) with profound and reverential satisfaction.[15]

Perhaps nothing is more notable in the designations of our Lord in these Epistles—James, Jude, 1 Peter,

John's Epistles and ' the Son of God.' 2 Peter,—than the dropping out of sight of the title ' Son of God.' Only in the single passage in 2 Peter in which

[12] That the passage is to be taken so is convincingly argued by Spitta, von Soden, and especially Bigg. Cf. Lightfoot on 1 Clem 2, where some of the patristic parallels are noted.

[13] The phrase " eternal Kingdom " is found here only in the N. T.; but cf. *Mart. Polyc.,* 20, *Clem. Hom.,* viii. 23 ; x. 25; xiii. 20, etc.

[14] Spitta, von Soden, etc. (cf. Wetstein) take the $\delta\varepsilon\sigma\pi\acute{o}\tau\eta\varsigma$ here of God the Father; Mayor hesitates. But cf. above on Jude 4.

[15] Cf. the statement of the christology of the Epistle by Bigg, p. 235.

the testimony of the Father in the transfiguration scene
is appealed to, is the term 'Son' applied to Jesus at
all. The case is very different in the Johannine Epistles. Of them the application to Jesus of the title
'Son of God,' in one form or another, is preëminently
characteristic.[16] He is called, indeed, simply 'Jesus'
(1 Jno 2^{22} 4^3 4^{15} 5^1), and 'Christ' without adjunct
(1 Jno [2^{22} 5^1],[17] 2 Jno 9); and also 'Jesus Christ'
(1 Jno 4^2 [4^{15}] 5^6, 2 Jno 7); and even 'Jesus Christ
the Righteous' (1 Jno 2^1);[18] and He is described in
the great phrases 'Word of Life' (1 Jno 1^1), 'Advocate with the Father' (2^1), 'Saviour of the World'
(4^{14}). But the favorite designations applied to Him
in these Epistles emphasize His divine Sonship. The
most common formula employed is the simple 'Son'
standing in correlation with God or the Father (1
Jno $2^{22,23,23,24}$ $4^{10,14}$ $5^{9,10,11,12}$, 2 Jno 9); but the full
form 'Son of God' occurs also with some frequency
(1 Jno 3^8 4^{15} $5^{5,12,13,20}$) and quite a variety of expanded phrases appear by its side, such as 'God's only
begotten Son' (1 Jno 4^9, cf. 5^{18}), 'Jesus, God's Son'
(1 Jno 1^7), 'God's Son, Jesus Christ' (1 Jno 1^3 3^{23}

[16] Cf. Westcott, *Epistles of St. John*, p. 131: "The title 'the Son' in
various forms is eminently characteristic of the first and second Epistles, in which it occurs 24 (or 25) times (22 or 23+2), which is more
times than in all the Epistles of St. Paul."

[17] In these two passages 'the Christ' is an appellative.

[18] The designation 'Lord' does not occur in these Epistles. Cf.
Westcott, *Epistles of St. John*, p. 131: "It is remarkable that the title
'Lord' (κύριος) is not found in the Epistles (not 2 Jno 3). It
occurs in the narrative of the Gospel, and is frequent in the Apocalypse. It occurs also in all the other Epistles of the N. T. except that
to Titus. The absence of the title may perhaps be explained by the
general view of the relation of Christ to the believer which is given
in the Epistles. The central thought is that of fellowship."

5^{20}), ' Jesus Christ, the Son of the Father ' (2 Jno 3).
By means of this constant designation of Jesus as ' the
Son of God,' John keeps before his readers His divine
dignity. He is not of the world, but has come into
the world (5^{20}) upon a mission, to destroy all that is
evil (5^8) and to save the world (1^7 $4^{10\text{-}14}$ 5^5), where-
unto He was sent ($4^{9,10,14}$), that all might have life
in Him ($5^{5,12,15}$) ; for God has given unto us eternal
life and this life is in ' the Son,' so that He who hath
' the Son ' hath the life ($3^{11,12}$). So closely is He associated with God the Father (1^3 3^{23}) that to deny Him
is to deny the Father (2^{23}) and to confess Him is to
confess the Father (2^{23} 4^{15}) and to abide in Him is to
abide in the Father (2^{24}, cf. 1^3). Obviously to John
the ' Son of God ' is Himself God; and what is thus
implied in the current use of this title is openly declared at the close of the Epistle, where of ' the Son of
God, Jesus Christ ' it is solemnly affirmed, " This is
the True God and Eternal Life " (5^{20}).

In this remarkable concluding paragraph the Apostle
is encouraging his readers in view of the sin which is
in the world and which they feel to be
working in themselves. " We know,"
says he, " that every one who has been
begotten of God "—that is to say, every truly Christian
man, who has been born of the Spirit—" sinneth not ":
not because he has of himself power to preserve himself
pure, but because " He that was begotten of God "—
that is to say, God's own Son, Jesus Christ—" keepeth
him and the evil one toucheth him not." This is but the
Johannine way of saying what Peter says in his way when
he assures his readers that Christians " are guarded by
the power of God through faith unto a salvation ready

*Jesus the
' True God '*

to be revealed in the last time " (1 P 1⁵). But John proceeds with his encouraging message. " We know," he adds, " that we are of God and the whole world lieth in the evil one. And we know that the Son of God is come and hath given us an understanding, that we know Him that is true, and we are in Him that is true, in His Son Jesus Christ." God is He that is true; and what is said is that if we are in His Son Jesus Christ, we are in God. Why? Because Jesus Christ Himself, being His Son, is Himself just this God that is true; and therefore it is just this that the Apostle adds: " This is," he says with the emphatic demonstrative,—" *this* is the True God and Life Eternal " (5²⁰). The upshot of the whole matter, then, is that those who are in Jesus Christ need have no fear in the midst of the temptations of earth: for to be in Jesus Christ is to be in the only real God, since Jesus Himself is this ' Real God,' and as such ' Eternal Life.'

Here, then, are two new descriptive epithets applied to Jesus, as the ' Son of God.' He is ' Eternal Life,' —which recalls the figurative designation of Him as ' the Life ' in the Gospel of John (14⁶ 11²⁵, cf. 1⁵,⁹, 1 Jno 1², cf. 1 Jno 2⁸). And He is ' the True,' ' the Real, God,' the God who corresponds in every respect to the idea of God, who is what God ought to be and is. There is " only one true God," John quotes his Master as declaring (Jno 17³), to know whom is eternal life: and now he tells us that Jesus Christ, because the ' Son ' of this only true God, is Himself this ' True God ' and this ' Eternal Life.'[19] He then who

---

[19] For the exposition of this passage see especially Weiss (Meyer, 1900), pp. 160, 161. But on the clause, " He that is begotten of God," see Westcott, p. 185, column 1.

is in Him is in ' the True God ' and has ' the Eternal
Life,—' the Eternal Life ' that was in the Father and
has been manifested in His ' Son Jesus Christ,' and is
now declared by the Apostle in order that his readers,
too, may enter into that fellowship which he was himself enjoying " with the Father and with His Son
Jesus Christ " (1^3).   The Epistles of John, also, thus
culminate not only in calling Christ ' God,' but in so
calling Him ' God ' as to throw out into emphasis
that He is all that God is.   James calls Him ' the
Glory ': Peter ' the great God ': Paul ' God over
all ': John ' the Real God.'[20] It was because he so conceived Jesus as God's unique Son (1 Jno 4^9) that John
is able to speak of the forgiveness of sins " through His
Name " (1 Jno 2^{12}), and of faith " in His Name "
securing eternal life (5^{13}, cf. 3^{23}), and even (3 Jno 7)
of the whole Christian course turning on loyalty to
' the Name,'—that is, obviously, Jesus' Name,—
without further definition.   Clearly, to him, ' the
Name of Jesus ' was the Name that is above every
name.[21]

Even a rapid glance like this over the designations
applied to Christ in the Epistles written by Christ's
How Our Lord's immediate companions will suffice to
Companions   show that the estimate put upon His
Thought of Him personality by Paul has nothing in it
peculiar to that writer.   There may meet us, as we
pass from Epistle to Epistle, varying methods of giving expression to the faith common to all: but it is
common to all to look upon Jesus Christ as a divine

[20] Dr. Westcott in an additional note on 1 Jno 3^{23}, p. 129 *seq.*, gives
a careful study of the names of our Lord in 1 John. Cf. also p. 189
seq., where he discusses the term ' the Christ.'
[21] Cf. Westcott, *Epistles of St. John,* pp. 129 and 232.

person. So far as appears it did not occur to anyone in the primitive Christian community to put a lower estimate upon His personality than that; and writer vies with writer only in his attempts to give his faith in his divine Redeemer clear and emphatic expression. If there was a more primitive conception than this of Jesus' dignity it had died away and left no trace behind it before the Christian community found a voice for itself. Whether that can be conceived to have happened in the course of the few years which intervened between the public career and death of Jesus and the rise of a Christian literature,—say, in James, —or, say, in Paul,—or, say, in the evangelic documents,—each one must judge for himself. But in seeking to form an opinion on this matter, it should be borne in mind that there intervened only a very brief period indeed between the death of Christ and the beginnings of Christian literature: that much of this literature credibly represents itself as the product of actual companions of our Lord: and that it was all written in the presence of such companions, reflects their opinions, and was published under their eye. That absolutely no trace of a lower view of the person of Christ is discernible in any portion of this literature seems in these circumstances not only a valid suggestion but a convincing proof that no such lower view had been prevalent in the Christian community: that, in a word, the followers of Jesus must be supposed to have been heartily convinced of His deity from the very beginning.

THE WITNESS OF THE EPISTLE TO THE HEBREWS

The Epistle to the Hebrews enters no claim to be the composition of one of our Lord's immediate followers. Neither does it represent the thought of a period antedating the composition of the Epistles of Paul. It synchronizes in its date rather with that of the later half of these Epistles (c. A. D. 64). It comes to us like its own Melchizedek, "without father, without mother, without genealogy," bearing its own independent witness to how Jesus was thought and spoken of by the Christian community in the seventh decade of the first Christian century; or, at least, by a special and very interesting group of Christians living at that time, made up of those Jews who had seen in Jesus the promised Messiah and accepted Him as their longed-for Redeemer.

In the designations it applies to our Lord in general, this Epistle reflects, of course, the usage of the first age of the Church, which has already been observed in the other Epistles: but equally of course not without its own peculiarities. As in the Epistles of Paul, the most frequently occurring of the simple designations is 'Christ' ($3^{6,14}$ 5^5 6^1 $9^{11,14,24,28}$ 11^{26}).[1] The simple 'Jesus,' however, is employed relatively much more

Prevalence of 'Christ'

---

[1] 'Christ' is used everywhere as a proper name—even when it has the article: cf. Davidson, *Ep. to the Heb.*, 73, note 1. In some passages the term 'Son' is almost or quite a proper name: cf. Riehm 272, Davidson, *loc. cit.*, note 2.

frequently than in Paul's letters (2^9 3^1 6^{20} 7^{22} 10^{19} $12^{2,24}$ 13^{12}): it occurs almost as frequently, indeed, as 'Christ.' Neither is, however, a common title in Hebrews (nine and eight times respectively), nor is the compound title 'Jesus Christ,' which occurs three times (10^{10} $13^{8,21}$), while 'Lord Jesus' (13^{20}) and 'Jesus the Son of God' (4^{14}) each occurs once. The simple 'Lord' also is only occasionally applied to our Lord (1^{10} 2^3 7^{14} [12^{14}]); and no combinations of it with other designations occur at all, except, as we have already intimated, the phrase 'our Lord Jesus' is once met with (13^{20}).[2] It is noticeable that in two of the three instances in which the term 'Lord' is employed of Christ (1^{10} 2^3) it is used in order to throw into prominence His superangelic dignity. The peculiarity of Hebrews is manifested in the free use it makes of the two designations, 'the Son' ($1^{2,5,5,8}$ 3^6 $5^{5,8}$ 7^{28}), or more fully the 'Son of God' (4^{14} 6^6 7^3 10^{29}), and 'the (or our) High Priest' (2^{17} 3^1 $4^{14,15}$ 5^{10} 6^{20} 7^{26} 8^1 9^{11}) or simply 'Priest' (5^6 $7^{3,11,[15],17,21}$ [8^4], 10^{21}), which form respectively the favorite ontological and the favorite soteriological designations of Christ in this Epistle.

It is chiefly by means of and in connection with the title 'Son' that this Epistle (in this, like the Epistles of John) gives expression to its conception of our Lord's person. There is no lack of recognition of the humanity of our Lord. Indeed, nowhere else in the New Testa-

Recognition of Jesus' Humanity

---

[2] Cf. Sven Herner, *op. cit.*, p. 41: "The usage by which κύριος is applied to Christ is not alien to Hebrews. We meet once (13^{20}) with the designation 'our Lord Jesus': and at 7^{14} we read 'that the Lord springs from Judah.' In 1^{10} God is represented as saying to Christ, 'Thou, Lord, hast laid the foundations of the earth,' and 2^3 speaks of

ment do we find the reality and the completeness of His humanity so fully expounded and so strongly insisted upon.[3] But it is the transcendent conception of Christ, which looks upon Him as 'the Son of God,' clothed with all the attributes of God, that gives its whole tone to the Epistle.[4] The keynote is struck in the very opening verses, where our Lord is set as 'Son' in contrast not merely with the prophets, the greatest representatives of God on earth, but also with the angels, the highest of creatures. All these are servants of God: He is His 'Son,' through whom no doubt God works (1^2), but as one works through a fellow in whom He is reduplicated; and whom He addresses by the great names peculiar to Himself, 'God' (1^8) and—its equivalent here—'Lord' ($1^{10}\ 2^2$).

That it is what is called the metaphysical Sonship, which is here attributed to our Lord is obvious in itself and is put beyond all doubt by the description which is given of Him as 'Son.'[5] In this description there are assigned to Him divine works, in eternity and in time: the creation of the world and the upholding of the

What 'the Son' is

---

the salvation which the Lord has announced. Finally Hebrews has a passage where we cannot decisively pronounce whether κύριος refers to God or to Christ, . . . (12^{14})."

[3] Cf. Riehm, *Der Lehrbegriff des Hebräerbriefes,* 1867, p. 271. "We shall see that the author emphasizes the true humanity of Jesus more than is found in any other N. T. book." Accordingly, cf. §§ 36, 37, 38, 39, for details.

[4] Cf. Riehm, pp. 270, 271: "He sees in Christ above all the Son of God in the eminent sense of that word."

[5] Cf. Riehm, *op. cit.,* p. 276: "There is already contained in what has been said the solution of the second question which we were to deal with in this paragraph—the question, namely, whether the uniquely intimate relation of Christ to God, which is designated by the name of

universe. But the most striking element of it tells us rather what the ' Son ' is than what He had done or is yet to do. He is, we are told, " the effulgence of God's glory and the very image of His substance "—which seems to be only a rich and suggestive way of saying, to put it briefly, that the ' Son,' as ' Son,' is just God's fellow. He is the repetition of God's glory: the re-iteration of His substance. By the " glory of God " is meant here just the divine nature itself, apprehended in its splendor: and by its " effulgence " is meant not a reflection, but, so to speak, a reduplication of it. The ' Son ' is just God over again in the glory of His majesty.[6] Similarly by the " substance " of God is meant, not His bare essence, but His whole nature, with all its attributes; and by " the very image " is meant a correspondence as close as that which an impression gives back to a seal: the ' Son ' of God in no single trait in the least differs from God.[7] In a word, what is

Son, is an ethico-religious or a metaphysical one. Since this name belongs to Christ on account of His pretemporal relation to God, the notion ' Son of God ' is plainly in the first instance a metaphysical one. . . . An unprejudiced exposition of the relative passages must lead to the conclusion that according to the doctrine of the author, it is precisely the metaphysical attributes which are attributed to Christ in $1^{2 \text{ seq.}}$ that make Him the ' Son of God.' "

[6] Riehm offers this illustration to clarify the notion of $\dot{\alpha}\pi\alpha\dot{\nu}\gamma\alpha\sigma\mu\alpha$: " Should all the light which proceeds from the sun be united again in a second body of light, which radiates it out again a second time, there would be an $\dot{\alpha}\pi\alpha\dot{\nu}\gamma\alpha\sigma\mu\alpha$ of the sun in the sense in which the author has used the word here. All the rays of the manifold divine glory unite again in the Son, in order in Him, joined together in a new glorious Light-Being, to present the divine glory a second time and to make it through this second presentation visible even to the creature" (p. 288). Cf. also Davidson *in loc.,* who judiciously echoes Riehm.

[7] Cf. Riehm, *op. cit.,* p. 284: " What the writer wishes is to emphasize in this second predicate that the nature of the Son corresponds precisely with the nature of the Father: that there is no trait in the

given to us in the ' Son ' is here declared to be God as
' Son ' standing over against God as ' Father.'[8]

It can cause no surprise, therefore, when the author
declares that it was of the ' Son ' that God[9] was speaking in the Psalm (45^6), when He said,

His Deity   " Thy throne, O God, is forever and
ever." This is only to apply directly to
the ' Son ' the name which is in the whole discussion
implied to be His: for undoubtedly the very point
of the whole argument is to the effect that Jesus Christ
as the ' Son of God ' stands infinitely above every creature just because He is ' God ' Himself.[10] We may
leave undecided the question whether or no the doxology at the close of the Epistle is to be referred to
Christ, treated here as the God He is recognized

nature of the Father which does not find itself in perfection also in the
nature of the Son, and *vice versa.*" Of the whole, he says (pp. 284-5):
" The Son is then, according to the doctrine of the Ep. to the Heb., an
independently existing Divine Person, whose substance is not created
by God, but has proceeded out of the glory of the Father's nature; a
Divine Person to whom in consequence the same glorious nature belongs, so that every attribute of the Father repeats itself in the Son,
and every attribute of the Son repeats itself in the Father; so that
through the Son the whole nature of God is completely revealed."
Cf. the long " Note on the Son " in Davidson's Commentary, pp. 73-79.

[8] It is noticeable, however, that God is not called ' Father ' as over
against the ' Son ' in this Epistle. Cf. Riehm, *op. cit.,* p. 272: " As the
author so frequently designates Christ as the Son of God, it is somewhat remarkable that he only a single time and that in a citation from
the O. T. (1^5) calls God the Father of Christ."

[9] For this is the significance of the formulas of citation to which 1^8
goes back.

[10] So Delitzsch, *in loc.* (E. T., p. 76): " The very point of the argument for the superiority of the Son above the angels, drawn from Ps
45^7 and foll., lies surely in the fact that He is here twice, or at least
once, addressed in the vocative as ὁ θεός." Hofmann and even
Riehm are unnecessarily subtle here.

throughout the Epistle as being. Certainly there is no reason why this author should not have ascribed "eternal glory" to the Being he had described as in His very nature "the effulgence of the divine glory,"[11] and for that very reason it may be a matter of indifference to us whether he has done so or not. Nor is much added to this picture of the divine Christ by his designation of Him, without qualification, as 'the Firstborn' (1^6), or by his noticing that God has "appointed Him Heir of all things" (1^2). 'Firstborn' and 'Heir' are little more than specially honorific ways of saying 'Son.' God's 'Firstborn' as such takes rank above all other existing beings: even all of the angels shall do Him reverence. God's 'Firstborn' is also naturally God's 'Heir,' an heir whose inheritance embraces the universe, and whose tenure stretches to eternity. All these declarations are bound very closely together in their common relation to the fundamental conception of our Lord's divine Sonship; and constitute items by the mention of which the contents of the idea of Sonship are developed. The statements of the opening verses of the Epistle seem to be arranged in a sort of climax by means of which the glory of the New Covenant, revealed in the 'Son,' is more and more enhanced. The glory of the New Covenant is that it has been introduced by God the 'Son'—that 'Son' who, despite His lowly manifesta-

---

[11] Riehm says (p. 286): "Still how can it occasion surprise that the author in 13^{21} praises Jesus Christ with the doxology, ᾧ ἡ δόξα εἰς τοὺς αἰῶνας, which, according to O. T. notions, is due to Jehovah only, but in the N. T. passages is also transferred to Christ? It is recognized by all recent commentators that the relative (ᾧ) refers to Christ and not to God." So also Bleek, Lünemann, Maier, Kurtz, Lowrie: contra, Delitzsch: *non liquet,* Davidson.

tion on earth, has been appointed heir of all things,—
that is, Lord of all: by whom, indeed, the worlds were
made in the depths of eternity,—that is, who is the
eternal Creator of all that is: who, in fact, is in Himself the effulgence of God's glory and the impress of
His substance—that is to say, all that God is: and by
whom, because He is all that God is, the universe is
held in being.

It is particularly noticeable that at this precise point
a mention of Christ's propitiatory work is introduced.

Soteriological Titles   This 'Son of God,' whose dignity has
been thus expounded, "made purifica-
tion of sins." The soteriological interest is present, therefore, even in this ontological
passage, and it is the soteriological interest, indeed,
which gives its importance to this ontological discussion in the eyes of the writer. The soteriological titles
by which he designates our Lord are therefore naturally as rich as the ontological ones. He is 'the Mediator of the New Covenant' (8^6 9^{15} 12^{24}) : He is the
Ground of eternal Salvation (5^9) : He is 'the Author
of Salvation' (2^{10}, cf. Acts 3^{15} 5^{31}) : He is 'the Author
and Perfecter of our Faith' (12^2) : He is our Forerunner into that which is within the veil (6^{20}) :[12] He
is 'the Apostle and High Priest of our Confession' (3^1) : He is 'the Great Shepherd of the Sheep'

---

[12] The αἴτιος of Salvation (5^9) is merely He who is the Cause or
Producer of Salvation. The ἀρχηγός of Salvation (2^{10}, cf. 12^2) is
commonly supposed to be He who has Himself trodden the pathway
over which our feet should pass, and to be so far equivalent to the πρόδρομος (6^{20}). So, e. g. G. Vos in the *Princeton Theological Review*,
July, 1907, p. 434, who classes ἀρχηγός and πρόδρομος together as
implying identification in experience, in contrast with αἴτιος in which
this is not present; but see to the contrary, Cremer, ed. 3 and subsequent
edd.

(13[20]) : and, above all (for this is a favorite conception of this Epistle), He is our ' Priest ' (5^6 $7^{3,11,[15],17,21}$
[8^4] 10^{21}) or more specifically[13] our ' High Priest '
([2^{17}] 3^1 $4^{14,15}$ 5^{10} 6^{20} 7^{26} 8^1 9^{11}). All these are great
designations : and we see at a glance that they reflect
in their substance the high estimate put upon our
Lord's person as the ' Son of God.' It is only because
He is the ' Son of God ' that He may be fitly described
in His saving work by these high designations. It is
also at once observable that the Messanic conception
underlies and gives form to them all. If Jesus is conceived by the writer of this Epistle in His person
fundamentally as the eternal ' Son of God '; He is
equally conceived in His work as fundamentally the
Messiah appointed of God to inaugurate the new order
of things and to bring His people safely into the experience of the promised salvation. As ' Mediator of
the New Covenant ' He gives His life for the redemption
of His people, establishing new relations between them

---

[13] Dr. Vos (*Princeton Theological Review*, July, 1907, p. 432),
supposes the use of the simple 'priest' to be due in general to the
appeal to Ps. 110 (5^{10} being exceptional), while 'High Priest' is the
real preference of the author, resting on a reference in his mind to
the entrance of the High Priest into the Holy of Holies on the day of
the atonement, which prefigures what is to him the central act of Christ's
priestly ministry,—the entrance into Heaven. "The Saviour is a high
priest because in the discharge of His ministry He enters into Heaven.
. . . The inference lies near that the whole discussion of the subject
ultimately serves the purpose of showing the necessity of the
heavenly state of existence of the Saviour." On the other hand,
cf. Davidson, p. 147: "According to the representation of the Epistle,
there is no difference in principle between priest and high priest";
and Denney, Hastings' *B. D.*, IV. p. 98 a: "In the New Testament
it is only in the Ep. to the Hebrews that Jesus is spoken of as ἱερεύς,
μέγας ἱερεύς and ἀρχιερεύς—terms which are not to be distinguished
from each other, the last two only signifying Christ's eminence in the
priestly character."

and God by means of His blood. As the 'Originator
of Salvation,' He tasted death for every man, receiving
in Himself the penalties due to them, not to Him. As
'Author and Perfecter of our faith' He endured the
cross, despising the shame that He might be not merely
our example, but our Saviour. As 'the Great Shepherd' He laid down His life for His sheep. As
'the Apostle and High Priest' He is the One appointed by God to make sacrifice of Himself for the
sins of the people,—for every High Priest must needs
have somewhat to offer, and this 'our High Priest'
has through His own blood obtained eternal redemption for us.

We see that the red thread of redemption in blood
is woven into all the allusions to the saving work of the

Christ our 'Priest'

'Son of God.' And we see that the chief
vehicle in this Epistle for the expression
of this high teaching is the representation
of our Lord's work as priestly in its nature, and the proclamation of Him as 'the great High Priest.' The
interest of this grows out of the circumstance that
here at last in the New Testament the conception of
Messiah as Priest comes to its rights. In their ab-
sorption in the conception of Messiah as King the
Jews gave scanty hospitality to the rich suggestions of
the Old Testament of other aspects in which His office
and work might be contemplated. It was characteristic
of Christianity, under the illumination thrown back
upon the promise by its fulfillment, to gather these
neglected aspects together and note their fulfillment in
Christ. Among them was the conception of Messiah
as a priest performing the priestly work of propitia-
tion. There seems to be little trace of the currency of

such a conception among the Jews. There is also little use made of it in other books of the New Testament. But in the Epistle to the Hebrews it is given its full exposition; strikingly illustrated from the same Psalm which declares the Messiah David's Lord not less than David's son,—" Thou art a Priest forever after the order of Melchizedek "; and made the vehicle ·for the inculcation of the fundamental doctrine of Christianity—the propitiatory death of Jesus, the reconciliation of God by His sacrifice of Himself, and His eternal intercession for His people. This is the great contribution of the Epistle to the Hebrews to the apprehension of the nature of our Lord's work.[14]

---

[14] On the conception of the Messiah as Priest, cf. Stanton, *The Jewish and Christian Messiah,* 1867, pp. 128-9; and esp. pp. 294 *seq.;* also Hastings' *B. D.,* III., 356 b: and cf. Swete, Hastings' *B. D.,* II., 406: " The Jewish Messiah, however, was chiefly the Anointed King; the conception of Messiah as the Prophet was less distinct, and that of a Christ-Priest (ἱερεὺς ὁ χριστός, Lev 4[5,16] 6[22]) entirely wanting, until it presented itself to the writer of the Epistle to the Hebrews (Stanton, *Jewish and Christian Messiah,* p. 293 ff.)." On the idea of our Lord's priesthood see the " extended note on the priesthood of Christ " in Davidson's *Com. on Heb.,* p. 146 *seq.;* and cf. Denney in Hastings' *B. D.,* IV., 98 *seq.,* and especially Vos, as above, pp. 423 *seq.,* who adduces the passages which show that although the term ' priest ' is not explicitly applied to the Messiah by the Jews, nor to our Lord elsewhere in the N. T., the idea is not alien to either the Jews or the N. T. writers.

THE WITNESS OF THE APOCALYPSE

The peculiarity of the Book of Revelation, as an Apocalypse, gives it the superficial appearance of

A Summary View of Early Conceptions standing apart from the other books of the New Testament in a class by itself. It requires little scrutiny of its contents, however, to assure us that this is true only of its form. In the matter of the designations it applies to our Lord, for example, the cursory reader is impressed by their novelty and astonished by the richness of their suggestion; but on analyzing their content he soon discovers that they embody in their splendid phraseology no other conceptions than those he has been made familiar with in the other books of the New Testament. Indeed, there is a sense in which it would not be untrue to say that the Book of Revelation, written as it was at the close of the first Christian century (c. A. D. 96), gathers up into an epitome and gives vivid, and we may say even emotional, expression to the whole century's thought of Jesus. A certain comprehensiveness is thus imparted to its christological allusions which has puzzled the critical student and been made by him the reproach of the book and even the occasion of denial to it of unity of composition.[1] It is in truth

[1] Cf. Holtzmann, *N. T. Theologie,* I., 467: "The Old Testament and Jewish conceptions of the Messiah form no doubt the fundamental basis of the christology, though they are on every side outvied and surmounted; so that such a conglomeration of all Biblical and even Jewish strata of doctrine results as is wholly without example else-

merely a witness to the unity of the conception of Jesus which characterized the whole Apostolic Church, finding, indeed, varied expression according to the idiosyncrasy of each writer, but remaining through all variety of expression essentially the same.

The long list of designations in which this conception of Jesus is at least in part embodied in the Book of Revelation may be perhaps somewhat **Two Classes of Designations** roughly divided into two classes. We say roughly divided because the separating line is an uncertain one and the two classes melt insensibly into one another. These two classes may perhaps equally roughly be discriminated as simple and descriptive designations: simple designations, that is to say, names merely designating our Lord, though, of course, no one of these names merely designates our Lord, but all have more or less of a descriptive element; and descriptive designations, that is to say, designations which are more or less elaborate descriptions of His nature and functions.

The simple designations are, in accordance with the general character of the book as a symbolical Apocalypse, both few and infrequently em- **Simple Designations** ployed.[2] In the formal opening of the book we have—as in the formal open-

where in the N. T., and has become one of the chief occasions for the current hypotheses which attack the unity of the composition." He quotes Bousset as speaking of the christology of the Apocalypse as a "confused conglomeration of the most diverse conceptions" (Meyer's *Com. on Rev.*, 161). Cf. R. Palmer, *The Drama of the Apocalypse*, p. 105, who complains that "the point of view of the seer is continually changing," so that it is impossible to obtain a unitary doctrine from him.

[2] Cf. Holtzmann's enumeration, *Theologie des N. T.*, 1, 467, and Gebhardt. *Doctrine of the Apocalypse*, p. 77.

ing of several others of the New Testament books (Mt $1^{1,18}$, Mk 1^1, Jno 1^{17}, Rom 1^1, 1 Cor 1^1, Gal 1^1, 1 P 1^1, 2 P1^1, [Jno 1^3, 2 Jno 3], Jude 1)—the full ceremonious name, ' Jesus Christ ' ($1^{1,1,5}$). In the formal closing verses of the book the place of this solemn designation is taken by the somewhat more descriptive designation ' the Lord Jesus ' ($22^{20,21}$, cf. however, v. r. ' Jesus Christ ' in verse 21). The simple ' Jesus ' occurs more frequently ($1^{9,9}$ 12^{17} 14^{12} 17^6 $19^{10,10}$ 20^4 22^{16}), and, if we may be allowed the expression, appears to be the more emotional, as distinguished from the more formal, simple designation of our Lord in this book. The simple ' Christ ' occurs only twice ($20^{4,6}$), although in what we may call its more descriptive form—that is in its appellative use—' the Lord's Christ (Anointed),' ' God's Christ (Anointed),'—it occurs twice more (at 11^{15} 12^{10}). The term ' Lord ' seems to be a designation of Christ at 14^{13}: and His Lordship is of course copiously recognized elsewhere, not merely by implication as in the designation of a day as " the Lord's day " (1^{10}),[3] but in a series of elaborately descriptive designations the simplest of which is perhaps ' the King of Kings and Lord of Lords ' (19^{16}), varied to ' the Lord of Lords and King of Kings ' (17^{14}, cf. 1^5 $2^{1,12}$ 3^7 5^5). Of the more common Messianic designations, besides the fundamental ' the Christ ' (11^{15} 12^{10}; and in compounds $1^{1,2,5}$) and ' Christ ' ($20^{4,6}$), only ' the Son of God ' occurs, and that but once (2^{18}, cf. ' my Father,' 2^{27} $3^{5,21}$; ' His God and Father,' 1^6; ' my God,' $3^{2,12}$), and accompanied by

---

[3] Such a phrase as ἡ κυριακὴ ἡμέρα could not have been framed unless Jesus had been to His followers ' the Lord ' by way of eminence. **Cf. 1** Cor 11^{20}, ' the Lord's Supper.'

descriptive adjuncts which give it its very highest connotation. Our Lord's own ' Son of Man,' however, has its echo in the description of Jesus in two visions as " one like unto a Son of Man " (1^{13} 14^{14}) : and by the preservation in this designation of the " like unto " of the Danielic vision (7^{13}) —strengthened from the simple ὡς to the emphatic ὅμοιον,—the seer manages to assert with great strength the essential deity of our Lord. He was not a son of man but only " like unto a son of man."[4] He even enhances this implication by interweaving into the description traits drawn not only from Daniel's " Son of Man," but also from his " Ancient of Days."[5] The Johannine designation of ' the Word of God ' (19^{13}) also occurs as the name of the conquering Christ, apparently with the implication that in Jesus is manifested the definitive revelation of God in which He addresses Himself to man with irresistible power.[6] Probably the " man child " (or " son ") of 12^5 (cf. 12^{13}, " the man ") ultimately refers to our Lord: and if so it also is doubtless Messianic, taking hold at once of Is 66^7 and Psalm 2^9, possibly even of Gen 4^1: in any event the allusion is to the conquest of evil by this Son of the woman.

[4] Cf. Gebhardt, *Doctrine of the Apocalypse*, pp. 78-9 : " De Wette and Hengstenberg find in the expression the superhuman glory of Christ; for, as De Wette remarks, to affirm of a man that he is like a man is to say nothing; or as Hengstenberg expresses it, if Christ only resembles a Son of Man, there must be another side of His nature which surpasses the human."

[5] Cf. Holtzmann, *op. cit.*, pp. 467-8 : " The Danielic Son of Man, $1^{7,13}$ 14^{14}, and even the Danielic ' Ancient of Days,' 1^{14}, shine through."

[6] The vision is the vision of the spiritual conquest of the world, and in such a vision the designation of our Lord as ' the Word of God ' is peculiarly appropriate.

The more elaborate descriptive titles which are applied to our Lord embody the same circle of ideas as
are more briefly suggested by the sim-
pler designations; and only more vividly and richly express their contents.
Some of these have for their burden the saving activities of our Lord and may therefore fitly be called
soteriological. A good example of these is provided
by the direct description of Him as " Him that loved
us and loosed us from our sins by His blood " (1^5).
But the most striking and at the same time the most
frequently employed descriptive designation of this
class is that which calls Him "the Lamb that hath
been slain " (5^{12} 13^8, cf. $5^{6,9}$ 7^{14}), or more commonly
simply "the Lamb " without express but always with
implied reference to the actual sacrifice ($5^{8,13}$ $6^{1,16}$
$7^{9,10,14,17}$ 12^{11} $14^{1,4,4,10}$ 15^3 17^{14} $19^{7,9}$ $21^{9,14,22,27}$ $22^{1,3}$).[7]
Indeed, we understate the matter when we say this is
the most frequently employed descriptive designation
of Christ of its class. It is in fact the most frequently
employed designation of Jesus of any
kind, and must be looked upon as em-
bodying the seer's favorite mode of
conceiving of Jesus and His work. He even uses it
in such a manner as to suggest that it had acquired for

Descriptive Designations

'The Lamb'

---

[7] The word is ἀρνίον, which is used 26 times of Christ in Revelation (in 13^{11} it is otherwise used). It is found elsewhere in the N. T.
only at Jno 21^{15} (plural), where it represents Christ's followers.
Jesus is called 'Lamb' (ἀμνός) in Jno $1^{29,36}$, Acts 8^{32}, 1 P 1^{19}, and
nowhere else except in Rev. (ἀρνίον). In the whole N. T. 'lamb'
(whether ἀμνός or ἀρνίον) occurs only of Christ except at Jno 21^{15}
(ἀρνία) [cf. Lk 10^3 (ἀρήν)]. On the use of the diminutive ἀρνίον
of Jesus see A. B. Grosart in the *Expos. Times*, II. p. 57, and cf. Gebhardt, p. 112; Swete, p. 77.

him much the status of a proper name, and suggested itself as a designation of Jesus even when the mind of the writer was dwelling on other aspects of His work than that most closely symbolized by this title.[8] There could be no more striking indication of the high significance the writer attached to the sacrificial death of Christ, and to the dominance of the fifty-third chapter of Isaiah in the framing of his Messianic conceptions; matters which are otherwise copiously illustrated by his language.[9] Other prevailingly soteriological designations advert especially to our Lord's resurrection,— such as that by which He is spoken of as 'the First-born of the Dead' (1[5]); and others still to His trustworthiness, such as when He is called 'the Faithful and True' (19[11]), or 'the Faithful Witness' (1[5]), and more elaborately 'the Amen, the Faithful and True Witness, the beginning of the creation of God' (3[14]); or again, 'He that is holy, He that is true,

---

[8] So Hoekstra, *De Christologie der Apocalypse,* in the *Theologisch Tijdschrift,* III., 1869, p. 4; and even Gebhardt, *Doctrine of the Apocalypse,* 1873, pp. 113, 114: "The seer in the course of his representation unquestionably often uses the expression 'the lamb' without any special signification, but only as a standing designation of Christ (cf. 17[14])."

[9] Cf. Holtzmann, *op. cit.,* I., 472: "This 29-[27-] times occurring Lamb, the most individual christological conception of the author (see Vol. II., 478) refers back most probably to Is 53[7]." Perhaps we ought to say it refers back proximately to Jno 1[29], and forms one of those subtle indications that this book is the composition of John—who was one of the two disciples (Jno 1[35]) to whom the Baptist pointed out Jesus as "the Lamb of God which taketh away the sin of the world." It has been too little observed to what an extent John (both in Gospel and Epistles and in the Apocalypse) was influenced in his conceptions by the Baptist. The thesis might be defended that the Baptist was his first and most impressive teacher in theology. In any event it is important to observe such hints of an underlying unity between Gospel and Apocalypse.

He that hath the keys of David, He that openeth and none shall shut and that shutteth and none shall open ' (3^7).

The transition from these soteriological designations to those which are more purely honorific, or perhaps

Accumulative Designations

we might better say, ontological, is very gradual, or indeed insensible: and nothing is more characteristic of the book than the sharp contrast into which designations of the two classes are brought by their immediate conjunction. Thus, for example, we read: "And I wept much, because no one was found to open the book, . . . and one of the elders saith unto me, Weep not, behold the Lion that is of the tribe of Judah . . . hath overcome to open the book. . . . And I saw in the midst of the throne, and of the four living creatures, and in the midst of the elders, a Lamb standing as though it had been slain, . . . and he came and taketh the book . . . " $(5^{4 \text{ seq.}})$. There is no question of mixed metaphors here: there is only question of bringing together in Jesus by the most varied of symbols all the aspects of the Messianic prediction, and the exhibition of these all as finding their fulfillment in Him. All these designations are distinctly Messianic in their ground tone, and the Messianic ground tone is taken from all forms of the Messianic expectation, but perhaps prevailingly from that associated in the Gospels with the title of 'Son of Man,' to which there is manifest allusion even in passages in which there is not only no adduction of that title, but no direct designation of our Lord from that point of view (1^7). The great opening description of our Lord as ' Jesus

Christ, the faithful witness, the firstborn of the dead, and the ruler of the kings of the earth' (1^5) unites already nearly all forms of designating Him employed in the book. Here is the simple name, the recognition of His dependableness, and the ascription to Him of the inauguration of life and of universal sovereignty. The Messianic ground tone is especially prominent in such designations as those which call Him 'the Lion of the tribe of Judah, the Root of David' (5^5), or 'the Root and the Offspring of David, the bright, the morning Star' (22^{16}), but passes more into the background in such as those which speak of Him as 'the Son of God who hath eyes like a flame of fire and His feet are like unto burnished brass' (2^{18}), or 'He that holdeth the seven stars in His right hand, He that walketh in the midst of the seven golden candlesticks' (2^1), or 'He that hath the seven spirits of God and the seven stars' (3^1). It is His Messianic function of judgment which is thrown forward in the description of Him as 'He that hath the sharp two-edged sword' (2^{12}); 'He that is the ruler of the kings of the earth' (1^5), 'whose eyes are like a flame of fire' (2^{18}), and who, since His dominion is universal, is 'the Lord of Lords and King of Kings' (17^{14} 19^{16})—although a greater than a Messiah is obviously here. The climax is attained in the description of Him as 'the First and the Last, which was dead and lived again' (2^8), 'the First and the Last, and the Living One' (1^{18}), 'the Alpha and Omega, the First and the Last, the Beginning and the End' (22^{13}), in whose hands are the destinies of men (1^{18} 3^7).[10]

[10] Cf. A. B. Davidson, *The Theology of the O. T.,* p. 165, on the high meaning of these phrases here applied to Jesus: "'The first and

It seems scarcely necessary to draw out in detail the wealth of implication of deity which these designations contain. The Apocalypse does not apply to our Lord directly the simple designation 'God.' But everything short of that is done to emphasize the seer's estimate of Him as a divine Being clothed with all the divine attributes.[11] This is generally allowed; and those who are set upon having the Apocalypse witness to a lower christology commonly content themselves with the remark that its language must not be taken at its face value. Baur, for example, contends that although the highest predicates are ascribed to Jesus, they are " only names borne outwardly by Him, and are not associated with His person in any inner unity of nature "; that

The Deity of Our Lord

last' (Is 44[6]) is a surprising generalization for a comparatively early time. It is not a mere statement that Jehovah was from the beginning and will be at the end. It is a name indicating His relation to history and the life of men. He initiates it, and He winds it up. And He is present in all its movements. 'Since it was, there am I' (48[16]). Even the last book in the N. T. has nothing loftier to say of Jehovah than that He is 'the first and the last': 'I am the Alpha and the Omega, the first and the last, saith the Lord, the Almighty' (Rev 1[8])." It is by these lofty designations that Jesus is spoken of in the Apocalypse. Cf. Swete on the passage.

[11] Cf. the brief but instructive sketch of the christology of the Apocalypse in Swete, pp. clv. *seq.,* especially the summary of the relations of Christ to God on p. clvii.: " (1) He has the prerogatives of God. He searches men's hearts (2[23]); He can kill or restore life (1[18] 2[23]); He receives a worship which is rendered without distinction to God (5[13]); His priests are also priests of God (20[6]); He occupies one throne with God (22[1,3]), and shares one sovereignty (11[15]). (2) Christ receives the titles of God. He is the Living One (1[18]), the Holy and True (3[7]), the Alpha and Omega, the First and the Last, the Beginning and the End (22[13]). (3) Passages which in the O. T. relate to God are without hesitation applied to Christ, e.g. Deut 10[17] (17[14]), Prov 3[12]

" inner connection between the divine predicates and
the historical individual who bears them " is lacking.[12]
In point of fact these divine predicates are there; and
whether the seer means anything by them may be safely
left to the reader to decide. Jesus is represented as
emphatically as God Himself, as the living one (1^{18}),
eternal (1^{18}), omniscient (1^{14} 2^{18} 19^{12}), the searcher
of the reins and hearts (2^{23}), in whose hands
are the keys of death and hell (1^{18}). If in
reminiscence of Is 44^6 where the Lord, the King
of Israel, and his Redeemer, the Lord of hosts, declares of Himself: " I am the first and the last: and
beside me there is no God,"—God is represented as
announcing: " I am the Alpha and the Omega, the
beginning and the end " (21^6, cf. 1^8), Jesus equally
(despite the strong monotheistic assertion of the original passage) is represented as announcing: " I am the
first and the last, and the living one " ($1^{17,18}$, cf. 2^8),
" I am the Alpha and the Omega, the first and the

(3^{19}), Dan 7^9 (1^{14}), Zech 4^{10} (5^6). Thus the writer seems either to
coördinate or to identify Christ with God. Yet he is certainly not
conscious of any tendency to ditheism, for his book is rigidly monotheistic; nor, on the other hand, is he guilty of confusing the two
Persons."

[12] So also substantially Köstlin and Hoekstra. See the refutation in
Gebhardt, pp. 86 *seq.* Bousset (Meyer's *Com. on Apoc.*), while representing the christology of the book as " a confused conglomeration of
the most diverse conceptions " (280), has yet to recognize that it is (in
some of its elements at least) " apparently the most advanced in the
whole N. T." (280). He says: " We have in it the faith of a layman
unaffected by any theological reflection, which with heedless naïveté
simply identifies Christ in His predicates and attributes with God,
while on the other side it calmly incorporates also wholly archaic
elements."

last, the beginning and the end " (22^{13}).[13] Indeed, in

the opening address we have one of those Trinitarian arrangements which betray the real underlying conception of deity in others, too, of the New Testament writers: " Grace to you and peace from Him which is and which was and which is to come "—that is Jehovah, of which this is an analysis,—" and from the seven Spirits "—that is the Holy Spirit set forth in His divine completeness,—" and from Jesus Christ who is the faithful witness, the firstborn from the dead and the ruler of the kings of the earth " ($1^{4\ seq.}$). In the presence of such pervasive and universally recognized ascriptions of deity to our Lord we need not stop to expound the significance of such designations as that by which He is called not merely the ' Amen[14] and the faithful and true witness,' but ' the principle of the

[13] Dr. B. W. Bacon, Hastings' *D. C. G.*, I., 43 *seq.*, endeavors to expound the application of these phrases to Christ as an eschatologico-soteriological adaptation, in which the metaphysical implication is lost: in them Christ would say " I am the primary object and ultimate fulfillment of God's promise " (4^3.). What is in its application to God, therefore, " a solemn designation of Divinity " becomes when transferred to Christ only an assertion that in Him the promised redemption is accomplished: " It is only in the eschatological sense that Christ becomes the original object and ultimate fulfillment of the Divine purposes and promises, 'the Yea and Amen,' 'the Alpha and the Omega, the first and the last, the beginning and the end'" (p. 45). The artificiality and inadequacy of this construction is manifest. Cf. on the other hand A. E. Ross, art. *" First and Last,"* Hastings' *D. C. G.*, I., 595 *seq.*, who frankly allows " that the title ' the First and the Last ' as applied to Christ in Rev. recalls and attributes to Him all that the O. T. writers had realized of the nature of God " (596 a). Cf. Dr. Davidson, as above, p. 318, note, on the essential significance of the phrases.

[14] On the ' Amen ' as a designation of our Lord, cf. J. S. Clemens, Hastings' *D. C. G.*, I., 51 a, and J. Massie, Hastings' *D. B.*, I., 81 a.

creation of God' (3^{14}) [15]—that is to say, the active agent in creating all that God creates. It is abundantly clear that the Christ of the Apocalypse is a divine person. [16]

[15] Cf. Gebhardt, p. 93, and Düsterdieck, *in loc.*

[16] Cf. T. C. Porter in Hastings' *B. D.*, IV., 263 a: "While angels are classed with men, Christ is classed with God; and various titles and expressions carry us beyond not only the Messianic but also the angelogical speculations of Judaism. He is once called 'the Son of God' (2^{18}), but see also 2^{27} $3^{5,21}$, cf. 1^6 14^1); once 'the beginning of the creation of God' (3^{14}), as only the Divine Wisdom is called in O. T. (Prov 8^{22}), and as Christ is called only by St. Paul in the N. T. (Col 1^{15}). He is called once also the 'Word of God' (19^{13}), and even this Johannine (Hellenistic) title is surpassed by the title of eternity, 'the First and the Last' $(1^{17}$ 2^8 $22^{13})$." Cf. Stanton, *The Jewish and Christian Messiah*, p. 163.

THE ISSUE OF THE INVESTIGATION

We have now passed in review the whole body of designations which are applied to our Lord in the

Fundamental Conviction of the Christian Community pages of the New Testament. We cannot fail to be impressed with the variety of these designations and the richness of their suggestion. It would be a pleasant task to develop all their implications. This would, however, take us too far afield for our present purpose. Let it suffice to observe that at bottom they seem to be charged with three specific convictions on the part of the Christian community, to which they give endlessly repeated and endlessly varied expression. Christ is the Messiah; Christ is our Redeemer; Christ is God: these are the great asseverations which are especially embodied in them. All three are already summed up in the angelic announcement which was made to the shepherds at His birth: "I bring you good tidings of great joy which shall be to all the people: for there is born to you this day in the city of David the Saviour, who is Christ the Lord" (Lk 2¹¹). The whole New Testament may be said to be an exposition and enforcement of that announcement: and in the course of this exposition and enforcement it teaches us many things. Above all, it places beyond dispute the main fact with which we have now to deal, this fact, to wit, that the whole Christian community, and that from the very beginning, was firmly convinced that Jesus Christ was God manifest in the flesh.

There really can be found no place for doubt of this fact. But upon its emergence as an indubitable fact it becomes plain that it is freighted with great significance. The fact that the whole Christian community from the very beginning held, as to its fundamental principle, to the deity of its founder, is a very remarkable fact, and surely needs accounting for. And it will be found difficult to impossibility adequately to account for it except upon the assumption that the founder of Christianity really was a divine person. This universal and uniform conviction of the deity of Christ in the primitive Christian body in a word implies the actual deity of Christ, as its presupposition. It cannot be supposed that the whole body of the first Christians firmly believed in the deity of their Master without evidence—without much evidence—without convincing evidence. The primary item of this evidence was no doubt our Lord's own self-assertion: and this is a fact of the first importance which is immediately given in the fact of the universal and uniform belief in our Lord's deity which characterized the first age of the Church. That belief cannot possibly be accounted for except on the supposition that it was founded in our Lord's teaching. As certain as it is then that the primitive Christians were firmly and without exception convinced of our Lord's deity, so certain is it that our Lord—as indeed He is represented to have done in the uniform tradition—asserted Himself to be a divine person. And now we must go further. As certain as it is that these two things are true, that the whole

[Marginal note:] This Conviction Presupposes Our Lord's Teaching

Christian community believed their Lord to be divine
and that Jesus taught that He was divine, so certain
it is that neither of them could be true if it were not
true that our Lord was divine.

We have already remarked that the Christian community cannot be supposed to have formed and im-
And Something movably fixed in their hearts the con-
More than His viction that their Lord was divine
Teaching without evidence—much evidence—
convincing evidence. We have also pointed out that
the primary item of this evidence was our Lord's own
assertion. But there certainly must have been more
evidence than our Lord's bare assertion. Men do not
without ado believe everyone who announces himself
to be God, upon the bald announcement alone. There
must have been attendant circumstances which supported the announcement and gave it verisimilitude,—
nay, cogency—or it would not have had such power
over men. Our Lord's life, His teachings, His character, must have been consonant with it. His deeds
as well as His words must have borne Him witness.
The credit accorded to His assertion is the best possible
evidence that such was the case. We can understand
how His followers could believe Him divine, if in
point of fact He not only asserted Himself to be
divine but lived as became a God, taught as befitted a
divine Instructor, in all His conversation in the world
manifested a perfection such as obviously was not
human: and if dying, He rose again from the dead.
If He did none of these things can their firm and pas-
sionate faith in His deity be explained?

Possibly we do not always fully realize the nature
of the issue here brought before us. Here is a young

man scarcely thirty-three years of age, emerged from obscurity only for the brief space of three years, living Including during those years under the scorn of the Something world, which grew steadily in intensity Very Conclusive and finally passed into hatred, and dying at the end the death of a malefactor: but leaving behind Him the germs of a world-wide community, the spring of whose vitality is the firm conviction that He was God manifest in the flesh. If anything human is obvious it is obvious that this conviction was not formed and fixed without evidence for it of the most convincing kind. The account His followers themselves gave of the matter is that their faith was grounded not merely in His assertions, nor merely in the impression His personality made upon them in conjunction with His claims,—but specifically in a series of divine deeds, culminating in His rising from the dead, setting its seal upon His claims and the impression made by His personality. This is the account of the great place the Resurrection of Christ takes in the Apostolic propaganda. It is the seal set by heaven upon the truth of His deity as proclaimed in His teaching. It is safe to say that apart from evidence so convincing the high claims of Jesus could not have been met with such firm and unquestioning faith by His followers. This very faith becomes thus a proof of the truth of His claims.[1]

[1] Cf. Stanton, *The Jewish and the Christian Messiah*, pp. 252, 253: "It appears to me that without the coöperation of the two main causes here indicated, first the impression made by the personality of Jesus, His works and His claims for Himself, before His crucifixion, and then the evidence which convinced His disciples of His resurrection, faith in Him as a supernatural Christ could not have been established so universally from the first."

And so, in fact, is the mere fact that He made these claims. We have seen that the fact that He made **Not Supposable** these claims is not only asserted by all **that Jesus made** His followers, but is safeguarded by **False Claims** their faith in His deity, which were inexplicable without it. But it is evident that He could not have made such a claim unless what He claimed was true. We are not absurdly arguing that the claim to be God is one which cannot be made by a human being untruly. What is it that the folly or wickedness of men will not compass? But why should we absurdly argue that Jesus may be supposed to have done whatever we think within the compass of human folly or human wickedness? Was Jesus the silliest of men; or the most wicked? The point is not that no man could make such a claim untruly, but that Jesus could not make it untruly! Many men there have been, and are, who might do so; some have done so— men who were vilely impostors or wildly insane. Is Jesus to be classed with these men? Are we to ask with Renan how far Jesus may be supposed to have gone in assuming a *rôle* He knew He had no claim upon? Are we to ask, with Oscar Holtzmann, was Jesus a fanatic? These are the alternatives: grossly deceiving; grossly deceived; or else neither deceiving nor deceived, but speaking the words of soberness and truth. He, the flower of human sanity; He, the ripe fruit of human perfection; can He be supposed to have announced to His followers that He was above all angels, abode continually in equal intercourse with the Father, shared with Him in the ineffable Name—and it not be true? As Dr. Gwatkin[2] crisply puts it,

[2] *The Knowledge of God*, I., 120.

" There is a tremendous dilemma here which must be faced: assuming that the tremendous claim ascribed to Him is false, one would think it must have disordered His life with insanity if He made it Himself, and the accounts of His life if others invented it." This witness is true. Neither Jesus nor His followers could have invented the claims to deity which Jesus is reported to have made for Himself: for the truth of these claims is needed to account both for Jesus and for His followers.

We have no intention of stopping here to argue these points; if indeed to establish them they need more argument than their mere statement. It was necessary, however, to suggest them in order to indicate the gain we register upon ascertaining, as we have ascertained, that the entire Christian community from the very first was firmly convinced of the deity of its Lord. That fact established, it carries with it the truth of the conviction. For the conviction, in the circumstances in which it was formed and held, cannot be accounted for save on the assumption of the existence of compelling evidence for it, and this compelling evidence must include in it the claims of Jesus, which in turn cannot be accounted for save on the assumption of their truth. Grant that Jesus was really God, in a word, and everything falls orderly into its place. Deny it, and you have a Jesus and a Christianity on your hands both equally unaccountable. And that is as much as to say that the ultimate proof of the deity of Christ is just —Jesus and Christianity. If Christ were not God, we should have a very different Jesus and a very different Christianity. And that is the reason that mod-

(marginal note:) The Issue the Sufficient Evidence of the Source

ern unbelief bends all its energies in a vain effort to abolish the historical Jesus and to destroy historical Christianity. Its instinct is right: but its task is hopeless. We need the Jesus of history to account for the Christianity of history. And we need both the Jesus of history and the Christianity of history to account for the history of the world. The history of the world is the product of the precise Christianity which has actually existed, and this Christianity is the product of the precise Jesus which actually was. To be rid of this Jesus we must be rid of this Christianity, and to be rid of this Christianity we must be rid of the world-history which has grown out of it. We must have the Christianity of history and the Jesus of history, or we leave the world that exists, and as it exists, unaccounted for. But so long as we have either the Jesus of history or the Christianity of history we shall have a divine Jesus.

INDEXES

These Indexes have been, with great kindness, prepared by the Rev. Dr. John H. Kerr, Secretary of the American Tract Society. Thanks are due to Dr. Kerr also for whatever accuracy has been attained in printing the text of the book.

INDEXES

II. INDEX OF PASSAGES OF SCRIPTURE

(The superior figures in this Index indicate the number of times a passage is cited on a given page).

(The superior figures in this Index indicate the number of times an author is quoted on a given page)